Finding Marshalls
A Genealogy Trip with a Black & White Twist

Kathy Lynne Marshall

FINDING MARSHALLS

A Genealogy Trip
With a Black & White Twist

Kathy Lynne Marshall

© 2022 Kathy Lynne Marshall

All rights reserved. Printed in the United States of America.

No part of this book may be reproduced or used in any manner whatsoever without written permission from the author except in the case of brief quotations embodied in articles or reviews.

ISBN #: 978-1-7375733-0-2

Library of Congress Control Number: 2022903657

First Edition

Cover design by Kathy Lynne Marshall.
Cover image of house with permission by Mike Buckner.

Kanika Marshall Art and Books Publishing
PO Box 1202, Elk Grove, CA, 95759-1202
Website: www.KanikaMarshall.com/books.html

TABLE OF CONTENTS

INTRODUCTION 1

PART I: GEORGIA 3

    Chapter 1: A Crazy Idea Forms 5

    Chapter 2: Rona Rolls In 11

    Chapter 3: Road Trip! 13

    Chapter 4: Sunday – The Journey Begins 21

    Chapter 5: Monday in Putnam 29

    Chapter 6: The Road to Talbot County 47

    Chapter 7: Tuesday in Talbotton 55

    Chapter 8: Wednesday Morning in Columbus 67

    Chapter 9: The Renaissance Couple 75

    Chapter 10: Thursday Exploring Grandpa's Hometown 97

    Chapter 11: Welcome to the Table 107

    Chapter 12: Car Talk+ 129

    Chapter 13: Another View of Georgia Race Relations 161

    Chapter 14: Guess Who's Coming to Dinner? 171

PART II: ALABAMA 177

    Chapter 15: The Alabama Backstory 179

    Chapter 16: The Archivist 185

    Chapter 17: The Courthouse 195

Chapter 18: Serendipity Strikes in Cotton Valley, Alabama 201

Chapter 19: Six Degrees of Separation 211

PART III: WELCOME FAMILY TO THE TABLE 213

Chapter 20: Plan Your Family Gathering 215

Chapter 21: Zoom Call With Cousins 221

Chapter 22: Lessons Learned 223

Chapter 23: Epilogue 229

ACKNOWLEDGEMENTS 231

ABOUT THE AUTHOR 233

Published by Kathy Lynne Marshall 234

Appendix A – Itinerary Example 235

Appendix B – 3X Great-Grandfather? 237

Appendix C – Trip Questions Example 239

Appendix D – Family Tree Chart Examples 241

Appendix E – Explore DNA ThruLines 245

Appendix F – Keep a Daily Diary 247

Appendix G – Solving Your Mystery 249

BIBLIOGRAPHY 263

END NOTES 265

INTRODUCTION

Have you ever wanted to journey across cultures? Explore taboo conversations? Visit places that carry the mystique of adventure? Capture priceless memories? Contemplate the reconciliation of past wrongs and hurts?

This book is a follow-up to *The Marshall Legacy in Black and White* about my paternal Marshall ancestors from the Deep South. DNA testing opened the secrets to my tangled historical past and scores of genetic relatives who had family trees dating back 1,000 years in Europe.

Normally, I travel by myself to research the locations where my ancestors lived, then write a twenty-page photo book about the genealogy trip. But my May 2021 trek to Georgia and Alabama was unlike any other. Caucasian DNA Cousin Amy wanted to travel with me. What resulted were some "Welcome Family to the Table" events with Black and White relatives who share the Marshall surname.

Imagine feeling free to ask family members whose skin tone and thinking differ from yours, questions about their lives, loves, and dreams. Breaking bread together at a meal and finding common ground can lead to a productive experience.

Oh? Are you also interested in taking a genealogy trip to your ancestral homelands? Well, this book presents snapshots of our journey and includes a plethora of *Lessons Learned*, as well as 16 steps that can help you structure a similar event for your family.

Part I invites you to tour Georgia with us as we trace the migration of our common Marshall ancestors. Part II explores Alabama, to illuminate the lives of my ancestors in Tuskegee after slavery expired. Part III contains several tools people can use to plan their own genealogy trip, family reunion, or Welcome to the Table affair.

Don't you think it's time to broaden our understanding of each other and write our communal stories? The ancestors are smiling!

PART I: GEORGIA

Highway 36, Talbot County, Georgia. 2021

Portrait by Margarita Chaplinska

Chapter 1: A Crazy Idea Forms

What is the scariest thing you've ever done? Jumped out of a plane? Gone scuba-diving with sharks? Hitchhiked at night in a foreign land? Mine was traveling 3,000 miles to Georgia and Alabama during a worldwide pandemic. Yep! In May 2021, I traveled there with a Caucasian descendant of my Black ancestor's slaveholders.

Amy and I visited plantations and courthouses. We compared family documents, laughed, cried, shared emotions, and even discussed taboo topics. We also met with other Black and White relatives to understand each other and our shared family history. Some genealogy circles call that type of racial healing a Coming to the Table[1] experience. Focused on racial healing, the group works toward truth-telling, liberation, and transformation.

Why take the health risk in my 60s? A passion for researching and writing family history, simple. I get goosebumps rummaging through old documents. I feel like Henry Louis Gates Jr. sleuthing facts about my ancestors' existence in the 1800s and earlier. It's a head rush to visit unknown places and chat with people who share the same joy of discovery. Why not take the chance while my brain is still healthy?

Over the past forty-five years, I picked up few hints about my paternal grandfather, Austin Henry Marshall; at most, enough stories to fill a one-page book. I needed to find his parents and grandparents, and what their lives were like. After decades of false starts and stops, I began *The Marshall Legacy in Black and White* on October 1, 2020. By 1900, an eight-year-old Austin was living with his grandparents at 618 Fifth Avenue in Columbus, Muscogee County, Georgia. His mother and four siblings lived there too. Where was his father?

It's embarrassing to admit I hadn't studied old maps of Georgia. I didn't realize Grandpa Austin's parents and paternal grandparents only lived twenty miles away in Talbot County in the 1800s.

Forty-five miles away, Grandpa Austin's mother and her parents were living in Tuskegee, Macon County, Alabama, in 1870. Ten years later, they were living in Columbus, Georgia.

> Lesson Learned #1: Examine old maps from the places where your family lived. County and state boundaries sometimes changed over the years. Even though your folks may have never moved, check adjacent county and state courthouses for official documents.

I uncovered no known free relatives in the 1860 Census. Therefore, I assumed we descended from enslaved people. It's hard to find documents that mention enslaved people by name, because they were treated like property. But extensive roots investigation produced a ton of word processing files, spreadsheets, family trees, inventories, and land deeds. But I stored them in a jumbled mess in boxes and digital files on my computer. Being disorganized kept me from creating plausible theories about my paternal lineage.

> Lesson Learned #2: Keep documents organized in one place, by family line, and chronologically by person within the family, so the information can be analyzed. Help the ancestral story shine through a structured approach to managing your genealogy records.

Lo-and-behold, the magic of DNA testing moved the pendulum from theory to proof. As the months ticked by, DNA revealed blood relatives whose ancestors also came from Talbot and Putnam in Georgia. Other relatives came from Macon County in Alabama. Genetic science took me further back in history than ever imagined. At last, I was getting somewhere with my research.

> Lesson Learned #3: Get yourself, your parents, eldest elders, and cousins DNA-tested NOW. This advice is critical for the descendants of enslaved people and adoptees. More than other groups, they know precious little about their family history. DNA, combined with traditional genealogical research, is a winning combination to unearth the ancestral story.

What? Our Marshall DNA matches were mainly with Caucasians who descended directly from our Marshall slave owners? Relatives who married those slaveholding Marshalls had surnames like Blount, Bunkley, Burt, Ligon, and Smith.

> Lesson Learned #4: Examine the documents of people who married into the family you're researching. Dowries often included enslaved people as gifts. Those records may be pertinent to your research.

The Elephant in the Room

Where's my deep chocolate sheen? For decades, the tinge of melanin in my sallow skin was unwanted. Now, I believe it might actually help me find my way-back ancestors. Caucasians had the power, influence, and education to write volumes about their lineage. Their family trees go back centuries. Identifying White ancestors might uncover blood relatives who fought in the Revolutionary War. Perhaps I could tack multiple generations onto my family tree. Maybe we could apply to the Daughters of the American Revolution (DAR). First, we must prove an unbroken lineage from me to a patriot.

Trust me, I had never aspired to join the DAR because of their past racist policies against minorities. But several respected Black women have fought to integrate that organization. Why not me, too? The lengthy approval process for other Black women is disappointing. But why not try for DAR?

Reaching out carefully, tentatively, I contacted White relatives met through DNA testing. I wanted to uncover our shared lineage. Sometimes African Americans wonder if the Euro American will hang up when the "slaves in the family" topic comes up. I rarely mention the "s" word until our third conversation. That gives me the chance to strike up a friendly dialogue about our shared heritage. The brass ring is glimpsing their historical documents before race becomes a potential stumbling block.

Thankfully, most of the White cousins I've met since 2016 have been nothing but gracious. In fact, when the topic finally pops up, it dismays some to learn their ancestors owned human beings. Some want to right past wrongs. I know my cousins weren't complicit in slavery. But I'm pleased as punch to help assuage their guilty feelings. You rub my back and I'll rub yours. It's a win-win.

My paternal family has no heartwarming stories about ancestors coming to America to become rich. We don't know of any genteel family members who owned plantations. My great-grandmothers didn't rock their days away in comfortable chairs or primp for cotillions and other social events. No, Honey. My Black family had to work six-and-a-half days a week! How did they survive so many hardships since 1619? That's when many historians feel slavers brought the first recorded Africans to the American colonies.[2]

I am the only one in my known family who has an undying passion to find the truth of our ancestral past. After retiring from a thirty-six-year career as a researcher, analyst, and technical writer for the California Highway Patrol, I was more than happy to take on the mantle of genealogist. I love being the guardian of our family history.

DAR, Here I Come!

Eddie was the first Caucasian Marshall relative who came across my radar. I jumped out of my chair when brother Greg's "Y-DNA" results became available in 2017. That's the Baby Daddy paternity test you hear about on smutty afternoon TV shows.

Eddie's Y-DNA proved he and my brother Greg shared 110 out of 111-markers, with one genetic distance. "What the heck does that mean?" In non-nerd English, it means there is a very close genetic relationship between my brother and Eddie. They could be as close as second cousins, sharing a great-grandparent, or as distant as fifth cousins sharing a four-times great-grandparent.[3]

I found no Marshall relatives past my great-great-grandfather, Samuel Marshall, who was born around 1830 in Putnam or Talbot,

Georgia. I was stuck behind a tall brick wall that obscured the magic answers. Exactly how were Eddie and my brother related?

I scheduled an appointment with a Family Search DNA expert after the 2021 RootsTech Genealogy Conference. Could he help prove a direct relationship to a patriot who fought in the American Revolution? Could DAR be in my future? The expert affirmed that Greg and Eddie's Y-DNA results should be all that's needed to prove our common Marshall patriot ancestor. But what was the name of the specific hero we shared? Sigh. DAR demands indisputable proof of lineage before they will consider opening their hallowed doors.

Eddie and I touch bases annually, but we could not find our familial connection… until March 2021. Slaveholder William Blount Marshall became my prime candidate for my family's owner and genetic ancestor.

William was born in 1796 in Halifax, North Carolina, and died in 1874 at the border of Talbot and Harris Counties, in Georgia. That's where my Great-grandpa, Henry A. Marshall, was born enslaved in about 1860.

Ancestry DNA confirms my family has over a dozen mainly White relatives who also have William B. Marshall, and/or his father, grandfather, and patriot great-grandfather in their family trees. Bingo! Did I finally hit the evidentiary jackpot?

Eddie's family tree contains a whopping fifty-six generations, thanks to his research diligence! It's easy to recognize our common ancestor as Captain John Marshall. John was born between 1710 and 1725 in Brunswick, Virginia. He died in 1782 in Mecklenburg, Virginia, a few years after his Revolutionary War service. I immediately called Eddie at work, excited with the news of our probable common ancestor. Laughter and cheers erupted from both ends of the phone. Thrilled beyond words, I plotted how to proceed on my DAR quest.

Chapter 2: Rona Rolls In

Most genealogy experts suggest visiting the courthouses, historical societies, and places where our ancestors lived, instead of just perusing online records from our comfortable homes. I normally plan a road trip for each of my heritage book projects. Those genealogy journeys are not cheap, each costing over $2,500 for plane tickets, hotel, car rental, and food for a week. The high cost is worth the knowledge gained.

There was an unexpected hitch with *The Marshall Legacy in Black and White* book project. "Rona"—also known as COVID-19, was large and in charge. The Coronavirus disease struck the world in late 2019 when reports of people dying started rolling in from Wuhan, China. Many in America dismissed the news as "China's problem" and life changed little in the United States.

Oblivious to the potential danger, my boyfriend, his daughter, and I took a fabulous five-day trip to Disneyworld in Florida, in late January 2020. It was kooky fun! But when we returned home, all news venues reported that tens of thousands were dying of the disease, and not just in China. Like AIDS in the 1980s, COVID started spreading to other countries. Older adults, and people who had severe underlying medical conditions, seemed to be at higher risk of developing serious complications and death.

What does all that have to do with this book? I planned to give two presentations about writing family story books in March 2020. The unthinkable happened instead: America shut down. President Donald Trump[4] declared a national emergency because of the ongoing COVID-19 outbreak. Most air travel stalled, to quell further outbreaks from other countries. That meant no genealogy trip for me in 2020.

Governments implemented various mandates to increase safety, like staying home, wearing face masks in public, and staying at least six-feet away from others. "Social distancing" became our new normal. Many employees worked at home using their home computers. Children stayed home from school and used the internet for distance learning. The world had stopped turning.

The only exceptions to the mandates were essential workers like police, firefighters, medical professionals, and grocery store and restaurant workers.

Science saved the day. A few pharmacies developed new vaccines to combat the virus. In early December 2020, the President issued *Operation Warp Speed* to vaccinate 100 million people before March 2021. Healthcare workers and the country's at-risk over-sixty-five population received the first vaccinations.

When President Biden[5] took office in January 2021, about 400,000 Americans had already died and two million worldwide had passed away from COVID-19. People struggled emotionally, physically, and financially. I was no different. Panic attacks, difficulty breathing, and heart palpitations became my new normal. Visits to the hospital emergency room, a battery of tests, and heart monitors found no physiological cause.

Was my "COVID Stress" from fretting that I was too young to get a COVID vaccination? Or was it sweating my July first editing deadline for *The Marshall Legacy in Black and White*? Or that I hadn't proven answers to my genealogy questions? Blah, blah, blah.

Scared and miserable, willing myself to believe the symptoms were all in my head, I convinced my brain to return to my normal positive, energetic self. Promising myself to relax after I published the *Marshall* book and pledged to skip the 2022 book project.

What? The airlines were opening their full flights to travelers in March 2021? You know what that means… ROAD TRIP!

> Lesson Learned #5: When the ancestors want their stories told, they will pave the way for you to get the job done, come sleet, or snow, or COVID plight! Their mandate is for you to do the research, writing, printing, and distributing their stories, no matter what.

Chapter 3: Road Trip!

I still had seven weeks to go before sending *The Marshall Legacy in Black and White* manuscript to my editor. Many credible theories rattled around in my head. But I still had not proven who the slaveholder was, nor who my great-great-great-grandparents were. Those were major goals for the book. A trip to Georgia and Alabama might reveal the needed facts. I craved to experience where my ancestors lived in the 1800s. I wanted to finish that book.

The remarkable breakthroughs in vaccinations allowed people like me—between fifty and sixty-five—to get vaccinated. I scored a blessed appointment at Kaiser Hospital's vaccination clinic on April 1, my mother's birthday. I got the second shot on April 22. Yay! Like the Grinch who stole Christmas, a glimmer of an idea crept into my brain. It caused me to grin from ear to ear. Maybe I *could* take a genealogy trip after all.

I assembled an itinerary of places and people to visit in Putnam, Talbot, and Muscogee Counties. I emailed the draft itinerary to some of my Marshall cousins. A few of them were the Caucasian sons and daughters of my ancestor's owners. Other cousins were the mixed-race progeny of those same planter Marshalls.

> Lesson Learned #6: Develop an itinerary of the places and people you want to visit on your genealogy trip (Appendix A). Ensure you determine the hours of operation and availability of venues. Schedule appointments before the visit. Share your plans with family. Maybe they'll want to join you on the trip, or supply ideas for more places to visit.

Guess what? A few of those cousins wanted to go with me to Georgia or share a meal with me. This was becoming an experience I'll call a "Welcome to the Table" event. Thrilled with that possibility, my heart flooded with adrenaline.

Date	Day	Where Activity	Open hours	Address & Phone
May 23	Sun	Delta 783 Sacramento to Atlanta	7AM Takeoff	SMF, 6900 Airport Blvd, Sac, CA 95837
May 23	Sun	Pickup Dollar Rental car #J75516101A0	3:15 PM	2300 Rental Pkwy, College Pk, GA
May 23	Sun	**Meet with cousin Eddie at Holiday Inn**	5 PM?	520 John B. Wilson Court, Lawrenceville, GA
May 23	Sun	Spend the Night at Julie's		Lawrenceville GA 30045
May 24	Mon	Pick up Amy. Drive 68 miles SE to Eatonton.	9:30 AM	520 John B. Wilson Court, Lawrenceville, GA
May 24	Mon	**Meet with cousin James Marshall**	11:00 AM?	104 Church Street, Eatonton, Putnam, GA
May 24	Mon	Drive to Eatonton County Clerk: plat, slaves	8:00-5:00 PM	100 South Jefferson Ave, Eatonton, GA
May 24/26	Mon	Find Marshall plantation site on Hwy 36		Bluff Springs Church & Marshall plantation site.
May 24	Mon	Drive to Hampton Inn	6:00 PM?	Hampton Inn, 7390 Bear Lane, Columbus, GA
May 25	Tues	Explore Talbotton courthouse **Vault**: deeds	9:30-5 appt	26 S. Washington Ave, Talbotton, GA, 31827
May 26	Weds	After lunch, chat with **Michael Buckner.**	1-4 PM?	Fielders Mill Road, Junction City, GA
May 26	Weds	Visit Waverly Hall cemetery		Highway 208, east of US-27, west of Talbotton
May 27	Thurs	Visit Marshall home in Columbus, GA		1710 Fifth Ave. Columbus, GA
May 27	Thurs	Visit 6th Ave. Train Station?		6th Ave and 10th Street, Columbus, GA
May 27	Thurs	Visit St. James AME Church Archives	Closed 1-2 PM	1002 Sixth Ave, Columbus, 706-322-8043
May 27	Thurs	**Early dinner with cousins**	2 PM	BoneFish, Veterans Parkway, Columbus, GA
May 27	Thurs	Leave Amy at Holiday Inn hotel		7336 Bear Lane, Columbus, GA, 31909
May 27	Thurs	Drive to Hampton Inn w/ Clevlyn?	6 PM?	2430 S. College St., Auburn AL 36832
May 28	Friday	Meet with Dana Chandler at Tuskegee	9:30:00 AM	1200 W. Montgomery Road, Tuskegee, AL
May 28	Friday	Visit Butler Chapel AME Zion Church & Zion		1002 N Church St, Tuskegee, AL 36083
May 28	Friday	Macon County Courthouse		101 E. Rosa Parks Ave. Ste. 300, Tuskegee, AL
May 29	Sat	Drive back to Lawrenceville, GA	2.5 hour trip	
May 30	Sun	DL 912 ATL to SLC, Res #F9JPS5	6:19-8:25 PM	6000 N Terminal Pkwy, Atlanta, GA

    I purchased airline tickets from Sacramento, California, to Atlanta, Georgia, for May 23, returning on May 30, 2021. I prepaid for a Dollar Rental Car with my Express Membership. That would allow me to go straight to the car lot, instead of standing in a long line of possibly sick people. My maternal cousin Julie, near Atlanta, invited me to spend the night. Voilà! The plan came together within a couple of hours.

Questions about the Marshall lineage

Person to ask	Day	Questions about the Marshall lineage
Eddie Marshall	May 23	What kind of family stories had you heard about growing up within 200 miles of our first Marshall ancestor?
Eddie Marshall	May 23	Did you only do the Y-DNA test with FTDNA? Tested with other company?
Eddie Marshall	May 23	Have you messaged other Y-DNA matches to find the common ancestor, like the one who has George Abner Marshall?
Eddie Marshall	May 23	Do you know which CHRs are for the Marshall line?
James Marshall	May 24	Who are your up-line Marshalls?
James Marshall	May 24	Some bios say William B. Marshall was a judge. Where would one go for higher education in Warren or Putnam?
James Marshall	May 24	Is the Farm Book and ANY mentions of slaves available from the Stephen B. Marshall (Sr. and Jr.) estate available?
James Marshall	May 24	Is there a plat map available for Stephen B. Marshall & Peter F Mahone?
James Marshall	May 24	Do you know what William B. Marshall looked like? Likely he had a gray beard?
James Marshall	May 24	What type of crops were grown in Putnam in the 1820s?
James Marshall	May 24	Was Tony Marshall's ancestor, John Marshall, the last son of David G. Marshall, born in about 1785? Is that why he moved Rebecca Burt to Putnam in 1810?
Michael Buckner	May 26	Where's Marshall plantation? Hwy 36 and Sarah Marshall Rd. Why Sarah?
Michael Buckner	May 26	Trying to figure out why my great uncles were named Wright, Searcy, Austin.
Michael Buckner	May 26	Any info about Marshall slaves? When did they leave? Any still here?
Michael Buckner	May 26	He said corn was planted for livestock. How much?
Michael Buckner	May 26	He said where the pines now are it used to be cotton.
Michael Buckner	May 26	Is there a sample of a grist mill left? Is there a sample of a cotton field left? Is there a sample of a cotton gin? Look at his pottery?
Michael Buckner	May 26	Was William B was in Talbot with indians? 1833? How long to build a house?
Michael Buckner	May 26	Did he say in 1860 there were 16,000 people? What proportion were slaves?
Michael Buckner	May 26	Said little towns disappeared when RR came, like O'Neals and Rough Edge?
Michael Buckner	May 26	Show plat map. What was planted where? Which sons given which plots?

Lesson Learned #7: Develop specific questions to ask local experts and notify them before your trip so they may have answers available during your visit (Appendix C).

Sign Up the Players

Lo-and-behold, DNA Cousin Amy Peacock, wanted to join me on the Georgia portion of my trip! We had chatted online for a year but had never met face-to-face. She would fly into Atlanta from her Utah home. Then DNA Cousin Eddie Marshall agreed to meet with me and Amy. He lived near Lawrenceville, where my maternal cousin Julie lived, and provided me a home for a few nights.

I emailed paternal Marshall Cousin Jocelyn to see if she could attend our party. Mixed-race Cousin Jennifer Owens agreed to share a meal with us at a restaurant in Columbus, Georgia. Black DNA Cousin Erika Thomas was a teacher living in Texas; she agreed to Zoom chat with us. White DNA Cousin Lori Ligon Hughes might meet us in Putnam, Georgia. The plan jelled quickly.

I emailed the Putnam Historical Society about my impending visit, asking for information about the Stephen B. Marshall family and their forced workers. The president, James Marshall, was more than happy to entertain my visit on Monday, May 24. *Marshall? Could we be related?*

Clevlyn Anderson is a cousin related to my paternal Grandma Daisy Dooley Marshall. Clevlyn wanted to join me in Alabama to meet with Dana Chandler, an archivist at Tuskegee Institute. He might help me find information about my Smith and Ligon great-great-grandparents, who lived in Tuskegee in the mid-1860s.

Two days before the flight, I stumbled across a new cousin online. Tony Marshall said his family history expert was his cousin, Jennifer K. She lived in Northern Georgia and would surely want to visit with us in Putnam. I forwarded my itinerary for him to give to her.

It felt like one of those old-time black-and-white movies from the 1930s and 40s. Plucky young Judy Garland and Mickey Rooney proclaimed, "You can get the band. I'll set the stage. You can make the costumes. I'll get the tap shoes. Then we'll have a show of shows in no time at all!"

Serendipity happened months before. I contacted the Lazarus Straus Historical Society in Talbot County, GA. A representative put me in contact with Mr. Mike Buckner who reportedly knows everything about Talbot County. I contacted Mike right away, not knowing whether he'd be receptive to my slavery-related goals. We chatted for an hour on the telephone. Then he mailed me excerpts from *A Rockaway in Talbot*, the ultimate book about my ancestor's homeland.

It's important to place my 2021 trip to Georgia and Alabama in historical context. In 2016, America was more politically divided than ever. Conservative Republicans wanted to elect the unpredictable and charismatic Donald Trump as President. He was a powerful American media personality and business executive who amassed and lost fortunes several times. More of the southern and midwestern states supported Trump. They thought the hubbub about COVID-19 was fake news, that the outbreak was planned, that vaccines were poisonous, and that wearing face masks was unnecessary.[6]

More folks from the east and west coast states thought Trump was a Nationalist, racist, and misogynist. They feared he would turn back the clock on racial equality, combating climate change, and maintaining positive communications with other world leaders.

The opponent, Democrat Hillary Clinton, won the popular vote by three million votes. But somehow Trump garnered 77 more electoral votes, making him the de facto winner.[7] As President, he quickly reversed many of the strides Barack Obama[8]—the first African American President—made during his eight years in office.

During the 2020 election, the ever-popular Trump barely lost to Democrat Joseph Biden. The new leader picked Kamala Harris as his Vice-President. Harris was the first woman Vice President, and the daughter of East Indian and Jamaican immigrants.

The 2020 election resulted in two key seats in the Georgia Senate races switching from Republican to Democrat. That change resulted in nearly equal power in the U.S. Senate and ignited animosity toward Biden, especially in conservative states like Georgia and Alabama. Those angry feelings fomented what some believe was a terrorist attack on the Capitol on January 6, 2021 after a Pro-Trump rally.[9]

What does all that political stuff have to do with me and this book? Well, I didn't know what kind of reception I would receive in the contentious states of Georgia and Alabama. On past trips to the Deep South, friends warned me to be careful. They said southerners thought Californians were nutty liberals—the devil-incarnate, etc. So, a California girl had to be prepared for anything to happen. I could also catch COVID because of the low vaccination rates in those two states. I hemmed and hawed, but gathering information for the Marshall book outweighed the dangers.

I worried for no reason. Nearly every person I contacted in Georgia and Alabama was ready, willing, and able to help. They put me in touch with experts who were as sweet as Georgia peach pie. The ancestors were working overtime on my behalf. They wanted their stories told and they would teach us players how to win the genealogy game.

How Are We Related?

My overworked brain couldn't remember how those new cousins were related to me. I constructed a graph to help us visualize who our common ancestors were. I color-coded the names of living people and their DNA connections to me in the bottom row in the following chart. We should read the chart from the bottom up. It shows each generation from the present up to the top line, which shows our common ancestry.

My unproven brick wall ancestor is in the second column from the left. I'm not sure whether William (b. 1796) or Jesse (b. 1809) or Enslaved Sam (b. 1813) fathered my great-great-grandfather, Samuel Marshall, born in about 1830 in Talbot, GA. Appendix C has a sample chart you can use for your family relationships.

I emailed the chart to my cousins, asking them to correct any errors in the information. I wanted to prepare them to discuss our common ancestry.

Common Ancestor: Robert Marshall Sr. (1642-1698, Bedfordshire, England)						Not Descended from Robert Marshall Sr.			
John Joseph? Marshall & Sarah Malone (1661?-1728)	John Marshall & Sarah Malone (1695?-1733, Isle of Wight to Brunswick, VA)	John Marshall & Sarah Malone (1695-1733, Isle of Wight to Brunswick, VA)				?	William Ligon Jr. (1682-1764, VA)		
Capt John Marshall & Mary Malone (1725-1782)	Capt John Marshall & Mary Malone?(1725-1782)	Capt John Marshall & Mary Malone (1725-1782)				?	Joseph Ligon (1704-1752, VA)		
Benjamin Marshall Sr. (1745-1818, TN)	David G. Marshall? (1740-1784, Halifax, NC)	David G. Marshall (1740-1784, Halifax, NC) Amy's 6xGGF				?	Joseph Ligon (1725-1780, VA)		
Samuel Marshall (1785-1857)	Stephen B. Marshall? (1767-1831, Putnam) & Slave Hannah? (1781)	Lucy Marshall (1758-1829) & William Blount 1755-1825)	Stephen B. Marshall (1767,NC-1831,GA)			?	Henry Ligon (1773-1856, NC)		
Stephen B. Marshall? (1767-1831, Putnam) & Slave Hannah? (1781)	**William B. Marshall (1796) or Slave Sam (1813) or Jesse Marshall (1809)?**	Richard Blount (1790-1841) & Ruth	William B. Marshall (1796-1874) & Rosa Marshall			Henry Marshall (b. 1830) & Mariah Bunkley	Wm. Jasper Ligon (mulatto) (1830-1889, Talbot, GA)		
William B. Marshall (1796) or Slave Sam (1813) or Jesse Marshall (1809)?	**2x=Samuel Marshall (1830-?) & Mary Wilkinson or Emeline Bunkley**	William Blount (1823,GA-1884,TX) & Martha (1823-1870)	Albert Marshall & Clara Marshall			Annie Marshall & George Owen	Joseph A. Ligon (1881-1938, Talbot)		
2x=Samuel Marshall (1830-?) & Mary Wilkinson or Emeline Bunkley	1x Henry A. Marshall (or Austin Marshall?) & Mary Smith	Oliver Marshall Blount (1857,GA-1924,TX) Emma(1865-1900,TX)	Mariah Marshall & John Walton			Lizzie Mae Owens & ?	Charles A. Ligon (1911-2009)		
1x Henry A. Marshall (or Austin Marshall?) & Mary Smith	Austin H. Marshall & Daisy Dooley	John F. Blount (1888-1969, TX) & Dora (1897-1981)	Walker Carter & Amelia Walton			Private	Private		
Austin H. Marshall & Daisy Dooley	Thomas Marshall & Mary Carter	Emma Blount & John Lyles	Private						
Thomas Marshall & Mary Carter	Private								
Private									
EDDIE__ Y-DNA to Greg 110/111	**KATHY,** Greg, Carrie, Pershell, Austin, Jocelyn, Lori, Michal, Carolyn, Matthew	**AZMINA,** 11 cM to KM	**AMY__** 4.1 cM to KM	**JP** & Nancy descend from Mathew Marshall and Rhoda		**ERIKA__** 6.9 cM to KM	**JENNIFER O**	**LORI,** 8 cM (to KM)	**LESLYE'S** Amanda Ligon Wood Boyd match Kathy's 2XGGM Laura Ligon
Tony & Jennifer K from Benjamin Marshall									

For 33 of my 36 years working for the California Highway Patrol, I developed and analyzed charts and graphs, and prepared research reports and other written outputs. Those robotic skills facilitate the deductive work needed for genealogy. Yet, normal people don't gush over charts like a dog with a juicy bone. In fact, their eyes glaze over at the mere mention of statistics.

I would soon learn that my genealogy trip would be less about data, and more about feelings, stories, perceptions, and dialog. Embracing that simplified trajectory helped all of us enjoy the process more.

> Lesson Learned #8: A genealogy trip with a Welcome to the Table twist doesn't have to be all about charts and graphs. It could be more about sharing family stories and exploring new feelings. It encourages people to examine new perceptions about how different people navigate their existence.

Y-DNA testing proves there are over a dozen blood ancestors who have Stephen B. Marshall in their family trees (Appendix D). Did that mean his son, William Marshall, was not only our slaveholder but also my three-times great-grandfather? Or was my direct-line ancestor one of William's brothers or uncles?

Does my brother Greg's Y-DNA match to Eddie Marshall cinch the deal that Eddie's two-times great-grandfather, Jesse Marshall, was also my two-times great-grandfather, Samuel's, father? Is your head spinning with the complexity? Mine is!

DNA testing confirms my blood relatives are Eddie, Amy, Erika, Azmina, Lori, and Leslye. I had hoped more Marshall relatives would take a DNA test in the future to help lend more proof of our relationships. My wish was partially answered during a Christmas visit to Hawaii to visit my grandchildren. My son and his wife agreed to DNA test their family, adding to the number of Marshalls whose genetic material could be compared to others in the Ancestry.com and 23andme.com databases.

Chapter 4: Sunday - The Journey Begins

Soaring like a mama eagle over the iron-hued Rockies, my radar honed onto a golden nugget. It glistened next to the turquoise river frothing through the gorge far below. Adrenaline pumping through my white-tipped wings, I dove like a rocket from the clouds onto my prey, talons grasping the tiny object. Without missing a beat, a rush of wind buoyed me back up to my perch atop a massive spruce tree on the hillside. I shed my feathered coat, then lowered myself with the grace of a yogi into my cozy nest. I opened my claw hand to examine the treasure. A golden mirror reflected my image, and that of another woman floating next to me. We smiled at each other with the knowledge of ages.

My musical alarm woke me at 5:05 a.m. in Sacramento, California, on May 23, 2021. I was still basking in the glow of that joyful dream. Perhaps it was a sign that everything would go well today. I got dressed, ate my favorite peanut crunch cereal, brushed my teeth, then placed a maroon silk cap over my braided silver hair.

Energized to begin today's adventure, I grabbed my suitcase containing eight days of clothes, snacks, and sundry items. A matching maroon Rick Steves hiking bag contained an iPhone, iPad, wallet, notepad, ink pens, and a one-inch, three-ring binder containing genealogy documents and my itinerary.

My boyfriend drove me to the Sacramento International Airport Terminal A, arriving at 5:45 a.m. He was worried about me catching the contagion on the plane but could not dissuade stubborn me from my plans. His kiss goodbye was passionate, and he reminded me to be careful every minute that I was away from him. How sweet… I put on my African-print cloth mask, slipped the bag's shoulder strap over my head, and pulled my purple carryon suitcase behind me.

I turned left inside the oh-so-familiar airport building, my doorway to world travel since the 1970s. As I rode the escalator, I admired colorful bird sculpture art installations sparkling through the glass windows in the bright morning light. I breezed through the Transportation Security Administration's pre-check screening line. "TSA-Pre"—which essentially was an $80 background check good for five years—expedites the usually invasive security clearance process implemented in U.S. airports after the terrorist attack on September 11, 2001. I glanced at the long security line for regular passengers, glad I did not have to remove liquids or the electronic devices from my bags or take off my shoes or jacket. Mine was a stress-free security check experience.

A large electronic monitor, descending from the ceiling at the end of the security line, contained departure gate information; mine was gate A-12. I purchased a bottle of water and a "Sacramento" souvenir mug at a gift shop before making my way to an empty table in "restaurant row." Retrieving cables from a special pouch in my hiking bag, I plugged in my iPhone and iPad into a nearby socket. I wanted to charge them for my four-hour, non-stop flight to Atlanta, Georgia. I only had forty-five minutes to wait before it was time to stand in the Delta Air "Comfort Plus" line. I felt confident that everything would proceed as scheduled.

Simultaneously, sitting in a plane 652 miles away at the Salt Lake City Airport, a five-foot, five-inch blond woman, who looked younger than her years, sent a text message saying her flight would be two hours late. That could put a serious wrench in our plans.

My newfound cousin, Amy Peacock, would join me in Atlanta for a genealogy romp through Georgia. Amy and I had only corresponded via email, but never met before then. We would be together for four days and three nights in Georgia, sleeping in the same hotel room, traveling in the same car. This trip to find our common ancestor would start up north in Gwinnett County, Georgia. Then we would travel to central-east Putnam County, then Central-west Talbot and Harris Counties. Our trip together would end in Muscogee County, along the Chattahoochee River, which bordered Alabama. Then I would explore Tuskegee, Alabama, on my own, for an additional few days.

What would happen when the Caucasian descendant of a Marshall slave owner (Amy) traveled through racially divided Georgia with a descendant of that slaveholder's enslaved African American *property* (me, Kathy)? As our planes barreled down their respective airstrips, my mind raced ahead to the interesting journey that awaited us. Would we cousin-strangers get along? Could we connect the dots to our specific lineage? Should we broach taboo discussions about race, religion, and politics while traveling together? Might we find common ground as Americans with differing backgrounds? That's exactly what we intended to determine. The best laid plans...

A Comedy of Errors

After landing at the Hartsfield-Jackson Atlanta International Airport, I maneuvered my carryon luggage to the airlines Sky Train tram. Staring out the windows, I enjoyed a scenic, five-minute ride to the Rental Car Center. It was a beautiful day in May with clear blue skies, albeit eighty-percent humidity and eighty-five degrees.

Leaving the tram, I followed signs which lead downstairs to the Dollar Rental Car office. I smiled at the forty-or-so people who had to stand in a long line to get their cars. I was a cherished "Dollar Express" member. That meant I got to go directly to the car garage, pick up my paperwork and car, then drive away carefree. Just to be sure, though, I asked a guy whether I had to stand in that long Dollar line even though I had already prepaid.

"No Ma'am." He pointed down the hall. "Cross the foot bridge to the car garage across the street."

Following his instructions, I left the crowd behind. But I neglected to ensure the man knew what he was talking about.

I crossed the footbridge leading to a darkened garage containing vehicles from various rental car companies. Hmm, the Dollar kiosk, where I retrieved my rental paperwork at other airports, was empty. In fact, there were no cars at all on the Dollar lot. *That's strange.* I maneuvered my wheeled suitcase toward the Hertz car lot, because

I heard Hertz had purchased Dollar. Nobody was inside that kiosk either. My "Spidey Sense"[10] was alerted.

I asked a garage worker wearing a Hertz emblem on his shirt to direct me to the Dollar Express line. He asked where my paperwork was, and I explained why I had none. The Express pickup process I used at other airports was to come directly to the car lot. He looked at the confirmed receipt stored in my iPhone, which proved I had indeed paid for a compact car. I guess I had an honest face because he readily gave me car keys to a silver Ford Fiesta.

He advised, "Just drive to the exit kiosk on the first floor. They'll scan the barcode from the confirmation email, then you'll be on your way." It seemed fishy. I had no paperwork. I willed myself to be calm, like my cool-as-a-cucumber younger son, Matthew, always appears. I willed myself to believe all would be well. I willed my heart to stop its scary, uneven pitter-patter.

Yay! Amy's flight had somehow come in on time after all. She text-messaged me that she had already picked up her luggage at the baggage claim and was headed toward the Rental Car Center. It's possible that everything would be alright, after all. I drove toward the stairs where Amy would descend from the Sky Train, so she could easily see me and *our* rental car.

Cousins Amy and Kathy meet for the first time in the Atlanta, Georgia, airport. May 23, 2021.

What a welcome we had! We hugged and laughed and hugged again, meeting at long last after sharing so many genealogy-related emails over the past year. We took selfie photographs, unmasked for a moment, then got her gigantic blue suitcase settled into the trunk next to my puny purple one. I drove us toward the exit kiosk, as instructed by the garageman. Oh no! There was a long line of cars inching forward lke caterpillars along a descending ramp, all waiting to exit the Rental Car Center. After ten or fifteen minutes of pleasant conversation, we arrived at the checkout spot.

"Where's your paperwork?" the gruff Exit Guy demanded, frowning when I explained the sequence of events. "You're not going anywhere in this car without paperwork."

Dread washed over my already damp brow. He directed me to re-park the car in the lot, stand in the long line to get the required documents, then come back through the lengthy exit line again. Frustrated, tired, and thirsty, I felt extremely embarrassed to involve Amy in this terrible chain of events. We needed that car, so I had to make things right. The next two hours would be a noir comedy of errors.

As instructed, I drove back up the long, narrow exit ramp, against downward flowing traffic. Back in the car lot, I parked near the base of the stairs where Amy and I first saw each other. Amy waited in the vehicle in that dark, stuffy garage. I took the car keys to prove to Dollar employees that I already had a car issued to me. I stood in two separate long lines—first at Hertz, then at Dollar. Don't ask.

Why were there only two attendants checking us in? There were at least forty impatient, unhappy people waiting in line. I felt like I was at Disneyland without a "Fast Pass," where four lines of impatient patrons stood, separated by heavy ropes, inching forward one after the other, moving one foot every few minutes. Arghh! Why couldn't I have rented a Budget car? There was no line there. I periodically messaged Amy when forty, then thirty, then twenty, then ten people were in front of me. Everyone in line was seething at the inefficiency of this crazy process. And guess what I learned from chatting with my angry compatriots? Everyone had prepaid and scheduled a pickup time for their vehicle, just like me.

Finally, there was only one person before me: a well-coiffed, Black woman in a conservative blue suit. She was having a verbal war with the tall, ebony male attendant. All of us in line could hear the conversation. It was shocking how rude he was to her, and she to him. When it was my turn, I struggled to keep my cool when the same rental car clerk accused me of intentionally being sneaky and purposely skipping the paperwork line. He even threatened to take back my car keys and make me wait an hour until they could ready another vehicle for rental.

After he checked my account on his computer, though, he suddenly changed his tune.

"You should have come directly to me to get your car," he scolded.

C'mon now, man. There was no way all those angry people would have let me crash the line. They had paid in advance, just like me. While I felt his contrite admission vindicated me, it did nothing to lighten my mood. I could only think about poor Amy, who had been waiting in that hot garage for over two hours. She trusted I had everything under control, having seen my detailed itinerary and scholarly explanations of our lineage. What an auspicious start to my carefully planned trip. I hoped this would be the only rough spot during our adventure.

> Lesson Learned #9: Ensure that you fully understand the car rental process for your destination airport. Practices may differ from place to place. Also, ensure that the people who provide you with information actually know what they're talking about. Bottom line: I will never use Dollar Rental Car again.

We were finally on our way at 5:30 p.m., two-and-one-half hours later than planned. The car air conditioning was running at full blast to combat the mugginess of an Atlanta afternoon in May. Amy inputted the address for the Holiday Inn Express in Lawrenceville into her smart phone Map App, and off we went. I was hot, tired, frazzled, and desperately thirsty, but relieved when we were finally on our way to Amy's hotel. I apologized repeatedly. Ultimately, it was all my fault for not knowing the Atlanta airport didn't honor Dollar Express' quick check-in. After a swig from my tepid water bottle, I relaxed a smidgen.

I guess I relaxed too much, missing the turnoff, and having to circle back around to the correct exit. That mistake would happen many times during our journey of discovery.

Dear reader, I do many things very well, but I am directionally challenged. A testament to Amy's forgiving nature and positive personality is that she handled this horrible first meeting with grace, assuring me that everything would be fine. Thankfully, she is also a delightful conversationalist, so the forty-five-minute trip to her hotel passed quickly.

Cousin Eddie

Amy and I had planned on meeting cousin Eddie at Amy's hotel at 5:00 p.m. He was another Marshall descendant who wasn't aware his ancestors owned human beings (see Chapter 13). His and my brother Greg's Y-DNA confirmed that my paternal Black family descends from Caucasian Marshalls from Europe.

As the car rental snafu escalated to Herculean proportions, I attempted to call Eddie to delay our meeting time. That's when I discovered I only had his work email and phone number. Hmm, Eddie had not responded to any recent messages about our dinner meeting. What happened? He had been so gung-ho about meeting with me and Amy. Did I misread his interest? Did the knowledge that he had Black relatives discolor his desire to meet with me? Days later, I learned Eddie and his family had contracted COVID. He had been on sick leave for weeks and hadn't seen the last few messages I had sent.

> Lesson Learned #10: Ensure that you have multiple ways to contact your relatives, such as cell and home phone numbers, email, home address, Ancestry account name, Facebook page, Instagram, etc.

Maternal Cousins to the Rescue

Depositing Amy at her hotel Sunday night, I drove to my maternal cousin Julie's house, twenty-five minutes away. By then, I felt like something the cat dragged in, zapped physically and emotionally. Breakfast was long past, and the two packages of almonds and cookies from the plane had not kept my hunger at bay. The three cups of water I had during that epic trip hadn't thwarted dehydration either.

My dear cousin offered me barbecued hamburgers, which I cut into chunks to top a fresh salad. I guzzled many glasses of cool water to rehydrate my body and brain. We chatted for a couple of hours, but my eyes drooped, and my synapses struggled to fire coherently. After a challenging eighteen-hour day, I said goodnight, showered, got clothes out for the next day, wrote a few pages in my trip journal, then fell into a deep sleep in their oh-so-comfy bed. My eagle dream started up again with Amy and me soaring through Georgia, meeting new relatives, and finding exciting clues to our shared heritage.

> Lesson Learned #11: Keep a daily diary of your adventures (sample in Appendix E). Describe your feelings and emotions, sights, sounds, and smells, as you found places where your family lived, or documents that contained family information. Typing your notes into a computer, laptop, or smartphone every day, instead of writing them longhand, saves you from having to retype them later. Use the photographs you took during the day to refresh the memory of your experiences. Most of all, enjoy the journey.

Chapter 5: Monday in Putnam

I awoke at 7:45 a.m. in a warm bed at Cousin Julie's house. It was Monday, May 24, 2021. Golden beams of light poured through slits in the white Venetian blinds, casting a cheery glow in her guest bedroom. This sunny greeting quelled my anxiety about today's hefty itinerary of driving, meeting with a history expert, then more hours behind the wheel.

That first full day in Georgia, I wore my most professional, short-sleeve flowered blouse over utilitarian-gray-cargo pants. We planned to meet with the President of the Putnam Historical Society.

While eating an efficient protein bar breakfast, Julie and I chatted about the day's plans. After brushing my teeth and applying lipstick, I packed the hiking bag and suitcase into my silver chariot. Plugging my iPhone into the car's sync socket, the Maps app connected to the car's navigation system.

Oh! I just received an email from James (Jim) Marshall, our expert guide for the day. He wanted to change our meeting place. I plugged the new coordinates into the navigation system: 114 N. Madison, Eatonton, Putnam County, Georgia. Cousin Amy and I were going to view the places where our common ancestor-slave-owner, Stephen Blount Marshall, lived from 1813 until his death in 1831.

Julie suggested I travel on local roads instead of the often-congested Highway 316. That preferred driving route appeared on a monitor in the car's dashboard. Siri[11] would tell me exactly when and where to turn on that circuitous route. The roads were winding and bounded by lush vegetation—almost like driving through England's tall hedgerows. I would never have been able to follow a paper map to get me to Amy's Holiday Inn hotel by 9:00 a.m. Thank goodness for technology!

"How was your room, Amy?" I asked when she came to the car with her suitcase.

She responded, "It was great. We get lots of perks with our Holiday Inn Express account. The rooms are always clean and contain helpful amenities, like a coffee pot, refrigerator and microwave, and there's a free breakfast. All reasons that keep us coming back."

Once we packed her large suitcase in the trunk, we buckled up and prepared to begin our day's escapade.

Amy is a talkative, upbeat person who uses lots of friendly emojis[12] in her emails and text messages. 😊 That gives people the impression she's always happy. Her lilting, emotive voice matches a smile that comes easily to her face. When she laughs, her eyes and nose crinkle. Family is everything to Amy, and she maintains close contact with her husband, children, and grandchildren every day. Her skin is pale and delicate, covered with a makeup containing sunscreen, which she applies a few times every day. Her straight, shoulder-length, honey-blond hair reminded me of the White girls on my school bus who could whip their hair around with a toss of their head.

I am olive-skinned with frizzy gray-white hair that becomes wavy with the application of a handful of hair lotion. My hair doesn't move much when I flick my head from side to side. I am five-feet six-inches tall in the morning, after a good night's sleep elongates my spine. There is little left of my once award-winning bodybuilder physique. I love speaking with people about genealogy or anything mechanical or creative. Otherwise, I am mostly a loner, preferring to research, write these heritage books, create steel-and-clay art sculptures, cultivate my vegetable garden, or work out in the gym. My sons and family speak irregularly, and more often via text and email rather than on the phone. But there are plenty of hugs and laughter when we get together. I am a focused, goal-oriented, cheerful person who has a self-imposed mandate to find out as much as possible about my Black and White Marshall ancestors. I shall publish this seventh book in March 2022.

Jim sounded so proper on the phone that I didn't know what to expect when we finally met. Hence, the reason I wore my best shirt that day. I needn't have worried. Jim met us at the "Bronson building" in the center of the county seat of Eatonton. He surprised me by wearing cute, pleated khaki shorts. He sported a short-sleeve plaid shirt tucked inside the waist. I instantly felt at ease. Jim is the President of the Putnam Historical Society, which is renovating that impressive white-columned structure. The placard out front describes its 1816 "Eagle Tavern Inn" origins. Over the years, the building had been a dentist's office, hotel, boarding house, private residence, and seven separate apartments, before the Historical Society bought it in 1985. It is now their headquarters.

Typical of a Greek Revival facade, it had five immense, fluted, white columns spaced evenly on the front porch which supported an overhanging roof. There were four windows on the second floor, and four on the first, which were bordered by black shutters. Five variegated-red-brick steps led up to the double-wide front door. It was beautiful if you like antebellum plantation homes. Inwardly, I always shudder at the ill-treatment often foisted upon our Black ancestors in those pristine edifices.

Jim proudly invited us inside to view their masterpiece being renovated. I needed a moment to assess the lavish foyer with its navy-blue and taupe patterned rug, under a hefty four-foot square table. A handsome flower arrangement of coleus, ferns, and ivy topped the table. Various chairs, a side table, and a floor lamp sat below three framed pictures hanging on the salmon-colored wallpaper. Four columns separated the foyer from the staircase and first-floor hallway. Despite it's age, it did not smell musty.

As happens each time I visit a former plantation house, the walls seem to whisper their secrets to me:

> *That's the hallway where Master fondled Sally's behind. Young Master spit on Yellow Bob from the top of those stairs. Mistress slapped Susie for taking too long to bring the sweet tea. Every day, it was humiliation after humiliation.*

Honestly, it is not my intent to sully the reputation of that beautiful building. I don't know whether any of those coarse behaviors happened on this property. It's just how I feel walking through these edifices from the antebellum, master-slave period. Plenty of slave narratives vividly tell of their experiences that shock the imagination.

Amy and I followed Jim into the salon on the left. Period sofas, loveseats, chairs, a piano, portraits on the wall, and a huge cranberry rug teased our eyes.

That Jim certainly knows how to break the ice! He held up a pair of crotchless ladies' bloomers and explained how women in the mid-1800s could relieve themselves. As a woman writer who finds bodily function details priceless, considering the layers of petticoats they expected ladies to wear, I loved his discussion about enameled chamber pots, pot chairs, and outhouses for guests. It helped me write Chapter 18 in *The Marshall Legacy in Black and White* manuscript, which I was preparing for my editor at that time.

"Say, Jim, how are you related to us?" Amy wanted to know.

Jim began reciting his family ties. "I come from a fellow known as 'John of the Forest' who died in 1752 in Essex County, Virginia. He was the son of Martha Jane Sherwood and Thomas Marshall." *Hmm... the same Sherwood Forest of Robin Hood fame?*

"Thomas was the son of Captain John Marshall—called 'The Immigrant'—who was born in Ireland in 1596. My direct ancestor was Mathew—with one 'T'— who came to Georgia in 1755. He applied to the Royal Governor in 1767 for headright grants,[13] which was a way they encouraged people to come into Georgia and settle. Then there was an Allen Marshall who got land in Talbot County and set up shop there." *What? Talbot? Where my great-grandfather was likely born?* "I descend from his son," Jim ended.

Whew! That was a mouthful! Amy and I looked at each other as if to say, "Did you follow all of that?" Thankfully, I had recorded some of the conversation on my iPhone. Later, I determined Jim, Amy, and I descend from that same "The Immigrant" John Marshall, through his son Robert Marshall, who was born in 1642 in Bedfordshire, England.

We ambled to the loveseat. Jim had set a framed color map of Putnam County, dated 1878, on the cushion. He showed us where

Stephen B. Marshall's house and the "Marshall Shoals" property were.

Jim's left index finger pointed to our current Bronson House location, and his right pointed to the Marshall property. He gave me a copy of the map to take home. We were soon to learn he had an interesting adventure planned for us.

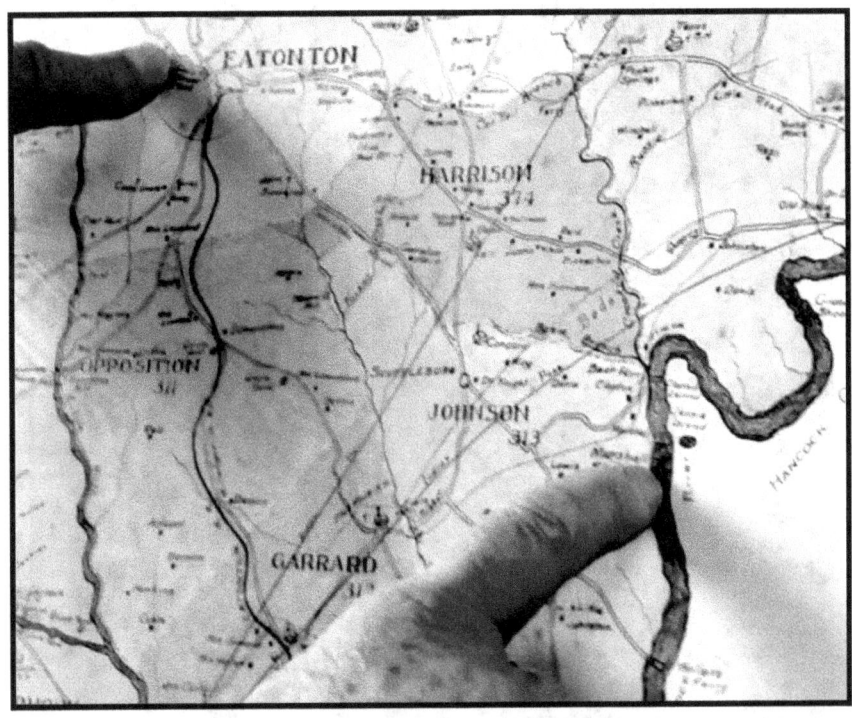

1878 Map of Putnam County, GA

Next, Jim pulled out a list of Putnam County marriages, Stephen B. Marshall's family tree, and a list of the Marshall, Blount, and Reid families buried in the Pine Grove Cemetery. Amy came from the Blount family, so her ears perked up. I recognized "Reid" as being a name possibly associated with my two-times great-grandmother, Laura Ligon, whom I would research in Tuskegee, Alabama that Friday.

Inside the Bronson House in Eatonton, headquarters for the Putnam County Historical Society, GA.

Another Marshall Cousin Surfaces

A few days before the trip to our Georgia homeland, I received a response to an Ancestry.com message I had sent to Tony Marshall, a cousin I met online. He had some of the same White Marshalls from Virginia in his family tree. When I revealed I'd be visiting Georgia the following Monday, he promised to notify his cousin, Jennifer K., of my impending visit. He bragged she had tons of Marshall family information stored in her brain. I gave him the meeting location in Putnam for him to pass along to his knowledgeable cousin.

About forty-five minutes after Amy and I started chatting with Jim in the imposing Bronson House, a buxom woman, wearing a delightful white and olive-green tie-die shirt, burst into the salon while we were looking at the 1878 map of Putnam County. Boisterous Jennifer was happy to finally speak with Jim. She said she had tried to contact him several times in the past with questions about her family, but without success. Now, she felt free to discuss her many questions about her family lines with our expert, distant cousin, Jim.

Inside, I must admit to a rather petty feeling, wanting Jim to get back to my questions. After all, I had traveled across the country to meet with him. Jennifer lived in Georgia and could visit anytime. *Calm down, Girl, your mama taught you to share.* Once Jim revealed where Jennifer's grandfather had lived in Eatonton, she felt mollified and ready to learn more about our common ties.

An Unexpected Road Trip

During our short time at the Bronson house, I took lots of photographs and videos to help me describe what might have been similar furnishings in the Marshall's plantation homes. Then the four of us piled into Jim's SUV, me up front, and Amy and Jennifer in back.

Eatonton is a beautiful town. Renovated antebellum homes gleamed behind greener-than-green landscaped yards. Jim knew the history of each building, and had helped their physical renovation, including bricklaying and wood working. Evidently, he and his wife are not only interested in history but are also capable restoration stewards. Impressive!

Jim drove us to the Pine Grove Cemetery in Eatonton. Section #1 housed three generations of White men named Stephen Blount Marshall (died 1831, d. 1864, and d. 1898). There were about a dozen of their Marshall descendants buried under the trees. Amazingly, there was no headstone for the family patriarch, Stephen B. Marshall, who was born in 1767 in Halifax, North Carolina. Neither was there a mention of his wife, Elizabeth Burt. Stephen's family had migrated to Eatonton by 1813. He died there in 1831, leaving sixty-eight enslaved people to be sold or split up amongst his heirs.

The $64,000 question became, "Were any of Stephen's forced workers my ancestors?" Y-DNA proves our male line comes from people surnamed-Marshall. Autosomal DNA shows that over a dozen people who are my blood-relatives have Stephen B. Marshall in their family trees. That may imply that my family descends from the eldest Stephen (died in 1831), or one of his brothers, or one of his sons. But which one *did the deed*? I couldn't find enough documented proof to draw an obvious conclusion.

"Jim, what happened to the deceased enslaved? Are they buried somewhere here?"

Sheepishly, Jim whispered, "They buried the slaves behind the cemetery, in what is now a snake-ridden bamboo forest." He pointed to the far end of the cemetery.

I started walking toward the invisible pull of souls who could have been my people.

"Wait, Kathy! It's dangerous back there!" Jim warned. He truly sounded afraid for me.

My camera continued to shoot video, as I ignored the well-meaning advice. The grass ended and sandy-brown weeds led me to a dark forest. At the edge of the bamboo, it was oddly beautiful, restful. No snakes in sight. I wanted to be alone, but Amy had followed me, and agreed to videotape my soliloquy to the dead. It was an emotional moment. I needed to process that some of my ancestors might be right there in the ground just beyond my reach. Lost, but not forgotten.

Pine Grove Cemetery, Putnam County, GA

Lesson Learned #12: Black lives and deaths did not matter in some cemeteries in the Deep South.

After that emotional moment at the cemetery, we proceeded to the next stop on Jim's driving tour: Stephen's early-1800s property along Lake Oconee, at the eastern border of Putnam.

This upscale lake area was picture-postcard beautiful, surrounded by lush trees and perfectly mown lawns. It was obviously a higher-rent district with its speed boats, colorful kayaks, and Skidoos helping folks enjoy the water. It was a paradise for those who could afford it.

Once I understood we were driving through the property that Stephen owned, I put two and two together. The enslaved souls listed on his 1831 property inventory were the same people who could have been my ancestors. They may have worked *right here*. I believe my family is listed at the beginning of Stephen B. Marshall's probate inventory list, with 18-year-old enslaved Sam, valued at $500. He was possibly my three-times great-grandfather, Sam Marshall. If my theory is correct, I needed to find out whether Hannah (age 50) and Essex (age 60) were also my relatives. That turned out to be a more difficult task than I ever imagined.

After that emotional moment at the cemetery, we proceeded to the next stop on Jim's driving tour: Stephen's early 1800s property along Lake Oconee, at the eastern border of Putnam.

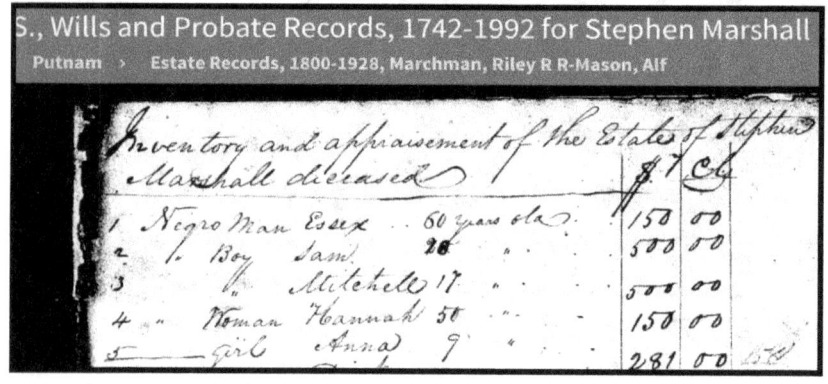

Stephen B. Marshall's 1831 partial inventory of enslaved, including Sam and Hannah, who may be Kathy Marshall's enslaved ancestors.

Jim parked the SUV on the side of the road. I got out and clicked scads of photos of the current modern house next to the water. I peered into every stand of trees or cleared piece of land, wondering if my relatives had worked there almost two hundred years ago. How could such a gorgeous place be the site of such bondage?

Cousin Jennifer, sitting in the back with Amy, mentioned there's an annual Marshall family reunion at Roosevelt State Park every September, right in this area. *What would happen if I crashed the party next year?*

This was part of Stephen Blount Marshall's property in Putnam County, GA, by the Oconee River. 2021.

I asked Jim what he knew about the Harmony Baptist Church which Amy and I had passed on our way into Eatonton. It surprised us to learn Jim was not only a member of that church, but that his great-grandfather was a preacher there for 57 years. Wow!

"John Borders was a slaveholder on my Grandmother Daisy's side. He instructed his brilliant, enslaved architects to build a Harmony Baptist Church across from his home in the Choccolocco Valley, in Calhoun County, Alabama. The architects were my great-great-great-uncles, Levic and Griffin Borders. John also had Griffin and Levic build an additional Harmony Baptist church in Noxubee County, Mississippi. That's where the slaveholder brought my Grandma Daisy's enslaved family from Alabama. The Borders let their enslaved worship at their Harmony Baptist churches." Jim did not comment one way or the other if his church had ever let the enslaved do the same in Putnam.

Jim asked, "Have you ever heard of Br'er Rabbit?" His eyes kept scanning the gently curving roadway that was leading us past stands of trees to another unknown location.

"Well, of course," Jennifer, Amy, and I replied at once. All people over the age of fifty know about Br'er Rabbit's antics.

Jim stated, "We're about to come upon Joel Chandler Harris's property. He wrote the Uncle Remus stories." Harris may have published the stories, enlarging his family's financial coffers, but it was likely the enslaved who created the stories, probably passed down from generation to generation in Africa.

"Look at that sign coming up. It tells all about the plantation where Joel Chandler Harris lived from 1862 to 1886, working there as a printer's apprentice." My ever-ready camera snapped away.

Jim continued, "People say it was the only newspaper ever printed on a Southern plantation. *The Countryman* was a weekly paper, edited and published by Joseph Addison Turner, owner of the Turnwold Plantation. Mr. Turner was a planter, lawyer, scholar, and writer who encouraged his youthful apprentice to use the large plantation library to write his stories. In the quarters for the enslaved workers, young Joel listened to the enslaved telling African animal legends and the true Negro folklore of the old South, which he immortalized in his *Uncle Remus* stories."

Turnwold Plantation is where Joel Chandler Harris captured the Br'er Rabbit stories were from the enslaved workers.

Weeks later, I determined that Joseph Turner fathered Martha Turner, who married William Blount Marshall, who was my family's owner in Talbot County. Close connections, indeed. Often, when women marry, they bring property into the marriage. A new question popped into my head: *were any of my family members enslaved on the Turnwold Plantation?*

Jim said, "There's another famous person whose family came from Putnam County. Have you heard of the author named Alice Walker?"

"Of course," I was the only one to respond. "She became famous for writing *The Color Purple*. Oprah Winfrey made the story into a movie starring Whoopi Goldberg. I've seen it many times. It's hard to watch, powerful, gritty, savage: probably authentic experiences for many Black families. Near the end of the story, it was joyful and heartwarming, with a smidgen of well-deserved retribution."

"Right," Jim replied. "Her people came from over there"—pointing at a sign on the right—"and her family attended the church over there," pointing to the left.

Time for Grub!

"Say, Jim, we're getting hungry. Is there a place nearby where we can get some local food?" Amy requested from the backseat, also offering to pay the tab.

In his quiet, measured voice, Jim said, "I know just the place." He drove us to a posh shopping center, to a flashy seafood place. Sadly, it was closed on Mondays. So, Jim doubled back to the Lake District, pulling into the "Georgia Butts BBQ" parking lot. Inside, the charming wooden, slat-walled restaurant, was peppered with southern memorabilia like flags, metal tools, tee-shirts, statues, etc. There were no overtly Confederate flags or lawn jockeys that I saw.

The menu had a good deal of meat-centered sandwiches like BBQ pork, smoked turkey, BLT (bacon, lettuce, tomato), brisket, ribeye, chicken, and hamburger.

Jennifer raved about how tasty fried pickles were. *Fried pickles?* Never heard of them, but Amy and I were game to try the Southern delicacy. Frankly, those battered and fried round pickle slices were yummy!

I ordered the pulled pork, fried okra, and fried cabbage with bacon. Definitely not the best lunch I've ever had, but the decor was festive, the bathroom was rustic and adorable, the conversation bright, and my new relatives made the experience memorable.

> Lesson Learned #13: Fried pickles are tasty! Trying local delicacies can enhance your genealogy trip.

Jim drove us back to the Bronson House in Eatonton. He encouraged us to stay in touch and to share any information we find about Putnam, for their records. A local organization has plans to publish a book of biographies of the original families who populated Putnam County in the 1800s. I showed Jim my draft of *The Marshall Legacy* book and promised to acknowledge his help and send him an autographed copy when published.

Before leaving his SUV, Jim revealed he had obtained a so-called "unreadable will" from Captain John Marshall's 1732 Virginia estate. Jim patched and repaired pieces of the will, so they were legible. He wanted someone in Virginia to include the repaired will in their archives, so I texted him my editor's contact information. Jean Cooper is the Principal Cataloguer at the University of Virginia Library. She might help him. We all promised to stay in touch, then went our separate ways.

Welcome to the Table lunch at Georgia Butts BBQ Restaurant

First Courthouse Visit

It felt like one hundred degrees in the shade when Jim dropped us off at our car. The air felt heavy, pressing on our heads and shoulders. We drank from our water bottles while sitting in our air-conditioned car for a few moments. Then I drove us around the corner to the courthouse. It was another stately red brick building in the Romanesque Revival style, anchored on each corner by octagonal towers. There was a wide, green lawn out front, and perfectly manicured bushes around the building.

"What's that?" I stared at an odd statue just off the path, halfway toward the massive front door. As we got closer, the answer was all too plain. Of course! It was a dapper Br'er Rabbit statue welcoming us to the "briar patch."

"Br'er Rabbit born and bred in the briar patch. He survives forever by his wit, his courage, and his cunning."

It was already after 4:00 p.m. and the courthouse closed at 5:00. We explained to Lisa McMillan, the clerk, that I hoped to find sales documents, which included the names of Stephen B. Marshall's enslaved workers. She escorted us into a diminutive room that housed the all-too-familiar red books that are found in every courthouse. Amy and I quickly looked through "Minute Book B" for the year 1831 but found nothing pertinent except the appraised value of Stephen's enslaved. I already had digital images of that list of 68 enslaved persons, #2 on the list being Boy Sam.

What I needed to know was who bought those people so I could prove where they lived after 1831. Did they all of them move to

Talbot County with William B. Marshall, or were they sold or given to Stephen's siblings after 1831? Disappointed, we found nothing helpful there. The clock was ticking.

At 4:45, the clerk brought out two folders of "loose papers" about Stephen's son, also named Stephen (of course!). The son died during a Civil War battle in 1864. I explained to Amy and Lisa that I was looking for recorded transactions worth thousands of dollars, because that's what the enslaved workers who made the planters wealthy were worth. It wasn't until five minutes before closing that we started seeing papers that listed high-valued enslaved persons by name. Finally! I photographed as many documents as I could, intending to analyze them later in the comfort of my home.

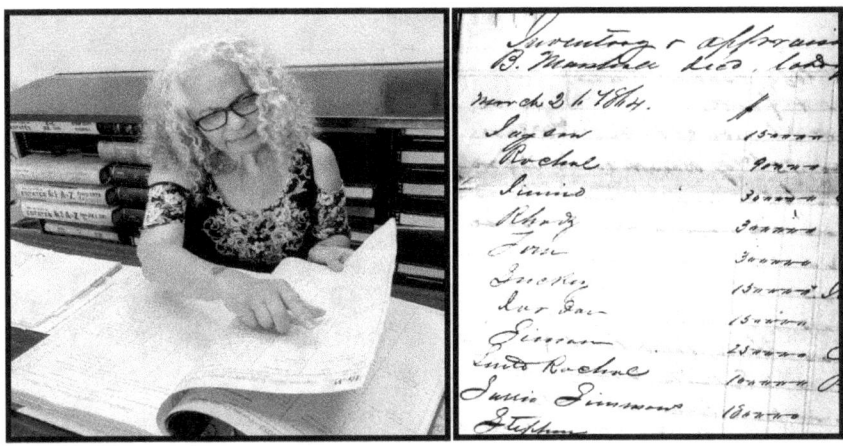

Kathy Marshall trying to find documents that listed the slaved by name and who they were sold or given to when Stephen B. Marshall Sr. and/or Jr. died. Eatonton, Putnam County, Georgia. 2021.

Dong, dong, dong! It was 5:00 p.m. Coworkers were going home and telling us to leave, too. I just kept snapping pictures like a crazy woman. Amy picked up on my intention to finish the photo-copying job no matter what, so she deftly kept chatting with the clerk. She mentioned we had traveled from California and Utah to find this information. That revelation may have encouraged Lisa to let us stay overtime for a few minutes. I hoped to see my family names documented, especially those named Sam, Hannah, Henry, Austin, Clifford, and Tom.

All those photos were likely extraneous, though, because they were people sold in the 1860s. I believed my family members were living in Talbot County by then, but I continued foraging anyway. I needed to know what happened to the enslaved from Stephen Sr.'s 1831 will. While the original "sold-to" information wasn't there, I had already captured online images of several "slave lots" back at home. I did not initially understand what those documents meant. Jim later confirmed that's exactly the data I needed to determine who received Stephen's enslaved people. Would I be able to confirm my theories that the William B. Marshall family passed the names Sam, Henry, and Austin down from one generation in their slaver family to the next?

> Lesson Learned #14: Take lots of photos and videos of courthouse documents. Don't discount any information gleaned from a genealogy pilgrimage. Note: Weeks later, after finding more corroborating DNA information, Stephen Jr., who died in 1864, might have actually had more to do with my family than I originally thought.

It had been an exhilarating day meeting cousins Jim and Jennifer, seeing where Stephen B. Marshall lived in Putnam, and experiencing the general area where his enslaved likely toiled. Jim sent us on our way with copies of maps, family trees, and marriage and cemetery records. We explored original deeds in the courthouse. Even though we discovered little additional data, it was a fabulous day of exploration.

Chapter 6: The Road to Talbot County

Hmm, there would be sunlight for another three hours. We didn't want to waste a moment. On the way to our hotel in northern Columbus, we had to pass through Talbot County. Great! We might cross a few more goals off my list that day.

Amy felt we should fill the gas tank, even though it was two-thirds full. Was she overreacting? I think not. We needed to monitor our gas tank. Ten days prior, a hacker had shut down a major oil pipeline in Texas had no gas. A panic ensued when the gas pumps went dry. Prices skyrocketed days before our trip. Inflated gasoline prices in the South were still at least one dollar-per-gallon less than normal prices in California.

The closest gas station, a Shell, was so full of cars, the waiting line extended into the street. We used the Maps app to find another gas station close by. Hmm, the driving directions took us through an economically depressed area. There were rickety trailer homes sitting atop overgrown grasses. We saw nary a person anywhere. I felt remorse wondering how those residents lived. I felt guilty about how comparatively easy my life was, 3,000 miles away.

The Maps app directed us to an ancient-looking gas station combo convenience store. I pulled in and parked next to a gasoline pump. My Spidey Sense[14] alerted. Why were the old-style pump handles full of spider webs? Why were old cars parked next to the pumps? Amy wanted to pay for the gas, but there was no mechanism outside to take a credit card. She began walking toward the store to tell the clerk which pump we wanted to use. I didn't feel comfortable with Amy going inside by herself. I locked our car and followed her inside.

> Lesson Learned #15: Trust your Spidey Sense and always be aware of unknown places and people. Remember where you parked your car. Look as though you know what you're doing. Don't be a victim.

The stench of marijuana and urine hit my nostrils as soon as we opened the door. I hate the smell of dope.[15] It reminds me of a ripe skunk. Amy walked to the back, searching for bottled water. While I was waiting in line, I became fascinated by a super-high fellow. He plopped a fifty-dollar bill on the counter for two bottles of beer and a stack of Lottery Scratchers. The rows of colorful games-of-chance tickets plastered on a three-foot glass wall mesmerized me. I felt sad the chap was wasting his money. His investments would be gone in a few hours. The beer would flow down the toilet and non-winning Scratchers would likely end up in the garbage. I felt sure this was the experience of many in that depressed community.

When Amy rejoined me, she expressed concern for the neighborhood. She found no plain water, only soft drinks and beer. There were long rows of candy, chips, and other junk food. I wondered whether there was any fresh food in that neighborhood. Many present-day African Americans have no clue how to grow nutritious fresh food for their families, even after centuries of our free Black labor used to toil the fields for rich planters.

Surprise! The cashier revealed they had no gasoline in their tanks. That explains the spider webs. They probably had sold no gas there for years. Amy paid for the flavored beverage she bought. Happily, we left the stench behind, gulping blessed fresh outside air. We drove back to the original Shell station, which now had an available pump.

A full tank of gas eased our fears of being stranded. On the route to our hotel, we spied the Bluff Springs Catholic Methodist Episcopal Church on Highway 36. Slaveholder William Blount Marshall was the postmaster of the Bluff Springs Post Office. I felt sure this Church was close to William's plantation house. It gave me goosebumps to know we were near where great-grandfather Henry and great-great-grandfather, Samuel Marshall, were enslaved workers. They may have even worshiped at this very church. We parked in the driveway and carefully walked through the mown grass to read the headstones. About one-third of the interred had Marshall surnames: Marvin, Vernoy, Jeff, Jonathan, Susie,[16] Willie Lee, and Annie.

I needed to investigate whether any of them were my relatives. Walking through patches of unkempt grass in the cemetery, Amy said, "I hope there are no chiggers here!"

"Chiggers? What are they?"

Amy explained chiggers were in the family of spiders and ticks. Their favorite spots are moist, grassy areas like forests and fields like we were standing in. "Adult chiggers don't bite. It's the babies that latch onto your pants and crawl around until they find a patch of skin. Then they use sharp, jaw-like claws to make tiny holes, then injecting saliva, which starts a feeling of uncontrollable itching. That results in bumps, blisters, or a hive-like rash."

I shuddered. Getting back in the car, I took off my shoes and tried to shake them clean of dust and chiggers. It was silly to think those actions would dislodge anything so tiny, but it made me feel better. Later, I would wash my pants, just to be sure.

> Lesson Learned #16: Be aware of particular animals, insects, flora, fauna, foods that you might be allergic to. Be sure to bring an inhaler or allergy medicines, or other medications with you on your trip. Consider packing a small first-aid kit and sewing kit.

William Marshall built his plantation house in 1833, and I was determined to find it. *A Rockaway in Talbot* mentioned William lived near Alabama Road. That was the stagecoach route from the Carolinas to Alabama, now called Highway 36. Looking at Google Earth mapping program, I noticed "Sarah Marshall Road" intersected with Highway 36, where William's home was located. I felt like one of those people in a reality detective show, developing theories of a buried treasure. We looked for clues, charted a course of action, then went on an exciting hunt for the truth. Driving at a 20 MPH pace, like the grandmother that I am, we peeled our eyes toward every sparse street sign on that rural road.

"There it is! Sarah Marshall Road!" I quickly pulled the car over to the sign, just off the edge of the narrow highway. The gravel road was way too rocky for a lightweight rental car, though. I didn't need a flat tire in that deserted countryside with spotty phone and internet reception. Parking in the middle of the graveled path was stupid. It would block any other car from entering the road (not that anyone would likely travel on that desolate road).

Sarah Marshall Road, Highway 36, Talbot County, Georgia. 2021.

Amy asked, "Who was Sarah Marshall?"

"I have no clue, but she was probably one of William's many descendants who remained in Talbot after slavery."

We got out of the car, my trusty iPhone camera recording our latest adventure. It was the Golden Hour—a photographer's dreamtime for taking outdoor pictures. The sun is just above the horizon, its rays imparting a golden glow over the land. We rested there a moment and took deep breaths. Enjoying the calm beauty of the scented pine forest, we relished the opportunity to stand in the place where our common ancestors lived almost two hundred years ago.

I snapped a few shots, then we began walking up the sloped road bordered by red Georgia clay, trees, and unruly grasses. Would we find the remnants of a plantation house at the top of the ridge, or would there be more trees? Amy and I began skipping like little girls, giggling. We pretended we were following the yellow brick road to the land of Marshall Oz. My breathing became labored, though, partly from excitement, partly from a racing heart, and partly from the muggy heat. How long was this road and where did it exit?

I didn't feel comfortable continuing our investigative stroll after spying a No Trespassing sign on a nearby tree trunk. We trudged back down the hill, jumped in the air-conditioned car, and drove toward our hotel. Adrenaline kept me alert for the fifteen-minute ride to the hotel. I later read the plantation was likely on the other side of Highway 36. Was it closer to Highway 208 in Harris County, Georgia? So close, but yet so far.

A Rockaway in Talbot said William's original house burned down from a lightning strike in about 1912. Amy said our DNA Cousin Erika read somewhere that William's grandson built a new house on the original foundation. Cousin Erika was the direct descendent of Rosa Marshall, an enslaved woman who bore four children allegedly fathered by owner William Blount Marshall.

In 1870, Rosa lived with her nine children by William and husband Ben. They lived next door to my second great-grandfather, Samuel Marshall. That's why I was so excited to learn that Erika and I shared seven centimorgan[17] of DNA. That means we had a common ancestor, most likely someone in the William B. Marshall family.

A mile from Sarah Marshall Road, Amy said, "I think that's the picture I have of Raintree Farms! Cousin Erika believed the bed-and-breakfast hotel called Raintree Farms Bed-and-Breakfast Inn was on William's original house foundation. Kathy, do you think that building is a reincarnation of William's house? Let's stop and check it out."

"Maybe, but honestly, Amy, my tank is on empty. It's been a long day of driving for me, and it is getting dark. Let's come back tomorrow, okay?" Amy nodded but looked disappointed.

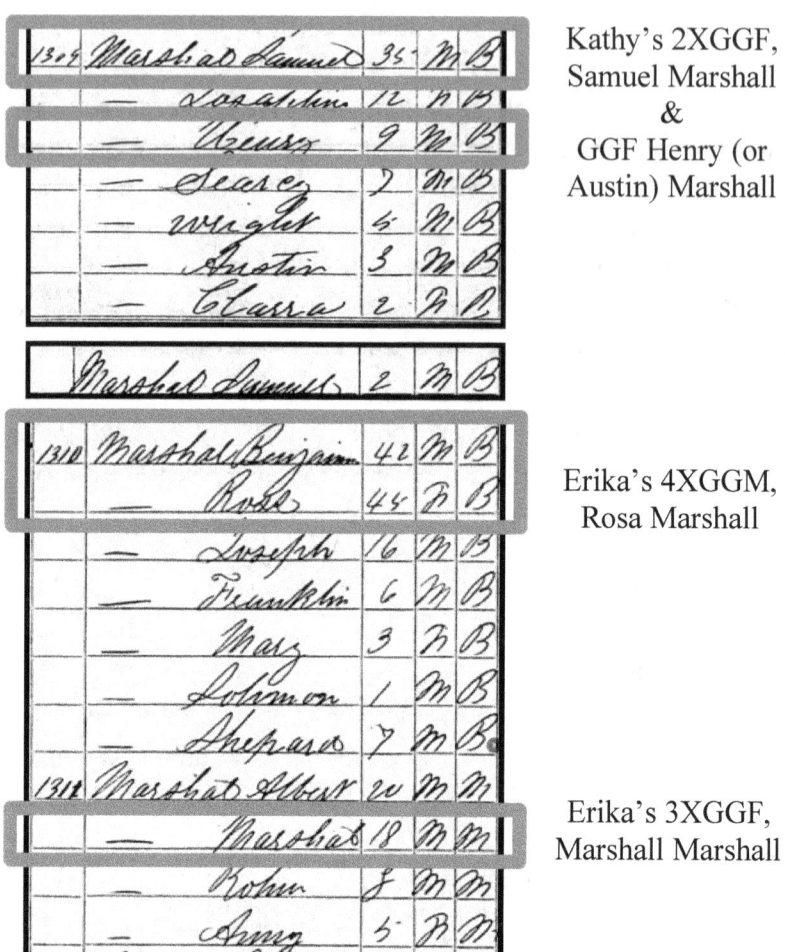

Cousins Kathy and Erika have ancestors living next to each other.
1870 US Census, Oneals District, Talbot County, Georgia.

    We checked into the Hampton Inn in North Columbus at about 9 p.m. We trudged our suitcases into the elevator, pulling them behind us to our fifth-floor room. Our home away from home was like any other mid-range hotel. It had two queen-sized beds, desk, chair, microwave, small refrigerator, closet, and TV.

Instead of going out to dinner at that late hour, I ate a protein bar in our room and Amy devoured a snack from her purse. I took a relaxing shower, put on my nightshirt, then began writing in my daily journal. Amy chatted on the phone with her family. For way too long, we reviewed the events of the day, finally getting to sleep at 11:30 p.m.

> *"What's all the commotion down there?" I screeched, awakened by the sound of clapping thunder after dawn. Zipping up my feathered dress, I soared, my eagle eyes focusing miles in the distance. Who are those upright creatures, and why are they pointing those thin branches at each other? Boom! Clouds of black smoke, but no fire. Screams. Loud days and nights. I wish they would leave me in peace. Bored, I flew back to my perch on top of a gigantic tree and slept for ages.*
>
> *The next morning, I awoke to a delightful smell. Those creamy white blossoms below my nest produce such a yummy aroma.*
>
> *Boom! I craned my featured neck to look down. It's one of those silly creatures making that annoying noise again! I rose, wings flapping, holding myself in place. Then I deposited a goopy, whitish gift on the offender, marking my disdain. Calling to my mate, we flew on to another adventure.*

On Mike Buckner's Property, Talbot County, GA

Chapter 7: Tuesday in Talbotton

Rise and shine! After dressing and primping, Amy and I took the elevator down to the hotel's breakfast room. The Hilton-owned Hampton Inn offered an efficient takeout breakfast. We could select from various prepackaged foods. Then deposit the choices into a takeout carton or paper bag. Or one could remain in the attractive lobby area designated for eating breakfast.

Efficient hotel breakfast bar.

I wanted more protein, opting for hard-boiled eggs, and yogurt with raisin bran at the table. I crammed a banana, orange, and two Quaker Oats granola bars into a paper bag for later snacking. Amy had eggs, a toasted bagel with cream cheese, yogurt, and an orange. We both took bottles of water for our big day of research; but would I remember to drink the water?

> Lesson Learned #17: Bring plenty of water and healthy snacks with you every day to keep your mental, emotional, and physical energy in tiptop shape.

We entered our Ford Fiesta and plugged my iPhone into the car sync socket. I set the GPS for Talbotton, then set off through the countryside to the Talbot County Courthouse. Lush, grassy fields and thick forests surrounded the undulating road leading us to 26 South Washington Street.

Talbotton Courthouse

The red-brick courthouse was the tallest building in Talbotton, which is the county seat. Its dramatic White spire reached six stories high. Two immense magnolia trees with fragrant creamy-white blossoms anchored the street corners. A large Confederate statue confronted visitors as they gained entrance to the building. I refused to sully my phone camera with that monument celebrating Black bondage. Oh! What's all that bird poop on the statue? I smiled, remembering my early morning dream.

Walking up a concrete ramp, we donned our anti-COVID face masks, entering the building through glass double doors. A uniformed African-American officer asked us to pass through the security gate, then he pointed the way to the Deed Room.

Massive magnolia tree with yummy creamy white blossoms.

We entered a bright office with a large window overlooking Washington Avenue. The woman sitting behind the desk was striking, unforgettable. She wore a bright yellow, form-fitting dress that emphasized her curves. Someone artfully styled the dark plaits on her ebony head like a Queen's crown. Her massive cat-eyeglasses signaled a vivacious personality. Chief Deputy Clerk Terri Jenkins of the Talbotton Research Center led us into the compact Deed Room lined with hundreds of weighty red books. Workers stacked behemoth tomes of land and vital records on shelves around the room. More books were underneath an immense worktable in the center of the compact space.

Looking at an index of probate records for a John Marshall.

I explained we were there to find information about William B. Marshall's enslaved workers. Where should we start? With the deeds? Vouchers? Minutes? Terri suggested we begin in the Probate Room. Their staff closed the office at lunchtime, so it was best we get started there first. She introduced us to Chief Deputy Clerk Shattara Powell in the Wills & Marriages office. We looked through ancient Minute Books, Wills, and other probate records for what seemed like an eternity but found little useful information.

Our eyes were bleary from reading antiquated handwriting. Despondent at not having found more documents than I hadn't already seen online from home, we took a lunch break.

We didn't see many open businesses. In fact, the town looked deserted. Walking across the street to a convenience store, I bought an ice cream bar covered with Oreo crumbles. Amy bought a healthier, fruitier option. We sat on a bench under a shady roof. The row of buildings across the street stood like historic sentinels. A pleasant, gentle breeze cut the humidity, and gray clouds helped us feel cooler.

Where were the inhabitants? Aside from a few logging trucks and cars that passed in front of our bench, we saw few people in this diminutive downtown area that surrounded the courthouse. It was eerie. I guess that's why I found no hotel rooms near Talbotton, thus the reason we had to stay in Columbus.

Our lunch time over, we walked back to the Deed Room. Terri brought in all four volumes of *A Rockaway in Talbot*, written by William H. Davidson. Everybody said it was the undisputed primo series about the history of Talbot's residents. I had already seen Volume IV at my local Latter Day Saints Family History Center in Sacramento. It contained detailed information about the William B. Marshall family. There was also an image of the original plantation house with William's son, James F. Marshall, and his family sitting out front. The author also included architectural details about the house and its many outbuildings, including a picture of one of William's cabins for his forced workers. In addition, he said William was a senator, representative, judge, postal officer, storekeeper, carriage maker, farmer, and slaveholder. That descriptive material helped me describe William's home life in Chapter 18 of *The Marshall Legacy in Black and White*.

My local Family History Center could locate none of the other three volumes; I chose not to pay hundreds of dollars for them on Amazon and eBay. It was a delight thumbing through the other three volumes of *A Rockaway,* for all the townships in Talbot County.

Amy descends from the Blount family. They married into and traveled with the Marshalls who migrated from Putnam County, Georgia, in the 1830s. Amy was none-too-happy to have slaveholders in her ancestral line. But I believe she found it interesting to see how and where our common ancestors lived in Georgia.

"Look at this, Kathy!" Amy reported in her lilting voice. It was an 1859 description of neighbor J. Rowland Mahone family's forced laborers.

```
Appraised Value of Distributees property re

Ariadna Mahone {  Lizzy        1000.00    George
                  Lavinah       705.00     Dozier
                  Josephine     545.00
                  Cornelia      375.00
                  Stephen       250.00
                              2875.00

Rebecca           Harriet      1312.50
Mahone            Asa          1190.00
                  Boy          1103.50
                  Mary          848.75    J Y Mills
                  John          212.50
                              5261.25

Galema            Emeline      1450.00
Mahone            Lillis        975.00
                  Sam          1470.00
                  Alice        1177.50
                  Millard       375.00
                              5447.50
```

J. Rowland Mahone's 1859 Will mentions Josephine, Emeline and Sam. Were Black family units mixed up?

She knew I was always on the lookout for the names of enslaved people. I didn't want to quell her excitement, but I had already saved the handwritten Mahone listing to my computer files. That interesting list had several of my family's given names, like Sam (my great-great-grandfather?), Emeline (Sam's second wife?), and Josephine (Sam's only child?). Were the people on the list my ancestors, sold to J. Rowland Mahone at some point? Were they kept together in their biological family units, or were they divided up, willy-nilly, to Rowland's heirs?

I wondered whether Amy was bored out of her mind, like a husband who sits patiently while his wife is trying on clothes in a department store. But she always presented a serene face, asked lots of questions, and helped me search for clues. Two more hours of fruitless research, and we called it quits.

The bright part of our day was chatting with Terri. She was a super-friendly, positive, engaging person. Too bad she had selected a boyfriend who didn't deserve her shine. Who were we to make such a proclamation, having only met her that morning? It shows how close we felt to her.

We said our goodbyes to the courthouse staff and took selfies. We exchanged business cards and gave air hugs through our masked faces (unmasked only for this photograph).

Amy, Shattara, Terri, and Kathy, Talbot County Courthouse, Georgia, 2021.

Amy and I exited the venerable building. We walked down the ramp past the enormous magnolia tree, then entered our car.

A few blocks away stood a dark-brown wooden church called the Zion Episcopal Church. Reverend Richard Johnson moved to

Georgia from South Carolina to open the church. His workers hand-carved many of the features in the building in the days before mills. They built the altar, communion rail, lectern, pulpit, and prayer desk from black walnut. They installed a Pilcher pipe organ from Philadelphia in 1850. It's still operated by a hand pump. The organ on the balcony had seating on both sides where the enslaved worshiped prior to the Civil war. In 1860, the population of Talbot County was half-Black, half-White, so the upper and lower levels were full of people.

Amy and I peered through the windows, taking pictures of the interior. I wondered whether my ancestors were among the enslaved members who sat on the balcony. That thought led me to write the dramatic end of Chapter 24 in *The Marshall Legacy in Black and White*.

I was enjoying a protein bar under the shade of the tree-lined street, trying to recoup my energy, which had faded fast at the courthouse. It was time to move on. My detailed spreadsheet itinerary had lots of potential venues we could visit if we had extra time. Driving around Talbotton, we observed many stately brick homes still in Talbot.

We tried to find where William B. Marshall was buried in the Waverly Hall Cemetery. Was the rumor true that someone buried his forced-concubine, Rosa Marshall, near William? Amy had dreamed of honoring Rosa's sacrifices by placing a rose on her gravestone. We had passed by the cemetery the day before, after the Putnam trip, so we both thought we knew where it was. Wasn't it parallel to Highway 36? My Apple map program just couldn't find it. We drove all over neighboring Harris County, it seemed, but we couldn't find the cemetery.

"Look over there!" Amy said. "How cute!" She pointed toward some salmon-colored umbrellas outside a Thai restaurant. Of all the restaurants to find in that rural place, we found a Thai food in rural Harris County.

The enticing restaurant stood at the end of a set of ancient buildings in a strip mall which looked more like a California Gold

Rush ghost town. The faded red and mustard-colored brick building could have been a jail in the past but is now an archery business.

I imagined the hustle and bustle of enslaved and free people walking along the sidewalk in the mid-1800s, shopping, chatting, drinking, sharing the news of the day.

Anyway, it was the "Authentic Thai" restaurant that caught our eyes and stomachs. Being famished, even though it was only 4:30 p.m., helped cinch our decision to stop and have dinner. Inside were artful baskets on the wall and an open kitchen on the right. Working there was an Asian cook, an older Black woman-in-charge, and a friendly, dark-skinned, Black man who took our order. We asked the employees and other patrons where the Waverly Hall Cemetery was. A fellow customer said, "Oh, it's just down Highway 208 a short distance."

The food was delicious, albeit brought to us in ordinary white Styrofoam containers. Our meals were pretty to look at, had a wonderful aroma, consisted of fresh ingredients, and tasted authentic. The eggroll appetizer was standard fare, but the main dishes were scrumptious. Amy ordered a super spicy-hot curry-over-rice dish. She liked it but needed something to cool her burning lips and mouth. The server brought her a can of soy milk which seemed to calm the burn. My dish was a heap of chicken pieces fried in a very light batter that was sprinkled with sesame seeds. The complex sauce under the ample helping of chicken was delicious. I ate the whole thing!

> Lesson Learned #18: Be sure to give into happenstance once in a while, even though it is not on your itinerary. Ask locals what their favorite restaurant is, where they would take their visiting family, or where to explore interesting local attractions. Leave some wiggle room in the itinerary to take advantage of unplanned experiences.

We went back to business after dinner. We were bound and determined to visit the Waverly Hall cemetery. Instead, I mistakenly plugged in the GPS address for Raintree Farms. I parked on the gravel in front of a wire fence beside the property. We walked up the driveway, then rang the doorbell twice. Nobody answered the door. Too bad, it would have been nice to see inside what could have been slaver William B. Marshall's remodeled plantation house.

We walked back to our car and got in. *Why does it smell so musty in here?*

"E-gad! We're in the wrong car, Amy!"

We'd unknowingly gotten into the resident's unlocked car. Lickety-split, we jumped out, ran to our own vehicle, and hopped in, seat belts buckled. I quickly backed the car out, then accelerated onto the highway before anyone called the cops! I wanted no trouble with the police in that neck of the woods (a refrain I voiced all too often for Amy's tastes).

Was this the moved and renovated William Blount Marshall Plantation? It certainly looks different than the original home at right.

Original William Blount Marshall Plantation, c. 1833-1898.

Could that have been William's plantation home we had searched for on Sarah Marshall Road? Perhaps we'll never know for sure, but that misadventure sure got our blood pumping.

Weeks afterward, I learned the Raintree Farms bed-and-breakfast went out of business in 2005. It's description online said, "Circa 1833, although it now rests on three acres, this early 19th-century home was once part of a large plantation, later moved to its present location. The grounds include a small lake and a garden.

They decorated the home in traditional style with some antiques." It sure sounds like it might have been William's property moved to this new location.

We finally found the Waverly Hall Cemetery. Nobody could miss William's grandiose monument to himself. I am glad he included the names of his parents, Stephen and Elizabeth. We had wondered why there was no appropriate headstone for them in the Pine Grove Cemetery in Putnam County, where they died.

Kathy Marshall next to slaveholder William Blount Marshall's memorial at Waverly Hall Cemetery, Harris County, Georgia.

Amy didn't want to take a picture next to William's monument, any more than I wanted to be in a photo with a Confederate statue. However, I wanted to have a photograph next to our blood ancestor, even though he owned my first great-grandfather, Henry A. Marshall, and my second great-grandfather, Samuel Marshall (and ninety more African American human beings).

We saw no evidence enslaved people were buried there. Amy was beyond disappointed. She wanted to leave a rose on Rosa's headstone. The enslaved not only had no headstones, but were often buried them haphazardly in undesirable areas, like the snake-infested swamp in Putnam County. *Unappreciated in life and discarded in death* was the enslaved person's epitaph. Saddened, we returned to our hotel.

I was beyond exhausted, my eyes drooping. Earlier in the year, I had contracted a severe irregular heart rhythm, combined with difficulty breathing. I tried to control the alarming symptoms using meditation, yoga, more sleep, and staying away from chocolate (my only addiction). Running on empty in both mind and body, I worried a cataclysm was coming our way.

> Lesson Learned #19: Visit cemeteries and take pictures to honor the ancestors.

Pushing those fears into the back recesses of my tired mind, I readjusted our itinerary, since we had accomplished more today than planned. We would get up by 8 a.m., have a leisurely breakfast, then arrive at St. James A.M.E. Church in Columbus by 9:30. I wanted to find proof of whether my family worshiped at that church, and whether my great-great-grandfather, Israel Smith, had been a Reverend there. Afterward, we would try to locate my grandfather's house at 1710 Fifth Avenue. Then we would drive forty-five minutes to visit Talbot expert Mike Buckner at his home at the southeastern edge of Talbot County. We went to sleep, knowing Wednesday would be a calm, peaceful day. Were we ever mistaken!

Chapter 8: Wednesday Morning in Columbus

We woke up at 8 a.m. and dressed leisurely, as planned. Amy applied her makeup, then we went downstairs to gather our takeout breakfast, repeating our meals from the previous day.

We hopped in our silver chariot and drove to the old part of Columbus, back to the era of the early 1900s.

Now I must admit how much I love the Travel Map programs on our smartphones. Just type in the desired destination address, then the program figures out two or three ways to drive there. Choose a route, press "Go", then follow the verbal and pictorial instructions shown on the car's monitor screen. Simple. Convenient. Except that I kept missing the last minute "turn right NOW" types of instructions. I can do a lot of things very well, but I am not directionally gifted. So, it always took a little longer to arrive at our destination than it should have. I was fortunate to be traveling with Amy, who never chided, nor seemed impatient with me for periodically screwing up at the wheel. We reached the St. James A.M.E. Church that I wrote about in the first chapter of *The Marshall Legacy in Black and White*.

Orange cones blocked most of the parking lot. *Hmm, what's going on here?* A woman sitting in a chair under a shade tree shook her finger when I tried to park the car. She got up and came to my window. "Do you have anything to drop off?" Evidently, we had come during a big food drive. The church would not be open that day for research.

We had to reprogram Maps to the next item on our itinerary, which was the old train station. No problem. We had plenty of time to burn before our afternoon appointment with Mike Buckner.

It only took a few minutes to reach the now-defunct train depot. We found a shady parking spot in front of a block-long brick building. I believe it used to be a warehouse for merchandise needed to be loaded onto, or taken off, the trains coming and going behind that building. We walked toward the Passenger Station sign at Sixth Avenue and 10th Street, which read:

> *"The Central of Georgia railroad station, designed by Bruce and Morgan of Atlanta, Georgia, was erected in 1901. Featuring massive granite arches, it served as the transportation hub of the city for over 70 years. Threatened with demolition in 1984, this landmark on the eastern perimeter of the original city, was saved through the leadership of the Historic Columbus Foundation..."*

Pressing my smartphone to the depot window, I captured inside images of the luxury which had delighted passengers during its heyday. We walked around to the backside of the depot. We stood at the edge of six sets of confounding tracks. My grandfather, Austin Henry Marshall, worked as an oiler, then a Pullman porter, from 1913 until about 1917. Then he registered for World War I and went to France to fight for our freedoms. It was an honorarium of his patriotic service, which I proudly documented in Chapter 6 of *The Marshall Legacy in Black and White*.

We walked toward the Machine Shop near a curve in the tracks. I thought we might get a tour of the facility, especially if I mentioned my familial nexus to the place. But no, a sign on the entry door indicated "COVID safety precautions forced the discontinuance of unscheduled visits."

I had to inner-process my being there. Was I standing exactly where Grandpa Austin stood at some point during his railroad career? I imagined the crowds of workers packing or unpacking the train cars into adjacent warehouses. They helped passengers with their suitcases and watched truckers bringing in or hauling away merchandise. It must have been incredibly busy, noisy, smelly, oily, and exciting all at the same time.

The Sixth Avenue Passenger Station where the author's grandfather, Austin Henry Marshall worked form 1913-1917.

I tried to picture being a young White girl in a frilly pink outfit and black patent leather shoes waiting on the boarding platform. She and her well-dressed parents were ready to hop on board when the right train rolled up. I could imagine being a young Black child in coveralls sweeping errant rocks and coal dust from that same platform. One child looked forward to an adventure on the rails, the other stared at the departing train, wishing she was on it.

We turned around, heading back toward the car parked a few blocks away. "Oh, what's that?" The welder in me drooled.[18] I noticed several bits of metal discarded in the gravel next to the nearest track. I picked up an enticing piece. Was it a one-half-inch thick door hinge or something else? It was hefty in my hand, rusted in its gravel bed. Forgotten. Is it stealing if one takes something that was discarded, or is it a kind of community service to remove it so people don't trip? It looked to me like an antique that wasn't being used or appreciated.

And speaking of old things... Amy noticed there was a store called "Vintage" across the street from the train depot. We drove over to see what they offered.

My cousin likes antiques: things that maintain their character. I wanted a souvenir to take home that represented my family's Columbus homeland. As soon as we entered the door, we both squealed like schoolgirls. There was so much interesting stuff hanging from the ceiling, perched on shelves, and freestanding on the floor. Our eyes couldn't focus because there were so many treasures to take in.

The owner, a pixie-haired woman named Stephanie, was vivacious, charming, funny, cute, and very welcoming. She was the epitome of Southern hospitality. The story of our journey, as told by Amy, enthralled our new friend.

Stephanie had lived a good part of her life in that very area. She regaled us with stories of her past and the general history of that part of Columbus. I asked her whether there were any African Americans who had lived in that part of town.

"Oh my, yes!" she chattered. "The Claflin School,[19] built for what were called colored people back then, is just around the corner a few blocks away, right before the overpass." She walked me to the window and pointed toward a tall church steeple, showing the school was close to that building. *Hmm, visiting the Claflin School had been on my list of things to see.*

Kathy and Amy at "Vintage" antique store at 1301 Sixth Avenue, Columbus, Georgia. Cotton bolls in green glass souvenir. 2021.

We toured Stephanie's large, well-organized vintage shop full of furnishings, knickknacks, household items, photos, dishes, candles, and more. I settled on buying three greenish glass containers that had little nodules of glass on the sides. I gave two of them to Amy, one of which she later mailed to Cousin Erika, a teacher living in Texas who couldn't join us during the school year.

I told Stephanie I wanted to get something that reminded me of Columbus, like some real cotton bolls. I had never seen cotton close up, never felt the stickery parts that made the picker's hands bleed, never imagined it could actually be an attractive plant. A few of the decorations in the store were garlands of cotton plants. She was kind enough to give me an eight-inch branch of the fluffy stuff to take home, for free. She was *so* friendly! We both loved her to pieces. I tried to pay Stephanie more than the six dollars she was asking for the three glass jars—a steal—but she wouldn't't hear of it. We left the store feeling charged with the store owner's warmth... or was it the already stifling temperature of a Georgia day in May?

> Lesson Learned #20: Purchase something that reminds you of the places you visited. This includes taking selfie photographs of yourself with the souvenir in front of well-known monuments and buildings, etc., to record your visit.

I should have had more water. Amy went through at least five bottles a day on our trip. I remembered to drink two, perhaps three. Hydration is especially important in a humid place like Georgia. Bad things can happen otherwise, such as heat stroke, dizziness, and incoherence. None are wonderful outcomes if one is driving. Thankfully, we had a lot of scheduled activities and probably wouldn't need to worry about such calamities... or would we?

Leaving the Vintage Shop, we headed east on Sixth Avenue toward the tall spire a few blocks on the left. But there was an overcrossing that blocked us. Hmm, I noticed the Linwood Cemetery was to our right, and a hospital complex across from that. I had read about that all-Caucasian cemetery so close to my family's home at 1710 Fifth Avenue, between Linwood and the train tracks. Or was their former home between Linwood and the new hospital? I couldn't remember, but I was excited to know we were near where my family resided. I called on the ancestors to guide me.

We circled around the big cemetery block, trying to reach the Claflin School where my grandfather attended class. His second wife, Vernelle Jones, taught there before becoming a nurse. Columbus originally built this schoolhouse in 1868 to educate the African American community, following the Civil War. This school became part of the Muscogee County public school system. They expanded its campus in 1921, when they added a larger masonry building. The Claflin School campus expanded again in the 1940s. Fire destroyed the original 1868 structure in 1958, but two buildings from the first half of the 20th century remain.

Former Claflin School, 1532 Fifth Avenue, where Grandpa Austin Marshall may have attended school in the early 1900s. Columbus, Georgia.

The city renovated the stately building for affordable housing. We parked in the back and Amy took pictures of me in front of the building and its marker. I tried to picture my grandfather and his siblings walking the few blocks from their home to this school every day. What must that have been like? How many students attended and what were the teachers and curriculum like? Did they bring their own lunches in metal lunchboxes? Did some children skip school to help their parents make a living? Was my grandfather a talented student? The Census only says he completed all four years of high school, which made me proud. It was unusual for most Negroes who ended up in Cleveland, Ohio like Grandpa did, to have finished high school.

We didn't have time to find Grandpa Austin Marshall's house that day. We had a date with a well-known history buff.

Chapter 9: The Renaissance Couple

The sun was high in the sky on Wednesday, the third day of our adventure. It was time to travel for forty-five minutes to today's main destination. We drove to Junction City, on the far east side of Talbot County, to visit with Mike Buckner, a renowned historian. We would soon learn he and his wife, Debbie, were much, much more. This would indeed become a day forever etched in my mind.

Talbot County was where my great-grandfather, Henry A. Marshall, was born and raised. He and his wife, Mary Smith, had eldest son Clifford there in 1889. This is a rural county. Its ambling, one lane-each-way roads curve around pine forests. The red clay soil contrasts with overgrown grasses and bushes that line the roads. Bucolic. Meditative. Beautiful, except for its marked history of slavery. We saw signs of places we were now familiar with: Talbotton, Waverly Hall, Geneva, and Woodland. The mapping program led us safely to the entrance of Mike Buckner's estate, which his Fielder family established in 1830, when Native Americans were still living there on their own land.

On the right, we passed archaic structures which could have once been barns, homes for the workers, or other outbuildings. Parallel to the left side of the road, beyond the initial line of trees, was a long stretch of dry, yellowish, plowed land. Was this a cotton field ready to be planted? That was on my list of things to see up close and personal during our pilgrimage. I kept stopping the car to take pictures out the window. I can't imagine what went through Amy's head with my constant photography.

A truck was driving toward us in the adjacent field. I got out of the car. The truck slowed and I shouted, "Are you Mike?"

A confirmatory nod, then he replied, "Sorry, I've got to take care of some unexpected business. I'll be back in fifteen." And off he went, leaving Amy and me on our own to explore his incredible plantation. The sandy, mile-long driveway ended near the main house. Amy and I explored the cabins.

c.1840, moved 1990s.

Playhouse, c.1911, moved 2000s.

Old kitchen, c.1830s.

Junction City house, c.1920s, moved early 1990s.

Smokehouse, c.1820, moved 1980s.

Willie Frank Sanders house, c.1920s, moved from Junction City

Outbuildings from nearby properties were moved here to preserve them. The book cover image was the home of Willie Frank Sanders for 25 years. He was born blind but was able to cut wood with a hand saw, shell peas, and perform other useful tasks, according to Mike Buckner.

"Hello there!" A female voice called out behind us as we took a bunch of pictures of cabins we suspected once housed enslaved workers. The Buckners later told us most of those structures were built elsewhere in the 1820s to 1840s, or early 1900s, which Mike moved to his property. He wanted to preserve those historical buildings, using some as homes for the aged people they cared for.

"Oh, hi. Sorry, we didn't know anyone was at home. While waiting for Mike to return, we were taking pictures and admiring your property," I responded.

The tall, dark-haired woman introduced herself as Mike's wife, Debbie. She invited us to follow her, as she walked across their circular, red-brick patio with a water fountain was in the center. We passed wrought iron furniture and hanging planters on the way, then entered the main house. It was dark inside, but we could see it was decorated with many interesting antiques. The Buckners didn't have air conditioning, so keeping the blinds closed during the heat of the day kept the interior cooler.

Debbie offered us some sweet, iced tea and introduced us to her son, a man with many building talents. Amy and I took our cool beverages outside, then followed our hostess into an unusual structure. We marveled at the huge, leaded glass window in the wall closest to the back door of the house.

Debbie said, "In the 1970s, many railroad depots were demolished. Among them was the Talbotton Depot. Its salvaged materials were recycled to build a replica of the waiting room. The leaded glass window was installed here, creating this solarium.

"One of Mike's aunts gave him parts of a much larger leaded glass window. Ken Barrett re-designed it into a window that fit the space of the replica of the Talbotton Railroad waiting room. Our solarium is filled with tropical plants and this humongous crystal chandelier." We three looked up at the intricate light fixture.

"We sometimes have parties out here. It's spectacular at night. The only drawback is having to clean the chandelier!"

I could have stayed there forever. Imagine being surrounded by lush plants in a cool, darkened space. It was relaxing, healing, mesmerizing. Only a chime or birdsong could make it more idyllic.

After about fifteen minutes, Mike returned from his errand. He wore a beige, button-down short-sleeve shirt under his blue jean coveralls. His work shoes were of sturdy leather. He was tanned and his skin as sun-spotted as mine. His blond hair was mostly straight and parted on the side, his face showing the signs of afternoon stubble. Initially, our host was all business, as he presented us with a glimpse of all four volumes of *A Rockaway in Talbot*. He spoke in a deliberate, soft voice, accented with a light Southern drawl.

Then Mike showed us some dignified paintings of Black folk painted after Reconstruction by William Akin Walker. He painted real people who would not have ordinarily been photographed.

The ice broken by preliminary conversation, Mike asked, "How about we go for a ride?" He showed the slightest hint of the mischievous boy who lived just below his serious visage. Amy felt riding in a car with a strange White man in the South was a little unsettling, so she was relieved when his wife volunteered to come along with us. We piled into his work truck and fastened our seatbelts. We had no idea where he was taking us. We put our full faith and trust in his plans to show us western girls a good time.

The dusty driveway turned onto an asphalt road. After five or ten minutes, he turned right to a dirt driveway and stopped next to a dozen pallets stacked with recycled, antique bricks.

A massive two-story building-in-progress was a renovation project Mike is constructing from an old house that had been trucked to this location. We took the opportunity to walk up the stairs and experience the incredible view of forests, with mountains in the distance. It was disconcerting, but fun, having no stair handrail and being able to look down into the first floor from above. We could also see spaces of light coming through the ancient wallboards. I couldn't believe he is doing most of the work himself.

By then, Mike had loosened up considerably. He was in his element: outdoors, creating, building, breathing fresh air, visualizing a bright future for his family. He was even hilarious at times. His intelligent, dark-haired wife was equally enchanting, but in different ways. She shared in the car that Mike was associated with various historical organizations including establishing the Patsiliga Museum and the Straus Historical Society, which had given me Mike's phone number months before.

One topic, in particular, sparked my interest. I think Debbie said it was Butler Island, off the east coast of Georgia. She was involved in an effort to help Black descendants save the island and preserve its history. Debbie and Mike made a good couple. Both yin and yang, both community-oriented, both builders and creators, both delightful to be around.

Prior to coming to Georgia, I talked with Mike on the phone, explaining that one of my main goals was to meet other descendants of the Marshall's enslaved workers still living locally in Talbot and Harris Counties. I had no clue he would drive us to a trailer home on Highway 208 and introduce us to a woman named Maybelle, a descendent of the Bunkley family and Sam Marshall who was born around 1899. My great-great-grandfather, Samuel Marshall, had a son named Sam in about 1868. In 1874, Samuel married Emeline Bunkley. Is that how Maybelle and I were related? Did my Great-Uncle Sam, born in 1868, have a son named Sam born in 1899 who was Maybelle's ancestor? My skin tingled.

We entered a typical mobile home trailer anchored to the ground. It was shady inside. Next to a bright window sat an attractive, ebony-skinned woman with a blue paper mask covering her face. She had experienced a stroke and had difficulty communicating, but Mike understood what she was trying to say and helped me to understand her responses.

Horrors! Everything started to cave in around me. The hot sun coming through the window, the warm air inside the clean home, and meeting a woman who could have been my cousin, threw me into a wall. I felt like a marathoner on mile 20, when the runner's glycogen is depleted and who feels unable to finish the race. For a few minutes, my brain literally stopped working. My thoughts were disjointed. I couldn't speak intelligently. I couldn't even remember my great-grandfather's name when asked. Was it Frank? No, my grandpa was Austin Henry Marshall. But what was his dad's name? No clue. It was more than a little disconcerting, I will admit. The lack of adequate hydration and sleep and being extraordinarily exhausted from planning and executing this trip, caused my mind to go blank. I felt like all eyes were staring at me, but I couldn't function. It was horrible… and embarrassing.

Finally, I remembered my great-grandfather's name was Henry Austin, the reverse of my grandfather's name. Shaken, worried my brain would never rev up again, I left my business card scribbled with the names of my father, grandfather, and great-grandfather on the back, along with my phone number. I hoped Maybelle would share my contact information with one of her relatives who knew more about their family.

Maybelle lived with her mother. Their home was clean and tidy, and she was shy and full of smiles. There was a long wooden ramp leading up to the front door which facilitated walkers and wheelchairs. It was a nice place, but in my mental turmoil, I had an overwhelming need to get outside. I felt light-headed and almost delirious when we got back to the truck. I finally guzzled all the liquid left in my water bottle.

> Lesson Learned #21: Stay hydrated at all times and eat nutritious snacks during the day to be at your maximum performance and avoid a medical emergency.

Back on the road, Mike admitted to periodically stopping by to see how Maybelle and her mother were doing. He honks if he sees them outside as he drives by. He also mentioned that the cabins in back of his house were used by several workers and older people he and his wife took care of when they needed a place to stay. Aww, what a nice guy and gal.

As you can tell by now, historian, contractor, humanitarian, and treasure hunter Mike Buckner was on a mission. He vowed to find where William Blount Marshall's plantation house was. The most obvious place to start was on Sarah Marshall Road where Amy and I had parked our car and walked one-eighth of a mile up the rocky trail two days prior.

That gravelly road reminded me of a harrowing trip my husband and I had taken along the south side of Maui in Hawaii. We were in a rental sedan that was not equipped for driving on the uneven lava beds. If our car broke down or popped a tire, nobody would find us for days on that isolated pathway. Thankfully, Mike had a sturdy truck which could handle the rocky terrain.

Our intrepid host drove slowly from one end of Sarah Marshall Road to the other. He said he'd never been on that road before, but he knew it was maintained by the county. The reddish hue of the rocky trail accentuated the green bushes on the left. Taller trees on the right cast sparse shadows on the road. We were traveling farther and farther from Highway 36, which worried me.

About one-half mile in, the forest thickened. Brown trunks of five-to-twelve inches in diameter, 30-to-40 feet tall longleaf pines crowded out the light. We noticed thick red duct tape on the trunks of some trees. Mike said those markers designated family property boundaries. The area is now used for logging, so there were several gates off the mile-long road.

Oh! There's a clearing to the right, with a metal gate leading to another sandy trail. Could this be the Marshall plantation? Nope, no plantation house was in sight. Mike called a local conservationist friend familiar with the area, but he didn't know who owned the properties along the route.

A Rockaway in Talbot indicated the original Marshall house was on the Alabama "Stagecoach" Road, which is now Highway 36. It indicated the house burned down in about 1912 from a lightning strike. Conversely, Cousin Erika was told one of the Marshall kids had built another house on that original foundation. Which story was true?

Mike Buckner searching on Highway 36 for a driveway that would lead to William B. Marshall's Talbot plantation. 2021.

Mike was bound and determined to find the renovated house. He did it by driving along Highway 36 and craning his neck to spy potential houses through the overgrown driveways and fences along the route. He occasionally swerved on both sides of the curvy, shoulder-less road in an attempt to discover the truth. There were steep areas alongside the highway and occasional oncoming traffic. It was a nail-biter adventure, for sure, but I was johnny-on-the-spot ready to grab the steering wheel if need be. Eagle Eye Mike knew the general area and found many places to explore on our quest to discover the Marshall stronghold. Being a passenger was scary and exciting, all at the same time.

"There it is!" Mike called out excitedly. "I knew I had seen it before." *What is he looking at?* I could see nothing but thick foliage. He pulled off the road alongside the fence next to another overgrown driveway. The rest of us stretched our necks to see if we could spot any buildings. "Nope. This isn't it," and he pulled back onto the road. My adrenaline stomped on my brakes, throttling down my excitement precipitously. I didn't know how much more my frazzled, thirsty nerves could take, but I wanted to continue the hunt. Absolutely!

More glimpses, swerving, and might-have-beens. Suddenly, he pulled off the road. We ordinary humans could see nothing special, but our intrepid driver inched the truck through tall weeds, around a slight corner, then, "Voilà!" A locked gate with an ADT security sign next to a thick tree trunk barred our passage.

From inside the car, we could see some sort of one-story house nestled behind several large, leafy trees. Then our eyes looked to the right, and I shouted, "There's the tall tree that was struck by lightning in 1912!" A large, blackened branch was dangling from one side of the trunk. Could a 109-year-old tree still be standing? My heart began beating faster. We could just make out a huge house with two-story white columns looming behind the tall trees.

Debbie had brought Volume IV of their *A Rockaway in Talbot* with us. She and Amy, who were sitting in the backseat, were reviewing the book for houses that matched what we were glimpsing on the other side of the gate.

I gasped, "It's a white house with green shutters, just how William B. Marshall's house was described in the book," I exclaimed. "This might actually be my heart's desire!"

Could this be William B. Marshall's house through the trees?

Mike exited the vehicle and so did I. We were on an expedition, a hunt for the place where my ancestors may have lived. This was the most excited I had been during this already incredible trip. I felt like journalist, political commentator, and former television host Geraldo Rivera, who made a live TV special called *The Mystery of Al Capone's Vaults*, looking for a treasure trove the gangster supposedly hid. I had dreamed of turning this trip to Georgia into a mini-documentary. This quest to find the plantation house might be the highlight of my story. I took plenty of video and still photos along the entire journey to capture the thrill of the experience for home viewing.

I whispered into my smartphone video camera, "This is my partner in crime." Mike giggled like a little schoolboy—his handsome blue eyes as big as saucers while opening Santa's presents. I looked conspiratorial and darn proud of it.

My PIC (partner-in-crime)

Inside my bones, though, I was a scared little Black girl. Remember, we were in rural Georgia, y'all. Lots of folks have guns here! It's where eight Asian worshippers were killed *the day before* during a mass shooting at their Korean Baptist Church in Atlanta, Georgia. I convinced myself that everybody knew Mike. He's a good ol' boy. They wouldn't shoot at him, or *us*. Right? I hoped my ancestors were watching over me.

In a low voice, I continued dictating into my phone. "He says we're gunna go see this place right now, and deal with fallout later." Caught up in the drama, I nearly forgot about Debbie and Amy until Amy said, "Oh my gosh!" as we walked toward a tall white structure peeking out from behind the trees. As we rounded the bend, we could see a huge Greek Revival antebellum plantation house. It had five tall columns equally spaced across the front facade. Four stone steps led up to a long porch that spanned much of the front. This may have been what my enslaved ancestors saw every day! My skin crawled.

Hmm, there was an odd bump poking out on the right side of the building, between the fourth and fifth columns. It had a window and green shutters, like the rest of the house. Mike explained that it was a self-contained room. Since the property was located on the Old

Alabama Road, the owners had built a Travelodge of sorts where weary travelers could rent the room and stay the night on their way from the Carolinas to Alabama. He said many houses had such an appurtenance for visitors.

Cousin Amy standing in front of what we thought was the Marshall house, then we guessed the Blount house, but it was actually the Bunkley's house.

Amy asked if I wanted her to take my picture standing in front of the building. Sure, although, in my bones I knew this didn't look like the Marshall plantation shown in *A Rockaway in Talbot*.

As I was getting ready to pose for posterity, Debbie spoke up. "Oops! This isn't the Marshall house. It's actually the Blount house." My emotions flip-flopped again. I was crushed that we didn't find the Marshall plantation, but happy Amy found her Blount ancestor's home. She begrudgingly stood in front of the façade while I snapped some photos. Amy wasn't the least bit happy to be associated with slaveholders.

We were ready to get back into the car when Debbie said, "Actually, I think this is the old Bunkley House. We all looked at the image in the *Rockaway* book and agreed. My disappointment transformed into gladness because Bunkleys *are* kin of sorts. Amy and my common cousin, Erika, had Bunkley ancestors. Additionally, my great-great-grandfather, Samuel Marshall, married Emeline Bunkley in 1874. (I am not sure whether Emeline was my great-great-grandmother, or it was a woman named Maria Wilkinson). I would later learn that Maybelle, whom we had just visited, also had Bunkleys in her ancestry. So, finding the Bunkley home became an even cooler adventure than we initially thought.

Imagine experiencing an original antebellum home built in the 1830s, almost 200 years ago, for a family line we all shared. I wished I had felt comfortable asking the current owners if we could peek inside for a moment.

We all piled back into the car, imagining our host couldn't possibly pull off anything more exciting out of his history-buff-hat than this. We underestimated his prowess yet again.

Back on the road, he took us to a cemetery for the Blounts and other prominent planter families. I noticed there were some Smiths buried there. The following evening, I would be driving to Tuskegee, Alabama, to explore my great-grandmother Mary Smith's family. Not knowing whether there was a nexus to the Smiths here in Talbot, I snapped a photo of John and Hugh Smith's headstones for future research.

"Ready to go home?" Mike said, a sly smile playing at his lips. It had been a HUGE day for us, having started that morning in Columbus before the Talbot adventure. It was a lot to take in, but I was ready for more. He drove us back to their home renovation. Amy and I got into our car, then drove behind Debbie in her car, while Mike stayed in his truck. We caravanned back to toward their property. But he stopped his truck about 200 yards before reaching the house.

What does he have up his sleeve now?

Months ago, when I telephoned Mike, he described the pottery kiln he personally constructed on his property. It was in remembrance of a potter who came from England to Talbot in 1827. That fellow served the county's pottery needs for decades. I've been a clay artist since 1980 and told Mike I would love to see his operation. I marveled that he, a non-potter, was able to build such a grandiose kiln firing operation. I would guess his kiln is 12 feet wide by 15 feet long by six feet tall (compared to my two-foot-cubed kiln).

A kiln is like a very hot oven that turns the dried clay pieces—called greenware—into stonelike pottery bowls, plates, cups, vessels, artwork, sewer pipes, or architectural cornices.

"The diminutive opening at the front of the kiln is so small," I said. How do you get the clay pieces inside the kiln to be fired?" Mike pointed to the steel roller bed in the base of the opening, and I peeked inside.

"Does someone have to go inside the kiln?" I asked.

He nodded. "A second person sets the dried clay vessels on the conveyor belt to carry them into the belly of the kiln. The first person, while inside the cavity, carefully places the unfired greenware in rows along the back wall. Ten-inch-high brick stints support fire-resistant kiln shelves. The potter places clay work to be fired atop the shelf, then another layer of stints and shelves and ware. This procedure continues until hundreds of pieces are inside. Then we stack cords of wood in the back, salvaged from old trees around this place. The wood is set on fire to achieve 2,000 degrees or more for a day, then cooling down for two more days."

Mike Buckner built this pottery kiln on his property.

"Wow!" Amy and I exclaimed. Then we got into our cars and drove an eighth of a mile to their house. Debbie and I parked in their curved driveway. Amy asked where the bathroom was. I waited outside, savoring the shade of the large trees in their front yard and the incredible view of the river below.

Where did Mike go now? Oh, there he is. He was walking up the slope of his front lawn with two bubble-wrapped packages in his hands, one for me and one for Amy. I unwrapped the gift and was delighted to now possess one of the lidded containers that had been fired right on their own pottery in Talbot, where my ancestors had been enslaved. Had any of my relatives worked in that pottery, making bricks or pots? Is that why I became a potter in California? Unlikely to ever know that answer, I put both containers in the backseat of my rental, then followed Mike up the steps through his front door to meet up with Amy.

The man of a thousand surprises said to me, "I bet I've got something you've never seen before." *What else could he possibly give me today?*

He escorted us into their dining room and invited us to sit. A few moments later, he returned with a big sheaf of papers. "This," he said, "is a work contract for the sharecroppers who worked for my Fielding ancestors, as well as day-to-day journals of expenses and revenues from their work."

I had seen an 1867 work contract for some of my other ancestors. However, I craved to see what President Thomas Jefferson called a "Farm Book" and others might call a Day Book or Daily Journal, which specified by name which enslaved workers were toiling in which fields. That would give me an idea of the type of work individual people performed.

"This has been so informative, Mike. I dare not ask anything else of you, but I noticed the big structure near the pond out front."

"Oh, that's the grist mill."

"I've read about them and how they work, but I've never actually seen one in action. Could we explore it for a hot minute before we leave?" I asked.

"Sure. Follow me." Amy and I grabbed our belongings and walked behind him toward the water's edge at the far border of his expansive lawn.

View from the Buckner's house toward the pond in front which provided an energy source for the grist mill.

Amy asked, "What's that?" We approached a statue that looked like a Black lawn jockey. We were shocked that the Buckner's would have such a racist sculpture. Before we could comment, Mike said, "Now, I know what this looks like, but it's not what you think. It is not the Black lawn jockey named 'Jocko.' Our statue is actually a White guy, a jockey commonly found at horse stables in Kentucky, manufactured in about 1920 by the White Oak Foundry.

Mike turned to the left and explained, "This is our church chapel. Most years in the fall, we host 'Harvest Days in Old Talbot' at our property. Hundreds of people come to see how our Fielder's Waterpower Grist Mill, a Draper Loom, and the pottery. Visitors of all ages parade through our house, which was built in about 1840. They enjoy demonstrations, exhibits, vendors, and activities."

Grist Mill on Buckner property

We entered the open door of the two-story wooden grist mill building and spent the next thirty minutes learning how corn kernels are ground into cornmeal. We dodged all sorts of machinery on the bottom floor, following Mike to a dock at the edge of a lake next to the mill. Every new thing Mike showed us was more extraordinary than the last.

He explained that turning what looked like a ship's steering wheel opened a gate under the mill, letting in a torrent of water from the pond through a turbine to power the mill. A water wheel on the backside of the building was put into motion by water exiting the mill. It was so peaceful watching it slowly revolve.

Under the mill, the water filled a square basin, churning against a one-inch vertical pipe which was attached to a turbine. That powered a long drive belt which turned the grinding stones on the second floor.

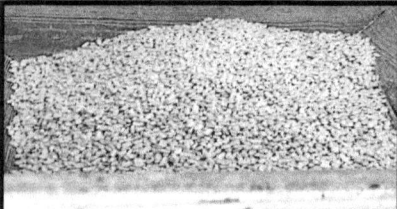

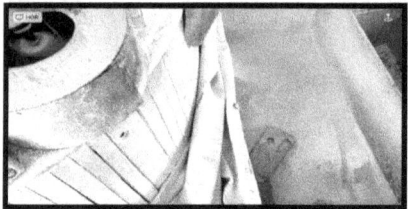

The water wheel-through-turbine powers the stone wheels which grind corn kernels into meal, which Mike scoops into two-pound bags of grits, that he sells under his family's "Fielder's Mill" label.

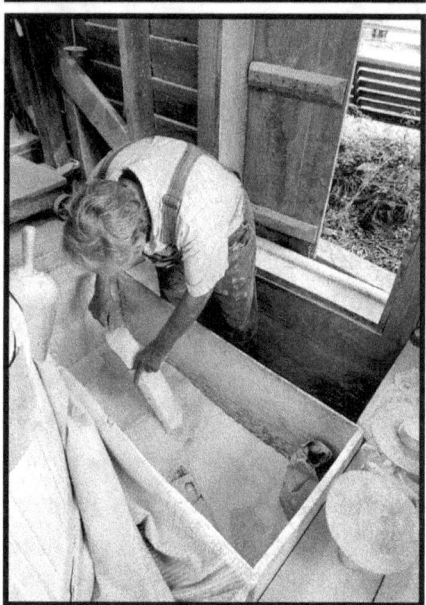

We ran up the stairs to watch Mike pour food-grade dried corn kernels into another square, wooden basin. Slowly the kernels were sucked through a hole in the center of the container, down between two stone wheels which ground the hard kernels more and more finely to the outer edge of the stones. Like a reverse vacuum cleaner, the ground-up flour shot out into a rectangular wood basin below the stones. Mike scooped the flour into two-pound paper bags, labelled with his family's "Fielder's Old Fashioned Water Ground Grits" logo.

Sitting next to a 500-pound bale of soft cotton. Thinking about my ancestors who may have been tasked to pick cotton back in the day.

Along the sandy, quarter-mile-long driveway was an empty field which is normally planted in cotton. Because of the COVID-19 pandemic, Mike didn't plant cotton this year. But he had a 500-pound bale of cotton in the grist mill. I looked none too happy standing next to it, knowing how many generations of my enslaved family had to cultivate it. It is deceivingly soft and fluffy, contrasted to the havoc it wrought on my Black ancestors.

After scooping a bag of newly-ground corn grits into a bag for me, and for Amy, Mike gave us a copy of the family cookbook full of recipes for cooking various grits dishes. Then the best date in Talbot escorted us back to our car. He directed us to use the pottery jars he gifted us to hold the bags of grits. Hugs of thanks and goodbyes signaled the end of our magical adventure.

We had been famished for hours, so eating dinner was number one on our agenda. We chose the BoneFish Restaurant twenty-five minutes away, arriving at twilight. The parking lot looked pretty full, but we had no problem getting a booth. The menus offered a variety of fish and seafood, as you might imagine from the name. We ordered an appetizer of Bang Shrimp®—crispy shrimp, tossed in their signature creamy, spicy sauce. They were to die for! I can taste those luscious babies right now! My main dish was filet mignon and Amy had a salmon pasta dish. Afterward, we rolled ourselves out of the restaurant and drove two blocks to our hotel.

"Oh look!" Amy exclaimed. "A blood moon." Indeed, the full moon was deep orange from a short-lived total lunar eclipse. What an interesting ending to an eye-opening day of discovery.

> Lesson Learned #22: If you are lucky enough to secure an expert guide (contact the local Historical Society or local library for recommendations), be sure to record, photograph, and videotape the tour. When you're back at home, you'll be happy you did.

Chapter 10: Thursday Exploring Grandpa's Hometown

My alarm rang at 7 a.m. I can shower, dress, put on minimal makeup and fix my hair in ten minutes, but I chose to write in my diary until Amy's alarm sounded at 8 o'clock. She decided to take her shower first this time. Quieting the worry that poked my palpitations awake, I zipped my lips, against my better judgment, and let her shower first. Taking the opportunity to email thank you cards to our Putnam and Talbot hosts occupied my mind for a while. My call to St. James A.M.E. Church to confirm our 9:30 appointment that morning went to voicemail. My text to Cousin Jennifer Owens to make sure she would still be able to meet with us for a meal at 2 p.m. received a prompt affirmative response.

Today, Amy and I would be visiting my Grandpa Austin's birthplace and hometown during his teenage years: Columbus, Georgia. Smiling, I remembered the previous two times visiting that charming industrial town whose border shares the Chattahoochee River with Alabama.

When it was my turn in the bathroom, I showered, got dressed, untwisted my nighttime locks, and applied minimal eye-liner and blush; there was no need for lipstick when wearing a mask all day. Hmm, my partner in crime still was not dressed. Glancing at the clock, it seemed to be ticking faster and faster ... or was that my wonky heartbeat?

"Amy, I left a message for the church saying we'd be there around 9:30 a.m. It will take us fifteen minutes to drive there." My unspoken request was, *Please hurry up!* Perhaps I could help things along by going downstairs to select my breakfast and snacks for the drive.

"May I bring you back something to eat?"

"Oh, how sweet. Sure. How about a repeat of yesterday's breakfast?"

Returning from the efficient takeout dining area, arms full, I found she still wasn't dressed. Dismayed, I sat on my bed eating hard-boiled eggs and a toasted bagel, impatient to get on the road by our 9:15 departure time. My roommate was enjoying her meal, reading her text messages, and applying sun-protective foundation to her pale face.

Too much a worrier, my blood raced from my left-hand fingertips through my body to the ends of my right hand, tapping my nerves like a spiteful child. I wanted to get on the road. I picked up my suitcase and volunteered to check us out of the hotel and wait for her in the lobby. By then, it was about 10 a.m. Focusing on meditative breathing, looking through my emails and Facebook messages. She arrived about fifteen minutes later.

Since the Holiday Inn Express Hotel, where she would be spending that night, was next to our Hampton Inn Hotel, we took a chance they would hold her suitcase while we were out exploring Columbus. Yay! They let Amy have her room before the normal check-in time. My grin appeared as I breathed a sigh of relief.

> Lesson Learned #23: Ensure you have given clear advance notice of itinerary timetables to everyone involved. Exercise patience and understanding to keep tempers cool.

Once in the car, I plugged in the coordinates for 1002 6th Avenue: St. James A.M.E. church. The plan was to learn whether my two-times great grandfather, Israel Smith, had ever been the Reverend at that church and whether my Marshalls worshiped there. After all, for fifty years, Grandpa Austin and Grandma Daisy had been trustees at the St. James A.M.E. church in Cleveland, Ohio. Many of their parishioners migrated there from Columbus, Georgia.

We chose a shady spot in the church parking lot. By then, it was about 10:45 a.m. and already stifling at 84 degrees and 84-percent humidity. Hmm, where was the church entrance? It was a grandiose brick building with many entrances, all of which were locked. The mercury inched up my internal thermostat.

"How do we get into this place?" We circled the building a million times, trying every door, with no luck.

Coming around the carved front edifice again, patient Amy took pictures of me standing on the steps of the church and in front of the historical church marker. Then that brilliant girl spied a sign that said," Deliveries go to the cream and burgundy." *What the heck did that mean?* She noticed that the house next-door was painted the colors of cream and burgundy. Great! We walked over and rang the doorbell.

A woman dressed in a cute blue outfit answered the door. She was the one who had been so kind to me on the phone two weeks ago. But today she looked a little angry, perhaps because I was ringing her phone so often trying to get inside the church building. This chain of events didn't start our visit on a good foot.

She escorted us to the Archives Room just inside the front door. It was full of photos and books about the history of that church, which was the largest of the 500 A.M.E. churches in Georgia.

"I'm hoping to learn whether my great-great-grandpa, Reverend Israel Smith, and my Marshall family were St. James parishioners."

The woman brought out a large red book, like the Deed Books we saw in courthouses. It held church records. This was the first time I had ever held actual church ledger records like this in my many years of genealogy research. That thrill and the fact we were in an air-conditioned setting perked us up. Could we find Israel's name, or any Marshall name, on the pre-1900 church attendance documents? Nope. Was my Israel a "visiting" Reverend? There's no record of him at that church.

Genealogy experts rave about church records and the useful information found in obituaries, but there was no evidence that my folks had been members in the St. James A.M.E. Church. We left a bit sad, but we could not spend any more time there.

Kathy hoping to find proof that her family worshiped here.

Our next destination was the house where my family lived from the 1890s until 1928[20] when my great-grandmother, Mary Smith Marshall, died. She was buried in the Porterdale Colored Cemetery off Victory Drive in Columbus, as detailed in Chapter 1 of *The Marshall Legacy in Black and White*. Their house was eight blocks from the St. James A.M.E. Church. Hmm, there were more churches closer to their home. Perchance it was St. "John" A.M.E. instead?

We drove to their 1710 Fifth Avenue address, but found no houses there anymore, just train tracks, the Linwood Cemetery, and some parking lots. Amy took a picture of me standing in the middle of the widened Fifth Avenue where I assumed the house used to be. As happens with some minority areas, their homes are bulldozed to make way for highways, or wider lanes, or for more lucrative real estate developments. Could our house have been one block from the current Metropolitan Baptist Church at 1633 Fifth Avenue, close to the Piedmont Physicians Pulmonary building?

Honestly, I didn't know whether Israel was a Reverend at an A.M.E., Baptist, or some other denomination church. A long train toot-toot-tooted as it barreled down the tracks next to where I believed my ancestors had lived almost one-hundred years ago. It was LOUD as it passed!

The cousin we were meeting that afternoon lives in the same general vicinity of my ancestral home, so I asked her where the 17th Street and Fifth Avenue neighborhood would have been. She said, "In the South we have this saying: Once you cross the tracks … that's where they put the Blacks. There used to be lots of homes there, but now there's just parking lots, a cemetery, a Black church, a Churches Chicken restaurant, and the Amos Cancer Center."

Later, searching the Google Maps app for pictures of houses a few blocks away near my ancestor's neighborhood, I found what a typical house looks like a few blocks away which may have been similar to Israel Smith's home from the early 1900s.

Typical house around 17th Street, Columbus, GA

We needed to kill some time before our Welcome to the Table event at 2 p.m. But when trying to drive to the Riverwalk historic quarter, we found ourselves crossing the Chattahoochee bridge into Alabama. The good thing about that is once we got back on the correct road, *facing* Columbus, we got to see the beautiful city skyline as we came back over the bridge. Too bad we did not take photographs of that magnificent view.

Driving past the Porterdale Cemetery, Amy could glimpse the *colored cemetery,* the final resting place where my Black Marshalls were buried. I pointed out how few above-ground monuments there were, but if a family had a little money, they might have an engraved two-foot by four-foot cement plaque on the ground. Otherwise, they had no stone and thus, no names at all, just red bricks that delineated where their remains were located. My horror at first seeing Porterdale in 2009 was prejudiced by what I thought was a substandard cemetery; I recorded my thoughts in the Preface of *The Marshall Legacy in Black and White.* That humbling experience taught me an important lesson that I would remember wherever I traveled in the United and States and the world beyond.

Austin Marshall family burial plot in Porterdale "Colored" Cemetery, Columbus, Georgia, 2009.

> Lesson Learned #24: Be more empathetic to the customs, sights, sounds, eatables, sanitation systems, people, etc., that I encountered on a genealogy or pleasure travel trip. Their ways are no less valid than mine.

The drive toward the Columbus Historic District, which meandered along the Chattahoochee River, would have been a perfect advertisement for the Columbus Tourist Bureau. We parked on one of the peaceful, tree-lined streets fronting beautiful historic homes, many of which were in the Greek Revival or Victorian style. The majestic Springer Opera House sat as a bright beacon at the entrance to this district.

Several streets were paved in red brick in an attractive herringbone pattern. I could imagine that inhabitants of this rich area hired many a Black woman to cook, clean, and take care of their laundry and their children. Those workers, like my ancestors, lived on the other side of town and may have hopped on a streetcar, the remnants of which were still visible at some street intersections.

Columbus Heritage Park along the Riverwalk, Columbus, Georgia.

History was all around us in the gentrified area near the Columbus State University. In Columbus Heritage Park, we took pictures next to statues of the pharmacist who created Royal Crown Cola, a life-sized bronze of a woman working in a factory, a Black man pouring molten metal into a mold, and a farmer standing in the grass. We peeked into a large beehive kiln and a house for an enslaved family; it was only outfitted with a bed.

We continued walking through the restful neighborhood, finding ourselves at the Chattahoochee Riverwalk, which is fifteen idyllic miles of historic monuments and markers alongside the wild beauty of the rolling river. We stood in a gazebo that commemorates the battle of Columbus with cannon and historical plaques. We kept exploring each new wonder, to the point where we lost our bearings and couldn't quite remember where we had parked the car. Oops!

Columbus Heritage Park along the Riverwalk, Columbus, Georgia.

Chapter 11: Welcome Family to the Table

We found our car several blocks away from the historic Riverwalk. After much-needed swigs from our water bottles, we decided to head toward the BoneFish Restaurant, eight miles away on Veterans Parkway, close to Amy's hotel. We made it to our destination with plenty of time to spare. My nerves were surging with excitement.

The Welcome to the Table the Table event we were about to experience was the culmination of this important trip. I felt like a little girl on Christmas morning, clamoring to start the joyous celebration. The original plan was to meet with Cousin Eddie Marshall for dinner on Sunday night, but he and his family had contracted COVID. Cousin Lori Ligon wanted to join us but couldn't get off work. Cousin Jocelyn was having troubles with her knees. Cousin Gloria Hardnett lived near Atlanta two hours away and had childcare issues.

Amy and I were fortunate to have had lunch with cousins Jennifer Kent and Jim Marshall in Putnam, on the first full day of our adventure. We were still hoping Cousin Erika Thomas would be able to video chat from Texas today with Amy, Jennifer Owens, and me.

Time for genealogy! I brought out my binder of documents we could discuss, including a chart showing the common ancestor for twenty of us cousins, a few questions about direct-line families, and printouts of our common DNA matches. As a researcher and analyst, I thought those technical documents would make for interesting conversation. Silly me. Thankfully, none of my boring plans panned out that day. Instead, it ended up being a lot less formal and a heck of a lot more fun.

Looking out the window from the red vinyl booth near the front door of the restaurant, my heart started palpitating as a big van pulled up.

"Oh, I think that's her!" A light-brown woman with a cane made her way to the entrance door. I stood up, camera in hand, ready to greet her from the darkened aisle.

"Oh, you are so adorable!" I uttered when five-foot-two Jennifer Owens came into view. She had a hint of Asia in her eyes. I flung one arm open to hug her, with the other holding my smartphone for a selfie photograph together. We COVID-vaccinated cousins are a hugging bunch.

Amy and Jennifer sat across from me. That made it easier to take their pictures and video our conversations. Cameras in the face are annoying, but they are great for documentation.

How Are We Related?

After a little social banter about the weather, Jennifer looked at Amy and me and asked, "So how do you know each other?"

"DNA," we responded at the same time, as though we were twins.

"Exactly how are your families related?" our new cousin asked.

I took the lead. "On the Marshall side. My great-great-grandfather was Samuel Marshall, born in about 1830 in Talbot County, Georgia. He was enslaved by William Blount Marshall, related to him by blood."

Jennifer uttered "um hmm" after each sentence, indicating she was listening with gusto, sopping up every word.

Amy piped in, "And my first cousin six-times-removed was the same William Blount Marshall. David Gregg Marshall is his grandpa—my sixth great-grandpa. William's dad, Stephen Marshall, is my sixth great-grand-uncle."

"That's great!" Jennifer chuckled, her eyes twinkling, dimples expressing her joy.

Amy resumed. "It's been fascinating learning about all this history."

"Thank you, Kathy, for all the work you've done to make this happen." Jennifer's compliment produced a ready smile which was infectious. We clasped hands across the table.

Pointing to Amy then at myself, I replied, "We have all been putting this history together in little bits and pieces, trying to figure it out. It's been as difficult to find answers as finding the proverbial needle in a haystack, but it's been so much fun meeting you all."

Amy nodded. "Another cousin may be calling us soon. Her name is Erika Thomas." Amy got out her smartphone and began searching through her Contacts. After a moment, Amy sighed, wrinkling her brow. "We had been communicating via Facebook Messenger, but I just noticed I don't have her phone number. I'll leave it on Facebook Messenger and hope she sees it soon." Erika's phone number was not in my Contacts either.

Amy explained to Jennifer that William made babies with his enslaved Rosa, and that Rosa was Erika's fourth-great-grandmother.

"Is that right?" Jennifer asked in her melodious voice.

"Yeah, it's crazy... and they had four kids together," Amy added, shaking her head in disapproval. "It's not something that I'm proud of, being related to him."

Looking at Jennifer I added, "That's why I was so excited to learn Amy and Erika are genetically related to me, even though the DNA connection is very distant. It lends further credence that my Black family is connected to those White Marshalls. For decades, I had no desire to be related to William or any slaveholder. But now, finding my European relations might reveal records for my Black ancestors."

The waitress came to take our orders just as our conversation was warming up. Jennifer chose the Cobb Salad with chicken, and pot-stickers as an appetizer we all could share. I ordered the Bang-Bang Shrimp Cocktail, which was so delicious the night before at the same restaurant. Amy chose the Baha Fish Tacos.

After the waitress left, Amy pulled up Erika's Facebook page to show Jennifer what she looked like.

"Oh, she's so pretty," Jennifer exclaimed.

"Yes, she's gorgeous," Amy affirmed. "I think she's close to your age, in your forties, right?" Jennifer nodded.

"Youngsters," I chimed in from my elder position. "Jennifer, you and your attractive sister are no slouches either. You have an exquisite Asiatic quality about you."

"I'm half-Filipino," Jennifer divulged. *That explains her exotic features.*

Amy took out her smartphone and showed Jennifer a picture of the probable common ancestor that Kathy and I have with Erika. "His name is Marshall Marshall. What a name, right? He's the son of enslaver William B. Marshall and his enslaved concubine, Rosa." She pointed at the photograph. "These are Marshall's daughters, Mariah and Susie."

"Isn't that interesting?" Jennifer exclaimed; one eyebrow lifted as the other eye winked. In an innocent feminine voice, she asked, "Who would ever guess how that came about?" Then she winked again. "And I wonder how he obtained that great photograph of his well-dressed daughters. It looks like it was taken before 1900, when photographs weren't something every African American could afford."

"Well, he *was* the son of the owner," I said. "Perhaps that's how he was able to get such a professional family photo. The 1880 Agricultural Schedule described their farm-related property indicating that Marshall Marshall and his brother, Albert Marshall, were doing pretty well, as the photo proves.

Marshall and his daughters, Mariah and Susie, c. 1900, Talbot, GA

"What I've been trying to find is William's will issued in 1874. I want to determine whether his children by Rosa were left any of Daddy Dearest's estate. I haven't found any confirmatory evidence yet, but that doesn't mean he didn't.

"You see, William's son, Samuel, and my direct ancestor whom I called "Black Sam" in *The Marshall Legacy,* both lived perhaps within a few minutes walking distance to one another in 1870. That's why I wrote Chapter 17 in *The Marshall Legacy* the way I did. Perhaps there was a close relationship between the two Samuels. They could have been good friends, or an owner and his property, or possibly even half-brothers. It's maddening not to have found a document that proves one of the Marshall planters had an enslaved son named Samuel, who was my great-great-grandfather. Y-DNA proves beyond a doubt we descend from that Marshall line.

"What we know for sure is that my brother's Y-DNA *proves* my paternal ancestors are from that line of Marshalls. It is scientifically true that either my Samuel's father or grandfather had to be a White man surnamed Marshall." Amy and Jennifer had heard it before, but if I kept proclaiming the theory aloud, someday the correct story would be proven.

Jennifer revealed, "There's a set of books called *A Rockaway in Talbot* in the Muscogee County library. It has a whole section about our Owens line in it."

"Yes, we were able to view all four volumes at the Talbot County Courthouse. You just have to make an appointment, though, because they're limiting entrance to two people in 'The Vault' at a time to review legal and land records. Those *Rockaway* books are with a doubt the best thing we found there, right?"

Amy agreed.

"I had already seen *Volume IV*, containing information about the Marshalls from Sacramento's LDS Family History Center, which also describes the White Owens."

Jennifer said, "Yes, that's the one I've seen. We were researching Annie Marshall, my third great-grandmother, and her husband, George Owens."

"Do you know where Annie died?" I asked.

"I don't know, but I think it could be Columbus, Georgia, because Annie's daughter, who took care of her, now lives in Columbus. I believe her mother is buried in Green Acres."

"Amy and I saw a headstone for someone named Annie Marshall in the Catholic Methodist Episcopal Cemetery on State Route 36." I replied.

"No," Jennifer contradicted. "I think my Annie is with her daughter and her children in Green Acres."

Amy said, "We heard Rosa was buried in the Waverly Hall Cemetery with William, but we couldn't find her there. We were by ourselves, though, so we could have missed it."

Sorry, Amy. There is no way the White Marshalls would commemorate William's Black family with a headstone, even if they were buried somewhere at Waverly Hall. Amy had been so disappointed, though, not to have found Rosa's headstone. After witnessing how the enslaved were treated in Putnam—buried amongst the snakes in a bamboo forest—I was not surprised in the least that we couldn't find Rosa buried near her enslaver/consort, William B. Marshall.

Jennifer revealed she used to work out there. "Not at the Waverly Hall Cemetery, but at a nursing home nearby."

"Did you ever eat at the Thai restaurant over there?" Amy asked.

"No," Jennifer replied.

Amy and I talked about how delicious the food was. In fact, Amy said it was the best Thai food she'd ever had. I wondered how many opportunities there were to sample different genres of food in her hometown in Utah. I hoped to experience them during a future visit with Amy's family.

"No, I never saw anything like that there, Jennifer replied. "You have to understand that it's kind of *country* out there in Harris County. So… you know how things have been here regarding the voting fraud allegations and Georgia barely turning *blue* in the 2020 election? Let's just say I don't stray too far into the *country* areas around here, at least not by myself."

Chuckling a bit, I told them about the dire predictions my African American genealogy friends warned me about driving alone in Alabama and Mississippi in 2019, when researching my Grandma Daisy's life. Oh, the grim predictions of death and rape! They made me promise to never drive by myself at night, or during the day in rural areas.

"In the car, we talked about those issues a lot. I would try to make a joke about the fact that there were so many sheriff cars out here, just waiting for an innocent Black person to come into view so they could be harassed ... or worse."

Amy said, "Yeah, she was driving me crazy with those tales!"

But I had to have my say because *it's true*. Some Koreans were killed in Georgia the day before our meal. "And each time I saw a police car, I'd say, 'Now don't be pulling me over, and don't give me any trouble, Dude.'"

Amy fake-laughed, saying, "And I was like, would you please stop?"

Yes, Driving While Black is tedious and frightening, but it happens all the time. Having conducted the *California Highway Patrol's Search Study* for three years, I understand how many police agencies *profile* brown-and-black-skinned motorists.

"Is it okay with you, Amy, if we change the subject?"

Laughing, she said, "Absolutely! If we never talk about that subject again, it will be too soon."

"Jennifer, here's my theory about your ancestor named Henry Marshall, who was born around 1830. I think he was the brother of my Samuel, also born around 1830. Have you found anything at all about Henry and where he was living in 1870?"

Jennifer shook her head. "No, sorry."

Amy said, "We've got to get you a DNA test."

So glad she brought that up, I wanted to "High Five" her.[21] I had tried for months to encourage Jennifer to get her folks tested so we could see if we shared enough DNA to prove we were related.

"I've got some test kits at home," Jennifer admitted.

"Have you taken it yet?"

Another head shake.

"Well, you've got to take it," Amy compelled. I don't think Jennifer likes being told what to do.

Jennifer said, "I'm on antibiotics for asthma, so I don't want to take the DNA test while taking medication. But I'm going to swab my dad because I got him a test kit, and one for my mom. She'll have to drool for me too."

We all laughed, knowing how surprisingly difficult it is to generate enough spit for the little tube that holds the saliva sample that most DNA companies require.

Doing the Happy Dance inside my head, I hoped Jennifer and her parents would take the tests and mail them in right away. Selfishly, I needed their results to be analyzed before I finished *The Marshall Legacy in Black and White* manuscript, which was due to my editor on July 1, 2021. Wouldn't it be great if DNA proved Jennifer, my, Amy, and Erika's genetic connection? That might lend credence to the theory that Henry Marshall was my Samuel's brother. That could possibly also explain why Samuel named one of his sons *Henry*—my great-grandfather who married who married my great-grandmother, Mary Smith, in 1888. Henry and Mary bore my grandfather, Austin *Henry* Marshall in 1892 in Columbus, Georgia. Jennifer Owens could be my key to documentation heaven. But I would have to wait on pins and needles for a couple of months before the results came in, after they spat in the tube.

Amy said, "My parents did it too. It's harder for older people to produce enough saliva."

"Well, you can refrigerate the partial sample, then try it again later to finish the job." Jennifer said.

"Oh really?"

"Yes, I read the instructions. For my dad, I ordered the My Heritage test, which is a cheek swab."

"I also use My Heritage, but not too many Black people purchase their test, for some reason. Did you say he has already given his sample?"

She shook her head, "No, he had a stroke in 2013 and now has dementia."

"My dad had dementia. I kick myself for not getting him the 23andme DNA test, which was also a swab test back then.

One of my biggest regrets in life was not getting his DNA sample before he died in 2014. My Marshall genealogy research would have been so much easier with his genetic sample. I am thankful my brother, Greg, has taken the 23andme, Family Tree DNA, and Ancestry tests."

Jennifer looked wistful. "It's hard work, taking care of them—the old ones, I mean. My mother is disabled, so I help her a lot. And I have my own health issues, so we take it day by day. My family comes first."

"It's wonderful that you have the choice to go back to work or not," I said.

Then Jennifer said something so very profound: "We always have a choice. We can decide on our course of action. Sometimes I'll make the wrong decision, just to see what happens. I can always pull back and maybe go in a different direction. We *always* have choices." I love her attitude and confidence.

Family Chat

"Oh, before I forget. I'll never forgive myself if I don't do this." I got up and squeezed into their side of the booth with my camera, to take some selfies with them.

Erika, please call right now. I hoped my request would make its way through the ether to Texas, and into Erika's brain so she would telephone us right away. Darn! No call.

Jennifer seemed to read my mind, wondering aloud, "How did Erika's family get to Texas, anyway?"

Amy shrugged but shared that her family migrated to Texas too.

"Kathy, your family went from Georgia to Ohio, right?" Jennifer asked.

"Yes, from Columbus, Georgia, to Cleveland, Ohio, where my dad and I were born. Then Dad was stationed in Seattle, Washington, for his military service in the Navy. He moved us down to San Diego, California, for another two years, serving as a Lieutenant in the Navy Medical Corps. After that, around 1961, we moved north to Stockton, California, to finish his medical residency. Once a bona fide doctor, he settled in the far eastern boonies of Sacramento, near Rancho Cordova, to start his obstetrics practice in 1964. He continued to work until 2000, when dementia forced his retirement."

"You're in California now?" Jennifer asked.

"Yep. I've lived in or near Sacramento since 1964."

"And you like it there? That's your forever home?" Jennifer asked,

"Absolutely," I smiled. "We are two hours from San Francisco and the Pacific Ocean, two hours from the snowy Sierra Mountains, six hours from Oregon in the north, and six hours from Los Angeles in the South. Winters are mild—generally above freezing as a low temperature—and summers are hot—which is great for growing vegetables. Yes, I love Central California."

"So where are your kids, Kathy?"

"Isaac, my oldest child, is in Okinawa, Japan, right now, in the Marines. He and his wife and three kids will be transferred next month to Hawaii, for a promotion to Master Sergeant."

"Oh wow! I've been to those places," Amy said, her smile suggesting fond memories of both islands.

"That will be his last billet and then he'll have earned his twenty years in the Marines. My youngest son lives in Sacramento and works for a State Department. This trip, this meeting," I extended my arms akimbo to encompass Amy and Jennifer, "is their legacy. You both are part of the legacy. I am thrilled you made the effort to be a part of this trip. I've been wanting to grt together with cousins for a long time."

Jennifer said, "One of the descendants of the owners of my Williams family had written a book about a lynching in Harris

County. The author had arranged for the White and Black family lines to come to the table, talking about their roots in racism and how they felt about it. I was able to meet the author. She had a reading at a bookstore, signed the book for me *and* ... she gave me the record of my enslaved ancestor!"

"How cool is that!" Amy and I both exclaimed.

"I was able to get so much more information for that side of the family thanks to that record. Kathy, you have Williams in your family too, right?"

"Yes, on my mom's side, though," I responded, a tickle prompted the genealogy folder stowed in my brain to open.

"But they're not from the South?"

Shaking my head, "Not that I know of, yet, *however*, with enslaved people being sold 'Down South' like cattle for slaughter, I can't say for sure.

What I do know is that Mom's immediate Williams ancestors were from Ohio, and Maryland before that. In fact, my first success as a genealogist was on that Williams line. In 2018, I wrote about the process in *Finding Otho: The Search for Our Enslaved Williams Ancestors*. I split off one of my five research goals—to trace the descendants of the enslaved Otho Williams—into a separate book called *The Ancestors Are Smiling!* which I published in 2017. There's still a lot more I want to know about our Williams line; perhaps there are more answers in the South."

Jennifer reminded us that Talbot, Troup, Taylor, and Harris Counties used to all be part of Muscogee County before 1827. "All of my relatives are pretty much from these parts, and we've been in this area for a long time. I guess it's easier for me to find my roots than most Black people."

I didn't want to admit how petty jealous I was of her good fortune. I lived 2,500 miles away from my relatives and had to spend the big bucks for travel and copies of documents to find crumbs of information. On the flip side, I was glad she had such great luck and told her I hoped that one day she'd have the time to write her heritage stories, too.

"Wherever we've gone on this trip I've asked people: "Do you have any Marshalls in your lineage, or Burts, Bunkleys, Ligons, or Smiths? Amy and I just learned yesterday that the woman who runs the 'Vintage' antique store across from the train depot on 10th Street has generations of relations in this area. She was kind enough to share a lot of history about that part of Columbus. In fact, the people here have been very open about their forced-labor history and how things are now."

Amy asked, "Kathy, you mean like where we were visiting today, trying to find the house your family lived in?"

"Yep, my family lived at 1710 Fifth Avenue, near Linwood Cemetery, from the 1890s until 1928," I replied.

Jennifer said, "I live about two blocks from there, on the other side of the hospital. Most Black folk lived in that general area."

My head was swimming, wanting to go to Jennifer's house right then and there and have her show me exactly where my family's home would have been before it had been demolished in favor of more profitable businesses. I wanted to know what businesses were there, as well as interview her live-in parents about the old days. But our time was short, and Jennifer had to leave soon to take her mother to the doctor.

The waitress brought our orders and Jennifer said grace. While we ate, Jennifer explained what her life was like taking care of her aged parents. Then she asked about Amy's lineage.

"We're fourteen percent Norwegian, eleven percent Swedish, Irish and Scottish, Welsh, and English. I have six kids and four of them are redheads. My husband is a redhead, but I'm not. I was always told that parents must carry the recessive redhead gene to produce children who have the trait. I don't know much about my dad because my parents divorced when I was little, so maybe Dad's side had the trait for red hair."

Was it Love or Lechery?

After a sip from her beverage, Amy cleared her throat. "We've had the best time in Georgia. People have been very helpful and friendly. Yesterday, we traveled with Mike Buckner, an expert from Talbot County."

Displaying a concerned look on her face, Amy continued, "And, by the way, I feel horrible that William B. Marshall was my ancestor, but it feels good to be part of this Welcome to the Table the Table adventure. It doesn't take away what was done in the past, but I'm glad to meet you both." Everybody smiled.

"I hate to talk shop," I began, after swallowing one of my delicious shrimps, "but I want to ask you about Rosa and *the guy*. You both had very astute observations about the love-or-force issue in *The Marshall Legacy* manuscript I sent for your feedback. I was playing both sides of the fence with how to portray William B. Marshall, the owner of ninety-some-odd human beings. I also asked Mike Buckner his opinion yesterday about how likely it was that William was a a decent guy or a lech.[22] Mike personally knew William's great-grandson, who was a telegrapher in Talbotton. Mike said the great-grandson and his wife kept to themselves. Some might call that behavior standoffish. I asked if that was an indicator of William's behavior.

"Mike took a moment, then replied, 'All I know is that a lot of his former enslaved workers kept the Marshall surname after slavery, and they didn't have to do that. I would think that if a slaveholder was cruel, his freed persons of color would scrap that surname and take another. Yet, many of the Blacks stayed in Talbot or Muscogee County and kept their Marshall name,' he concluded."

Jennifer said, "Kathy, I think you should be sensitive about how William is portrayed in the book, since you don't know the truth about his actual demeanor toward his enslaved property. Remember that future readers, young and old, Black and White, might learn about William through your words. You have to be careful with the stories you write."

Amy nodded and several times uttered, "Yeah, yeah," as Jennifer was giving her opinion.

But Amy was not as willing to give William an understanding "pass" because of his slaveholding behavior. She brought up a scene from the *Underground Railroad* TV series where she saw a slaveholder forcing an enslaved man to couple with an enslaved female in order to *grow* the owner's crop. That man was called a "breeder," purchased like a stud horse to procreate strong Black babies who would become laborers for the plantation owner. Or the enslaved offspring could be sold like a commodity.

Amy frowned. "I was horrified to learn the slaveholder often watched the couple to make sure the seed had been planted. I'm used to married folk being loving, monogamous couples. I absolutely hate being related to William Marshall, who created a known Mulatto family with his enslaved Rosa."

"And he possibly had kids with my Black Marshall family ancestors," I added. Amy's pure understanding of monogamous marriage was not always possible for the enslaved, whose bodies were not their own. But bless her for being so indignant toward some of her ancestor's behaviors.

Jennifer and I listened, already knowing that the voyeur behavior Amy described was true and happened with regularity. According to our research, peppered with some actual family tales, slaveholder actions were often much worse than just watching the act.

Black people whose pale skin looks like mine have many female ancestors who were likely accosted by White men to produce us mixed-race children.

This topic epitomized the beauty of a Welcome to the Table the Table experience. White people, who have little knowledge of what it means to be Black in America, can learn the truth of normal African American daily life which is never taught in schools. Of course, there is a Bell-shaped curve of socioeconomic reality amongst the African Americans, from the very wealthy—think Oprah Winfrey—to the very poor. The news media often portrays the most negative elements in the Black community, not the regular folks who are hardworking, family-oriented people who navigate systemic racism the best they can.

Jennifer and I explained to Amy that forced workers had no rights to make choices for their lives. If two enslaved people were in love and wanted to "jump the broom,"[23] they had to get permission from their owner(s). Legally, enslaved persons could not marry, and it was rare they could live together as husband and wife if they were owned by different masters. A husband from a different plantation might be allowed to visit his wife on specific days only.

When enslaved babies were born, the female's owner usually visited the newborns right after birth to give them an official name, which was logged in the family Bible or a property ledger. The enslaved could rarely name their own children, but it was common for parents to give them nicknames. Those nicknames make genealogy research difficult for their present-day descendants to find their official names. Enslaved people of all ages were owned by the slaveholder to do with as they pleased: to keep or to sell, to name, or to maim.

Jennifer and I were still not sure Amy was buying what we were selling. Some things are just too heinous for a religious White woman who isn't exposed to the ugliness that many minorities endure every day.

Monogamy in marriage doesn't always happen. We all know that. Planter/owner William B. Marshall was married to Mary Annice Flournoy. His concubine, Rosa, was married to his enslaved worker, Benjamin Marshall. It is likely Rosa had no choice but to couple with William whenever, wherever, and however he wished.

To keep things in historical perspective, Mike Buckner suggested that Rosa's family may have received more clothes, better food, a nicer house, easier jobs, etc., in exchange for her favors to the master. I've read the same thing in different texts. Amy expressed disgust at the very concept—bless her pure heart.

I believe Rosa may have actually exercised a measure of power to improve the living conditions for her husband and her nine children (five Black children with Benjamin and four Mulattos with

William). We will never know the truth. So, in Chapter 18 of *The Marshall Legacy in Black and White*, I tried to present both potential sides of the coin, leaving it to the reader to judge Master William Blount Marshall's true character.

Clearing the air, Jennifer piped up. "It's just like my Owens line. Their descendants are still living in Talbot County, carrying the Owens name, like many enslaved Marshalls did. The same given names were also doled out from one generation to the next."

We could tell Amy still wasn't convinced that William could be considered a decent human being, while owning over ninety enslaved individuals at one point. She couldn't quite grasp that he could be *my* three-times great-grandfather and that I wasn't fighting mad about it. In Amy's experience and understanding as a follower of the Church of Latter-Day Saints, a man loves one woman, and that is his wife (which is weird to me, because Mormons were known to be polygamists back in the day).

Amy couldn't fathom why Jennifer and I seemed to be okay if a pretty Black woman used her beauty to get a better life for her children.

This situation reminded me of the Black matron in "The Underground" TV series who controlled her master sexually in the bedroom but served as the dutiful lead housekeeper during the daylight hours. Horrendous? Maybe, but the enslaved were not allowed to participate in their own lives. If some of them found creative ways to get what they wanted and what their families needed, I would say, "Go on with your bad self!"

Another disconcerting conversation was whether a woman forced to be a concubine could actually love her enslaver. In general, I think Black women put in that position did *not* love the White man exercising his power over her. They were forced to submit. That's the definition of rape, pure and simple. It's comforting for some Mulattos to believe those master-slave ancestor relationships were consensual. I wasn't there; maybe some of them were. There have been recorded cases where a White man pretended to be a Negro because he wanted to be married to the Black woman he loved.

Miscegenation–reproduction by parents of different races–was illegal until the late 1960s in many states, even though there were some loving Black-White relationships before then. But for the most part, I do *not* believe Black women who were forced to make babies liked it or asked for it.

However, I believe people can love more than one person in a lifetime (and even at the same time). In my playbook, William could have loved his wife *and* Rosa at the same time. A lot of White men were, and are, attracted to Black women. It's possible that Rosa wasn't a total victim, that she played the master's game so her Black family could live more comfortably. That power-play concept is abhorrent to some, but a necessity to survival for others.

That Amy struggled so mightily with this contradictory material made me love her all the more. She and I could *not* have gotten along as well if she felt like many in this country who chant for non-Whites to go back to where they came from ... even though they feel it's okay for them as Euro-immigrants to stay in the land they appropriated from indigenous people. Amy definitely tries to be an enlightened person, and that's half the battle.

Taking the Speaker Stick again, it was time for a little genealogy. "I have a theory about the plight of enslaved Hannah, who may have lived in William's household when he was growing up. His dad, Stephen B. Marshall, married Elizabeth Burt in 1793. She was given an enslaved girl named Hannah from her father, Joseph Burt.

Elizabeth BURT was born on 20 January 1774 in Halifax County, North Carolina, daughter of Joseph BURT and Elizabeth (?).

Elizabeth BURT was named an heir in the will of Joseph BURT dated on 20 June 1788 in Halifax County, North Carolina. "I give and bequeath to my beloved Daughter Elizabeth Burt one negro girl named Hannah to be delivered to her when she comes to the age of Eighteen Years old or sooner if she marries, and also one sorrel mare..."[1,2]

Elizabeth BURT appeared on a census, enumerated 2 August 1790, in the household of Elizabeth (?) in Halifax County, North Carolina.[3]

Elizabeth married Stephen MARSHALL, son of David MARSHALL and Mary DAVIS, circa 1793 in Halifax County, North Carolina.

I believe Hannah was Joseph's Mulatto daughter—or the daughter of one of his sons. Why? Because my family has over twenty DNA relatives who indicate they descend from that Burt family line. When Stephen's wife died in 1820, Hannah became Stephen Marshall's *property*. He never remarried, so it's my theory that Hannah could have been Elizabeth's half-sister. Hannah could have become Stephen's concubine when Elizabeth died in 1820, taking care of his children *and* him (if you know what I mean), until he died eleven years later in 1831.

It cannot be assumed, though, that Hannah loved Stephen if my theory is correct. She likely had no choice in the matter. In fact, according to Stephen's 1830 Will, an enslaved woman named Hannah was married to a man named Essex, and their children were Sam, Mitchell, and Annie. Was that Sam my three-times great-grandfather and Hannah my four-times great-grandmother? One day, I'm hoping to prove or disprove that theory.

On that same Stephen B. Marshall 1831 Inventory List of property, there was a woman named Oney (27), a man named John (30), and a daughter named Rose (10). That Rose may have later been called Rosa, who was forced to become Stephen's son, William B. Marshall's, concubine. It's definitely a bird's nest of possibilities.

Am I light-skinned because multiple, Caucasian, three-times great-grandfathers made Mulatto babies with their enslaved women, and I descend from those forced concubines? DNA says my genetic mixture is half-African and almost half-European, with a tiny bit of East and North American Indian. It's an ugly truth that many African Americans must carry to this day.

Cousin Jennifer K.—who joined Amy and me on the first day of our adventure with Cousin Jim Marshall in Putnam—had a different view of who Hannah might have been. She thought Hannah might have been light-skinned enough to marry one of the Burt sons who migrated to Pike County, Alabama. Jennifer descends from the Burt and Marshall lines and is the history expert in her family. I was all ears to absorb whatever Jennifer wanted to tell me.

Amy is a very intelligent woman who is a strong proponent of inclusivity. She explained to me in the car that her LDS religion preaches "embrace-all-cultures" concepts. But her eyes opened wide many times during Jennifer and my revelations at lunch, as she attempted to understand that her optimistic view of the world is not as rosy for all people.

Cousin Amy says she has lived in the poorer parts of Indiana and feels she knows a thing or two about the treatment of people living in socio-economically-depressed neighborhoods. But her sunny outlook on life was rattled during our Georgia trip of discovery. I hoped she would take what she learned from the Deep South back home to her flock, to continue enlarging their understanding of how some people are still treated in America. I'd love to see more White people become antiracists—actively encouraging their racist friends to become more understanding and inclusive to people who look different from what they see in the mirror.

Jennifer said, "I've had great luck in finding my ancestors. I credit my ancestors with helping me to find answers to our family history questions. I sure hope DNA will determine whether my Henry and Kathy's Samuel Marshall are brothers. They were both born around 1830 and both married Bunkley women, you know."

It was time to change topics. "You'll never believe the thrilling sleuthing trek that Mike took Amy and me on! He had us scrutinizing every driveway off Highway 208, trying to find the Marshall plantation. He parked his vehicle on a weed-choked gravel road. And we both shouted, 'That's it!'" I related our adventure using my best 1960s slow-and-deliberate *Dragnet* TV show voice and showed Jennifer the pictures we took.

"Once we consulted the *Rockaway* book, we became convinced it was the Bunkley house instead. But that was still cool because Jennifer and I have Bunkleys in our family history. In the video I took on the premises, I wondered aloud if I was walking in the footsteps of our respective ancestors in that very yard." I think all of us got goosebumps just thinking about it.

Coda

Jennifer ordered a fish dinner-to-go for her mother as we were finishing our meals. We asked the waitress to take pictures of us together. After an armload of hugs, and me holding back tears, we said goodbye.

Life is so weird. Within sixty seconds of Jennifer leaving the parking lot, Erika finally called. Darn! "Missed it by that much," as Agent 86 of the *Get Smart* TV show used to say when something went a little bit off plan. We chatted with Erika for about ten minutes via Amy's smartphone before Erika had to get back to work. We told her about the wonderful time we had with Jennifer and that we missed her, our Texas cousin.

Wanting to be sensitive, I took this opportunity to ask how Erika wanted me to present the master-slave relationship between her direct line ancestors, William and Rosa Marshall.

Erika replied, "Just tell the truth: that Rosa was owned and had four children by her owner. Enough said."

OK, I got the desired clarification. I like to ensure that people mentioned in my books approve of how I portray them or their family before I press the "print" button.

After hanging up with Erika, Amy and I sat for a few more minutes, talking about how to interpret a few DNA results. Then we rehashed our entire experience together: the highs and lows, the scary and funny, the heartwarming and the disgusting. I was sad that our adventure together was going to end too soon. We drove a couple of minutes to her Holiday Inn Express hotel. Amy would fly back to Utah the next day. More hugs and promises to stay in touch, then I wished her adieu, and got on the road to the next leg of my Deep South journey.

My destination was a Hampton Inn Hotel forty minutes away in Auburn, Alabama. During my drive, alone for the first time in five days, I reminisced about the interesting conversations Amy and I had during our days and nights together. The topics we discussed while traveling in the car were the most memorable and interesting, and some were downright taboo.

In upper right photo: Cousins Kathy Marshall, Jennifer Owens, and Amy Peacock. Bottom center: Erika Thomas on a video chat with Kathy and Amy.

> Lesson Learned #25: A face-to-face or online meeting can go very far in fostering a loving, familial relationship with people of different backgrounds. Stories may be shared, differing upbringings brought to light, and the healing of wounds caused by racial divides secured.

Chapter 12: Car Talk+

What does "Car Talk+" mean, anyway? What would two women from different racial backgrounds talk about while driving long distances in an unfamiliar state, meeting new relatives, and grappling with the unpopular topic of slavery? What follows are myriad interesting talks in the car, the hotel room, and with people we chatted with during *and after* our May 2021 trip to Georgia: sentimental, scintillating, salacious, shocking, saddening issues. These topics stretched the imagination and forced us to come to grips with America, then and now.

    This is the reason I decided to write an entire book about this genealogy trip, instead of my usual twenty-page photo book, was the exciting fact that several new Black and White cousins wanted to join me in Georgia and Alabama. My car mate Amy, in particular, was aghast that her Marshall and Blount ancestors owned Black people. She wanted to do everything in her power to help me and other enslaved descendants in her Marshall line. I think she believed this trip was a kind of "Christian mission," helping her atone for her ancestors. Even though I know she had nothing to do with those enslaver behaviors, I was delighted to help her feel good about helping me. It's a win-win, right?

So what? Who cares?

Our country is divided. Nationalism, climate change, COVID vaccinations, and voting rights are divisive issues right now, as is continued racial and sexual discrimination. Kindness and civility have given way to a cancer fed by mistrust and hate. If we don't come to a truce soon, the sickness could result in a dystopian Civil War. We need to listen to one another and come to enough of a consensus to avoid cataclysm.

These types of discussions are doable attempts at healing our country and our world. This chapter is divided into three groupings: 1) Slavery and Being Black, 2) Black and White Issues, and 3) Religion and Family.

How would *you* present these sensitive issues to your relatives, especially those who have disparate opinions about these topics?

Do you have the typical Caucasian fears, like "What if I accidentally say something racist? What are the acceptable (PC: politically correct) terms nowadays? What if my family finds out I'm sharing our personal information with "those people" (e.g., Blacks, Asians, Hispanics, Native Americans, gays)? What if those new cousins want to meet with us face-to-face?"

Or, do you have the typical African American fears like, "What if they hang up the phone, and block me from viewing their online family tree and their DNA results, once they find out I'm Black? Will they respond to my request to chat about our common ancestry? Will they send the KKK after me?"

These car talks are the most important part of this book. The purpose of sharing these stories is to shed light on what real people's lives are like, not the fluff presented on the nightly news. They may help explain the reasons why there are still economic, educational, and social differences among various groups of people in America. This information is not taught in the history books. It's hard to learn about others if one has no concept of their day-to-day reality. Amy,

Erika, Jennifer O., Jennifer K., Eddie and I talked about the following issues to try to forge a common understanding.

The intent of this book is to encourage people to listen to one another, to try to be understanding of the other person's viewpoint, and to act civilly. I may be naive, but could Welcome to the Table-types of discourses save our world from internal destruction?

The Time of Slavery and Beyond

My Ancestors Owned People! What Should I Do?

Kathy: A lady in one of my writing groups revealed she found bills of sale, wills that bequeathed Black people to family members, personal letters mentioning the enslaved, and other evidence that some of her ancestors were slaveholders. She was shocked and dismayed.

Amy: I know, right? That's why I feel better being here with you, helping you in any way I can to find our genetic connections.

Kathy: Believe me, Amy, all of us appreciate your willingness to share your genealogy documentation with us. But my writing friend did not know how to proceed. She wanted to pass on her information to the enslaved's descendants, so I offered her the following suggestions:

> First, understand that the descendants of slaveholders are *not* responsible for slavery. Things our ancestors did in the past should not automatically reflect on their progeny.
>
> Use the "Member Connect" option in Ancestry.com to note whether any African Americans are searching for those slaveholding ancestors; those searchers may be the descendants of the forced workers.
>
> "Check the DNA results of the slaveholding family. This could include DNA "matches" (i.e., relatives) from the various DNA testing companies, or Ancestry.com's

ThruLines[24] to see if those descendants are genetically related.

"Create a spreadsheet of the enslaved people's names, slaveholder names, locations, etc., found in family documents. Also include the sources where enslaved data was found, like from the Will of deceased's name, date, location, any of the slave's names also listed, age, complexion, skills, monetary value, etc.

"Check ancestry.com, 23andme.com,FamilySearch.org, and social media outlets like Facebook, to see if the descendants have contact information.

"Contact the descendants with a short email saying something like: "Hello. I was reviewing my family's genealogy records and found some information that might be about your ancestor's name who lived in this place in this year. I'd be pleased to share that information if you are interested. You may contact me at ___ (include your contact information)."

"Provide your slave-related information on blog posts and online genealogy groups in specific states and counties.

"Post your information onto genealogy-oriented Facebook pages, such as: Slave Names - Found and Shared in Genealogy, My Enslaved and Enslaver Ancestors, Beyond Kin: (https://beyondkin.org/), and email Sharon Morgan of Our Black Ancestry at morganoba@gmail.com.

"If your African American DNA matches contact you with questions about how your Caucasian family connects with them, please answer with as much information as possible. It is as difficult to trace the histories of the formerly enslaved as it is those who were adopted.

Is Peonage a Kind of Slavery by Another Name?

Kathy: Did you know that peonage–unpaid prison labor–is allowed by the 13th Amendment of the U.S. Constitution? It says: "Neither slavery nor involuntary servitude, *except as a punishment for crime whereof the party shall have been duly convicted*, shall exist within the United States."

Amy: Peonage? No, I never heard of it.

Kathy: Also called debt servitude, peonage is a system where an employer compels a worker to pay off a debt with work. Convict leasing was a system of forced penal labor which was often practiced in the Southern United States and overwhelmingly involved African-American men.[25] In the town where my grandfather was born and raised, each day the Columbus Consolidated Government dispatches about 425 inmates for outside work detail and, around 150 inmates remain inside their facility to provide services and to maintain City property. Replacing the inmates with regular city employees would cost more than $10.5 million annually.[26]

Amy: That's crazy. It *does* sound like slavery still exists in the Georgia city where your grandfather was born.

Forced to Eat from a Pig Trough?

Kathy: In my research of slave narratives and biographies, I learned that the cruelest owners sometimes forced their enslaved to eat their meals from a trough, like how pigs and horses were fed. This was more common for planters who had a lot of enslaved workers to feed. No plates or eating utensils were provided, so the people had to kneel at the trough and scoop the food into their mouths with their hands. I learned from Gloria Hardnett—a cousin of Maybelle's, whom the Buckners let us visit—that their great-aunt worked seven days per week for a White family in Talbot. She was paid one can of sardines per week as her compensation and ... she was forced to eat her employer's leftovers while kneeling at a trough in the backyard. This horrendous, unbelievable, unacceptable behavior occurred in the 1930s in the township where my great-grandfather was born and raised.

Amy: That's AWFUL! I remember the Buckners sharing an interesting story that illustrated that slavery was carried out differently in different places. She revealed that on Sapelo Island, there was an African American overseer who was more flexible with the schedule. He gave the slaves an opportunity to work their own plots of land or fish.

Kathy: It's always important to remember that slavery was not a one-size-fits-all thing, although we hear many more of the horrific stories than the humane ones.

House and Field Negroes

Kathy: Historically, more light-skinned Blacks were used as "house Negroes" serving as cooks, waiters, chamber maids, wet nurses, and babysitters. This is often contrasted with darker-skinned Blacks who were more often forced to work in the fields. A famous history expert named E. Franklin Frazier argued that Mulattoes—Blacks with White progenitors—led a more privileged existence when compared with their "pure Black" counterparts. During slavery, these fair-skinned Blacks were at times emancipated by their White fathers. After slavery, their kinship ties to Whites gave them an advantage over other Blacks in obtaining education, higher-status occupations, and property.[27]

Amy: My understanding is that house Negroes had lighter workloads and perhaps a possibility of nicer clothes than field Negroes. However, did that also make the women working indoors more accessible to their owners to rape or sexually abuse them!?!

Kathy: I think so. Some women who were the object of the master's advances, like our cousin, Rosa Marshall, probably had no choice but to do what her master demanded, whenever they demanded it. Rosa had four children by her owner, William B. Marshall, while she was married to Benjamin Marshall, with whom she had five more. I don't think Rosa had a choice, and I don't think she loved William. But based on a photograph I've seen of her Mulatto son, Marshall, it's possible that she and her Mulatto children *did* receive better clothing, and more food rations, and better work opportunities. I suspect Rosa and Benjamin would have preferred NOT to have a White man sniffing around, but perhaps they didn't suffer physically as much as other Blacks on the plantation. We'll never know whether Rosa loved William and her husband, or not, will we?

What is Colorism?

Kathy: All my life people have been asking, "Are you mixed?" And I would reply, "No, I'm Black, can't you tell?" Light-skinned African Americans who look like me, but don't have a known White relative, assume that an owner (or other White man) had their way with our enslaved female ancestors. I have a specific story in *The Mystery of Margaret Booker* about my three-times great-grandmother, Margaret Booker, and how her Mulatto children were conceived.

Being light-skinned does not guarantee me tons of friends in the Black community. Even though my art business is called Kanika African Sculptures, for many years the Black community did not accept me as a Black artist. So, I have experienced White and Black racism. Waah, waah, waah (whining). I know I've probably had an easier life than many darker-hued people, and it's understandable that I might incur their wrath, but I don't have to like it.

A dictionary explanation of "colorism" or "shadeism" says it's a form of prejudice and/or discrimination in which people who share similar ethnic traits, or perceived race, are treated differently based on the social implications that come with the cultural meanings that are attached to skin color.

Amy: What I remember about this topic was that you didn't like people asking why you were so light and were offended that they might suggest that you had some Caucasian blood in your family tree. It seems that was something that kept you from truly feeling accepted by darker African Americans. You also hated Whites because of what you had seen with all the discrimination and racism and did not want to be part of them especially by blood! I say that with all empathy, as it is completely understandable! 🩶

Who Names Enslaved Babies?

Kathy: One of the research crumbs I am trying to piece together is the use of first "given" names from one generation to the next, noting the commonalities in the names of the Marshall owners and the names they gave their forced workers.

Amy: What do you mean?

Kathy: From all I've read or heard about for decades, it was generally owners who named the enslaved newborns, often naming their young human property after their family members or their Caucasian friends and business associates. For example, my great-great-grandfather, Samuel Marshall, may have been named for owner William's Uncle Samuel; and William named his son born in 1841, Samuel. The children of my Black Samuel who were born during slavery were:

- Josephine (1858–?): possibly named after William's Aunt Josephine Burt or family friend Ella Josephine Ligon who was living in next door Harris County, GA?

- Wright (1862–1923): maybe named after William's friend surnamed Wright?

- Searcy (1860–?): possibly named after William's fellow plantation owner surnamed Searcy?

- Henry (1861–1897?): perhaps named after a Black Henry born in 1830 or son of Henry Malone Marshall?

- Austin (1864–?): My grandfather was named Austin Henry Marshall Sr. and he named his son Austin Henry Marshall Jr, and his son was Austin David Marshall. That propensity to carry on the father's name continued to this day.

- Samuel's last two babies were born after emancipation, so it is likely he and his wife were able to choose their children's first and last names, as follows:

  àClarra (1868–?): was the name derived from Clarra, a possible enslaved woman living on William's property in 1880?

  àSam (1868–1934): was derived from his father, Samuel.

Amy: Why does it matter who named the children or why they were named that way?

Kathy: Well, if I can show a pattern of naming in my Black Marshall relatives, it might help prove that my relatives were indeed enslaved by, and maybe related to, a specific Marshall. That helps direct my investigation into the probate and tax records of specific owners. Additionally, in combination with DNA testing, naming conventions may help me prove who our White genetic relations are.

Amy: I assumed the enslaved could name their own children, so this is an eye opener.

Kathy: The enslaved were rarely given that power, I'll wager. Everything in most slave's lives was directed by his or her owner. The enslaved rarely had a say in decisions made on their behalf. If the master wanted to call the baby CooCoo or Craphead, that's what their name would be.

Like in the story *Roots: An American Family,* by Alex Haley. The teenaged teenager named Kunta Kinte was stolen from his home in Africa and beaten within an inch of his life by his new master. Why? Because Kunta refused to accept the new name "Toby" that his master had given him. Most masters changed the Africans' names to something more anglicized—easier to pronounce.

Amy: I honestly did *not* know that owners gave babies their first names, until our trip! I knew they were forced to take the slaveholder's last name and I knew freed people of color could change their surnames after slavery.

Is Driving While Black a Real Thing?

Kathy: One day, it seemed every twenty miles there was a police car parked at the side of the highway, just waiting for a reason to stop the few drivers on the road. Each time, after passing the car I would make a comment like, "Whew! I dodged a bullet with that one!"

Let me preface what I'm going to say by reminding you that I worked for the California Highway Patrol for 36 years. I loved my job there and had a lot of respect for many of the officers and uniformed management during my tenure. With that said, I explained to Amy that most Black parents teach their children to be extra careful when they're driving a car. We caution them to keep their hands on the steering wheel if they are stopped by a police officer. If the officer tells them to retrieve their car registration and that registration document is in the glove box, we counsel our children to keep their hands on that steering wheel at all times. There have been way, way, way too many instances where a police officer shoots the innocent driver, then says something like, "I feared for my life when they reached for the glove box," even though it was the officer that forced the driver to reach for the glove box!

We urge our children to be safe behind the wheel: no swerving, no speeding, no drugs or open alcohol, no goofing off. But many times, it's not enough to be following all the rules. If an All-Points Bulletin alerts the police to "An Armed Black Man Driving on Interstate 5 South," any Black man could "fit the description" of the generic "wanted man" and be pulled over and searched. Or worse.

Three years in a row, I was the analyst who prepared the "Search Study" of law enforcement practices for the California Highway Patrol. I know what a "pretext stop" and "probable cause" means. The line between a legal stop and an illegal stop is a fine one. Police must have either witnessed a violation of the law or have *probable cause* to stop a vehicle in order to do so. Some police officers aren't really that interested in the low-level traffic violation used as a *pretense* to stop the motorist, like a broken headlight, or missing registration tag on the license plate. The officer is after a drug bust, not a traffic ticket. If after making the stop, they can make a case for a DUI (driving under the influence), they will do so with glee, for it may count as a "work activity" if their department has work quotas. Being suspected of a drug violation almost always results in an embarrassing physical search of the vehicle and the driver. We know from the nightly news what sometimes happens to nonwhite drivers in America who are pulled over on a pretext stop. It's a practice that happens all the time, often with deadly results. I don't want that for my children or for me.

So, every twenty miles on Amy's and my trip in Georgia, when we saw another police car waiting by the side of the road for a potential victim, I made a joke about it. I would express fear about being stopped Driving While Black, then chuckle, saying, "Oh, I was kind of kidding." But it *truly was* a concern of mine. I was in the South, after all. Its reputation for not valuing Black lives precedes it. I know it got on Amy's last nerve. But there was one instance when I almost did have a big problem.

Most of my friends feel I drive like an old grandma. I do not exceed the speed limit by more than five miles per hour, preferring to maximize fuel performance. On this trip, I was so enthralled with everything around me, I had to remind myself to press the accelerator to *achieve* the speed limit. Well, this one time, I was approaching a steep hill and I was afraid my little Ford Fiesta rental wouldn't have enough giddyap, so I floored it. The Fiesta raised up on its hind legs like a stallion getting ready to race! Thankfully, just before I reached the top of the hill, I released my foot from the accelerator. Just on the other side of the hill's apex was a police officer waiting at the side of the road. Sweating BBs, I didn't turn my head toward him as I drove past, hoping I had slowed down enough. I didn't hear any sirens and didn't see him in my rearview window. "Whew! I escaped another one," I gasped to Amy.

Apologizing for bringing it up again, I was glad I was not pulled over. What I was unable to say to her—and was angry at myself for fearing her retribution—was that I was worried each time we passed a police car in Georgia. I was the Manager of the California Highway Patrol's Selection Research Program, providing recruiting and hiring statistics to management, as well as conducting evaluations on various law enforcement programs. I know the statistics. And like everybody else who watches the nightly news, I know what too-often happens on the road to Brown-and-Black-skinned people, so I was angry that I felt the need to apologize for my feelings and concerns.

Amy: What I gleaned from our conversation that really opened my eyes was that because of racial profiling, law enforcement officials often target individuals for suspicion of crime based on the person's race, ethnicity, and religion. When this occurs, the police rely on a group of characteristics they believe to be associated with crime. Examples of racial profiling are the use of race to determine which drivers to stop for minor traffic violations (commonly referred to as "Driving while Black, Asian, Native American, Middle Eastern, Hispanic, or Brown"), or the use of race to determine which pedestrians to search for illegal contraband.

When a society adopts racial profiling, as the United States of America has, and the penalty for the crime is deemed convict labor; this can set intergenerational patterns. For example, Caucasians continue to suspect that persons of color are involved in deviant behavior. Persons of color then have children who grow up seeing their family members, often males, serving in convict labor. They have the image in their minds that is what life is supposed to look like for the adults and they don't aspire to more. Convict labor also puts the Caucasian race in a master-like position, overseeing the convicts in their prison issued jumpsuits, performing the forced labor.

Kathy: The girl gets it!

The Angry Black Woman

Kathy: "Cousin Amy, you've never raised your voice in anger, rolled your eyes, or told me to stop venting about the continued unfairness toward minorities. You've always had a positive attitude, were upbeat, had an endearing smile and kind words. I have to tell you something that I am embarrassed to share. That last morning in the hotel, I was pacing, upset that you were taking so long to get dressed. Later, I redressed myself for being so angry that morning. You had certainly borne more inconveniences than I on this trip, especially that horrible first afternoon in Atlanta [see Chapter 4]. But like my Caucasian boyfriend, on that Thursday morning, subconsciously, you had become the scapegoat for all my pent-up anger that comes from doing incredibly difficult research on enslaved ancestors, 24-7. I had become the Sharon Morgan of our trip—the angry Black woman—as described in her excellent *Gather at the Table* book that she wrote with Thomas Norman DeWolf. As a presenter at the virtual 2021 RootsTech Genealogy Conference in Salt Lake City, Utah, Sharon described how she almost killed her trip mate.

Amy: Yeah, I watched Sharon's RootsTech presentation, and wondered what the White guy did to make her so very angry at him. I feared that I would be regarded in the same light by you, Kathy.

Kathy: Those fears crossed my mind, too, not knowing how we would get along. I'm kind of a loner who has never traveled with anyone else on a genealogy trip. But to answer your question, I did contact Sharon after her presentation and asked her what terrible thing he had done to make her so angry with him. Here is her answer:

Sharon: How could Thomas not understand why most Black people are still struggling in America? How could he not know America has a different set of rules and laws which intentionally restrict Black freedoms? How could he be so clueless? How could he not understand how we feel? There was never a break from the smiling White face sitting next to me who didn't comprehend a thing. They want to be understanding, but there's no way they can ever "get it."

Kathy: Sound familiar? My mind has often raced through all of those same questions with the White people I encounter every day, including my Caucasian significant other, who has *never* sided with the White nationalistic ideology. I sometimes feel bad about feeling so mad. Then I feel madder that I feel bad about being mad. Why *can't* Black folks be angry at White privilege, at people who simply don't get what it's like to experience racism or sexism or ageism. Every day on social media and the news, we hear about racial minorities, LGBTQ, and women who are subjected to unequal treatment by, especially, White males in power.

Why do we have to walk on tiptoes and be nice and understanding and tell White folks, "You're one of the good ones," when a Caucasian treats us as an equal? Why do we have to back off our demands for equal treatment, when some White folks now feel bad that true and complete American history is starting to be told? How the truth of their ancestors' barbarous actions toward Native Americans, Asians, Latinos, LGBTQ, and Blacks is being unveiled for all the world to see. People like me who are writing our family histories, and Black filmmakers who are telling our stories on the big screen and social media?

Why can't "Critical Race Theory" be taught in schools to tell real history which includes the contributions of non-Whites to the greatness of our wonderful nation? Why can't our Black children read about the positive accomplishments of their ancestors? Why is only White history sanctioned for schools? Why can't we marginalized groups point a finger of blame at Caucasians for their colonialism, their sexism, their racist laws that were made to keep Black and Brown folks in line, the lynchings, the refusal to hire us or grant our home loan applications, and on and on, ad infinitum?

Why do we Black folk always have to be the ones to turn the other cheek, to be grateful for the "good (White) ones" to befriend us? That's what drives some of us up a wall. That's what makes the Black Woman angrier than a hornet's nest.

What adds to the discomfort is the fact that many of us feel our only hope, Obi Wan Kenobi, is to befriend the "anti-racist" White people, those who want to understand our angst and help fix the problem. We suspect they *are* the true answer to this dilemma. They must preach antiracism to their less tolerant pale friends, in their churches, in their businesses, at their social gatherings, and within their family units.

Perhaps the "good ones" can put a wedge into the high percentage of White folks who still grasp their almighty power majority. They're like a dog with a bone in its teeth, unwilling to let it drop, so non-Whites can have a taste. The I-wanna-keep-my-power mongers are passing voter suppression laws, and laws that quell the teaching of inclusive American history in public schools. They don't want their White children to learn that *some* of their Caucasian Founding Fathers had been cruel and inhumane to make America what it is today. To "Make America Great Again" means to turn back the clock, when non-Whites were constantly under the thumb of White people, in the lowest of low jobs, and perpetually uneducated and unwanted.

It's important to make clear that I love America and being an American. I've traveled many places in the world, but I prefer living in California, in the good ol' USA. Most Black people love America too, even with all its *many* foibles which make it woefully difficult for us to live a full life here. Our patriotism for this country is clear. That's why so many Black folks fought in the Revolutionary War (9,000 were American patriots), the War of 1812, the Mexican American War, the Civil War (200,000), World War I (700,000 registered, but were forced into segregated camps), World War II (1.2 million), the Vietnam War (400,000, most of whom were assigned to deadly combat units), and Iraq (including my son, Isaac). Even so, our patriotism is constantly questioned, leaving us to wonder *why* we try so hard to make White Americans recognize us as equals.

What's so interesting is that I was pretty much raised in a nearly all-White neighborhood. It wasn't until junior high school, then being bussed to a mixed-race high school in Sacramento, California, that I had non-White friends. Am I being indignant for something I haven't largely experienced for myself? Am I being hypocritical to rail against White folks who don't understand, when I don't have a lot of the background myself? I think doing this investigative genealogy work has opened my eyes to my privilege. My Black and Mulatto ancestors withstood the indignities of rape and poverty. My parents and their parents worked hard to grab a piece of the American pie. They taught us to shoot for the moon, work hard, don't accept "no", set goals, be a good citizen, and make life what we want it to be. They climbed the ladder, ignoring the insults and roadblocks along the way, in order for me to have the fabulous life that I live in America. It has been my mission to impart those lessons to my children and grandchildren so they can continue the climb toward Martin Luther King Jr.'s mountaintop.

Amy: I know for 100% sure that the Ancestors are guiding us! They want us to know their names and their stories. Doing this genealogical research and connecting with our living family/cousins—especially on this Marshall line—brings all of us healing. Healing to our own families and perhaps a greater understanding for our communities at large, to try to make the changes we so desperately still need, to help establish the laws, and policies that can benefit ALL races. Helping to bring people of color to the SAME COMMON ground with their privileged Caucasian brothers and sisters.

Kathy: I feel so much better to get that off my chest. I appreciate you, Amy, for listening and sharing your views. That's what this experience is all about.

Black & White Issues

Economic Disparity

Amy: Why do you think there is still such an economic disparity between Blacks and Whites in America?

Kathy: Wouldn't you think there would be economic and social parity between the races by now? I think the most obvious reason is systematic racism which started with slavery. I am a numbers girl, so let's look at historical *facts*. By 1619, Africans were being brought into the Americas. A small percentage were indentured servants, but most were stolen/bought from their African homelands and enslaved in the English colonies which would become America. For 250 years, eighty to ninety percent of *all* Black people in America were enslaved at some point in their lives. During that time, it was against the law in most states to teach the enslaved how to read or write. It was against the law for enslaved people to own property. The condition of the mother indicated the condition of the child, so if a mother was enslaved, so too would their children, in perpetuity.

Amy: That's awful!

Kathy: Yep! When slavery was dismantled in 1865, a twelve-year period of grace, called Reconstruction, was the first glimmer of hope that African Americans would be treated like our great Constitution purports. The Freedmen's Bureau was established to help the former enslaved and poor Whites acclimate to a more inclusive America. Black men were able to vote, and some were voted into political positions of power. Blacks could purchase property and even legally marry for the first time, and their children could start attending schools.

Unfortunately, Reconstruction didn't last long.

Starting in 1877, Whites began enacting tons of heinous Black Codes and Jim Crow Laws which prohibited Black folks from voting, and from living a comfortable or profitable life. Those laws resulted in jail time for the smallest of offenses, for African Americans alone, like standing on a sidewalk for longer than five minutes (loitering) or looking a White man in the eye (disrespect). Those unequal laws further encouraged the police to apprehend Blacks for the skimpiest of reasons. These practices have continued to the present day.

Laws have been roadblocks to Blacks being able to catch up to Whites in most areas. It wasn't until 1954 in *Brown vs. the Board of Education* that African Americans could, by law, attend *quality* schools. The Civil Rights Act wasn't passed until 1964 and the Voting Rights Act in 1965. So, it's only been about sixty years that Blacks have enjoyed a semblance of equal treatment under the law, in America.

Of the 400 years spent in this country, 350 of them—six-sevenths of that time—Blacks had been treated like second-class citizens or, truer-still, like non-citizens, even non-humans! How can African Americans be on the same educational par today, or have generational wealth, when only one-seventh of their time in this country has allowed them to participate on a theoretical equal footing?"

Amy: OK, I see how systematic racism continues to pervade all aspects of our society, and therefore has a built-in negative affect for minorities related to housing, employment, education, etc.

Why Didn't Blacks Rebel More?

Kathy: Did you know that a separate Bible was created just for enslaved people?

Amy: That's preposterous.

Kathy: It may be, but it is true. Check Google. The so-called *Slave Bible* told of Joseph's enslavement but left out the parts where Moses led the Israelites to freedom. While slavery was legal in America, its planter proponents often justified it with a verse that tells servants to obey their masters. Most of the Old Testament is missing, and about half of the New Testament remains. The reason? So that the enslaved Africans in the Caribbean islands of Jamaica, Barbados and Antigua couldn't read or be read anything that might incite them to rebel. The *Slave Bible's* editors highlighted portions that would instill obedience in the forced workers, to keep them from running away; that was the only way they could get into Heaven.

Being indoctrinated into the Christian religion, along with encouragement to be docile by various leaders like Booker T. Washington and Martin Luther King Jr., Black folk were encouraged to turn the other cheek to systemic racism. All of those reasons may have extinguished many rebellions. After all, God would make things better by and by if you prayed hard enough.

What other reasons could there be that Blacks did not more actively attempt to overturn their captors? Eight out of ten Black Americans surveyed affirm they are Christians, compared to seventy percent of Whites. Even so, many Caucasians are scared to death that Black folks will rise up against them. Could that be the reason for the high incidence of police shootings of innocent Black people?

Highways Displaced Minorities?

Kathy: Another reason why Blacks are economically depressed is that cities often choose to bulldoze minority neighborhoods to build new roads or freeways, medical centers, department stores, government buildings, public utilities, and railroads. Even if minorities owned the property they lived in, "eminent domain" allows governments to take their property and transfer it to a private third party for redevelopment. Minority neighborhoods are more often deemed "blighted" or an "impediment" and are the first to be considered for redevelopment.

Amy: I read that the 1956 Federal Highway Act offered to cover 90 percent of the costs of modern highways and roads from cities to the fast-growing suburbs. However, it seems many African Americans found it nearly impossible to move to the suburbs. They were more often denied home loans by the federal government, via a practice called Redlining. Laws were put into place preventing White homeowners from selling to minorities. They were also denied jobs and other opportunities that would have made it possible to afford to buy a house.

Kathy: You're right, Girl. In Sacramento, many Asians and Blacks living and working their businesses downtown were *redeveloped out* during the 1940s, to make room for new government buildings around Capitol Park. My ex-husband's grand-parents, Isaac Charles and Louise Anderson, owned a popular nightclub in the middle of what is now Capitol Mall, from about 1942 to 1949. The Andersons were able to buy it when, during World War II, the successful Japanese business owners were forcibly removed, their property seized, and their families forced into concentration-like camps in the most desolate areas of California. Why? White Americans thought their Japanese neighbors were spies for Japan, even those born in America. It was a travesty.

I believe most of those artificial impediments to home ownership are less prevalent today.

White Baby, Black Breast

Kathy: OK Amy, this is a tough one for me to talk about. If enslaved Black women were considered subhuman, as was evidenced by the ill treatment they received from many of their White owners, then why did so many slave-owning White women suckle their babies at the Black "mammy's" breast?

What I don't understand is if Black people are subhuman, and therefore not fit to eat with or use the same facilities as Whites, then why in the world would you put your precious White baby at the breast of a Black woman? Why would you trust your children to be raised by them, then later teach that child to scorn, belittle, and devalue their Black nursemaid? Well, I guess if Black women are thought of like cow animals. We drink milk from cows. Perhaps that is why some people thought it was OK to milk a Black woman's breast for White babies. Can someone please explain that logic to me?

Amy: No comment.

Which is More Beautiful? Black or White?

Kathy: In the 1940s, psychologists Kenneth and Mamie Clark designed and conducted a series of experiments to study the psychological effects of segregation on African-American children. They used four dolls that were identical, except for skin color, to test children's racial perceptions. Children between the ages of three and seven were asked to identify which color doll they preferred. A majority of the Black children preferred the White doll and assigned positive characteristics to it. The Clarks concluded that "prejudice, discrimination, and segregation" created a feeling of inferiority among African-American children and damaged their self-esteem.

Amy: I remember this conversation. We were in the St. James A.M.E. Church, or was it the Talbot courthouse vault? There was a drawing of Jesus with children, and all the children were White. You said that little girls wanted a White baby doll because they thought it was more beautiful than the Black one. I found this shocking and so sad! ☹

Are White Women and Black Men Still Taboo?

Kathy: During the Civil Rights movement of the 1960s and 1970s, Black men felt the ultimate freedom from White rule was to rule White women. For so many generations enslaved Black men could not keep their wives safe from predatory White owners, overseers, and buddies. The White woman became the ultimate prize.

It became a goal of many Black men to have a White *lady* on their arm. It didn't matter whether they were ugly; if they were White they were all right. And blondes were the biggest prize because that is perceived as the ultimate in Whiteness and purity. That meant there were few Black men available for relationships with Black women. A percentage of Black men were in jail, a percentage were gay, and a percentage chose White women. What did that mean for the Black woman wanting a mate?

Amy: All I remember about this subject was that I said that I didn't feel that my grandmother (who helped raise me and died two years ago and would be 100 years old this year) was racist. Yet when I became an adult, we had a conversation which she let me know that she did not think it was okay for Blacks and Whites to marry. When I said this, you said that the feelings were just as strong from a Black family, when one of their family members married a White person.

Are Black Women and White Men Taboo?

Kathy: I had never wanted to be in a relationship with any other race that African American. I am more attracted to brown-skinned people who are generally more muscular and athletic than other races. Their shoulders and arms are defined, and they are generally not barrel-chested or flabby. Brown-skinned men are generally less hairy than White men. Maybe their musculature became genetically enhanced due to all the hard physical labor they were subjected to in America? Whatever the reason, when I was in the dating scene as a 37-year-old divorcée, I advertised that "I prefer Black men" in a personal ad. Unfortunately, Black men weren't interested in my profile, so I gave up and, for the first time, considered dating outside my race. Plenty of White men were interested in my profile, but I still felt weird even contemplating going out with any of them, until one day in 2006 ...

Amy: And? You can't leave me hanging, Kathy. What happened in 2006?

My former husband and I used to pal around with a White coworker of mine and his Japanese wife, who went to high school with me. I was present for the birth of their daughter, and they brought us home with our first child. We were friends. They divorced in the 1990s as did we, then my ex-husband was killed by a drunk driver in 1998. So, due to a crazy fluke, my old friend and I ended up as a couple. But I had to go to counseling to allow myself to date a White man. Funny, as soon as I started showing up at social events with him, suddenly some Black men in my art circle started to take notice and were all of a sudden interested in me. Go figure!

Amy: You sound like you have a very good relationship and have known each other for a very long time.

Kathy: Yes, fifteen years together, but I am not interested in getting remarried.

There are lots of White men who enjoy the company of women of color. Generations of mixed-race children have been born from those mixed-race liaisons and marriages.

Could mixed-race progeny be the knife in racism's heart? Those children may be less hateful toward people of various racial and ethnic backgrounds because they themselves are from different races. How can you hate part of your own genetic combination? *I should ask myself that same question.*

Religion and Family

Mormons vs. LDS: What's the Difference?

Kathy: We shouldn't talk about politics or religion, but I am really interested in knowing what the difference is between a Mormon and LDS.

Amy: The name of my church is The Church of Jesus Christ of Latter-Day-Saints. That is the name of it because Jesus Christ is who we worship. The Book of Mormon is another testament of Jesus Christ just like the Holy Bible. We believe both are Holy Scripture. We believe the Book of Mormon is a record of God's dealings with mankind on the

North, Central, and South American Continents. The Holy Bible is the record of God's dealing with mankind in the "old world". We believe both are the word of God. So Mormon is a nickname given to us because of the Book of Mormon.

A couple of years ago our current prophet, President Russell M. Nelson, asked us to stop referring to ourselves as Mormons. He said we need to call the church by whose name we worship. Mormon is the name of an ancient prophet that wrote and abridged the Book of Mormon; although we respect him we do not worship him. Jesus Christ is who we worship, and by keeping the name of our church clear in our head, instead of our nickname, we should be better at being a witness of Jesus Christ and trying to do what He would have us do: to try to love and serve others as He would do. LDS is simply the initials of the last part of our church's name: Latter-Day-Saints.

Kathy: That explanation makes a lot of sense! Thanks for clearing that up for me.

Amy: Yes, that helps us remember that this is the same church that Jesus Christ organized while He lived on the earth. They were called Saints or Christians. We are Christians and we find it very offensive when people say that we are not Christians. We love Jesus Christ and worship Him as our God, along with our Heavenly Father. We also believe in the Holy Ghost and that when we follow Jesus we can have the Spirit of the Holy Ghost to lead and guide us. We believe that both Jesus and the Heavenly Father have resurrected and glorified bodies of flesh and bone, but the Holy Ghost is a personage of spirit.

How are LDS "Missions" Different from Other Denominations?

Kathy: How is an LDS "mission" different from an Episcopal church mission, like what Cousin Jim Marshall was talking about at lunch in Putnam?

Amy: Now this one I am shooting from the hip. I have not belonged to an Episcopal church so I would not presume to be an authority on their religion or their missions. I do have many Christian friends in other religious denominations who have been involved in missionary work.

I think most Christian Denominations including members of The Church of Jesus Christ of Latter-Day-Saints do have what I might group as Humanitarian Missions. These types of missions cover a wide variety of needs, for example: clean water, building schools, teaching farming, teaching, and educating individuals to help them enter the work force and have better life skills to be self- reliant, mental health counseling, medical doctors, clothing, and food distribution, helping to clean and rebuild a place after a natural disaster, teaching people to read, etc.

I would guess that the LDS church is the only church that does Family History/Genealogy Missions. The LDS missions for young adults last eighteen months to two years. LDS missionaries pay for their own mission ahead of the time they go to serve their mission. If the individual can't fund their own mission the church will pay for what that person cannot. During an LDS mission the missionary leaves everything else behind: work, school, family, and they are not married and do not have children during or prior to their missionary service. Older or just retired adults, married and unmarried, can serve missions as well.

Kathy: Are people on a mission paid for their service? How do they live?

Amy: I cannot speak for other Christian denominations, but I can for mine. Missionaries are not paid. They save the money prior to going on their mission. If this is not possible, the church pays for the individual's mission. The young adult LDS missionary life is celibate, focusing solely on service to the Lord and their fellow men in the field. They have a code of honor to help them focus fully on this. No dates or movies, even the literature they read and music they listen to during this time period is supposed to be focused on serving God and service to others. Older retired adults do not have to be celibate if they are married.

How Does the LDS Church Feel About Gay Love?

Kathy: I've seen some of the good things the LDS Church does as far as African Americans are concerned. They allow anyone to search their Family History Centers and Family Search website for genealogy records for free. The Sacramento LDS Church sponsors an annual Black Genealogy Seminar and other free community events throughout the year. I am a fan of their generosity! But like most Christian sects, there seems to be a bit of strain when it comes to accepting gay relationships into the church. Am I mistaken? How would you treat someone close to you who happened to be gay?

Amy: Well, that might be a little of a sticky. First, let me share a little foundation of LDS beliefs as I answer this question. First, we don't just believe in one heaven, and we believe that hell is a pretty hard place to get sent to! We also believe in a Heavenly Father and a Heavenly Mother. We believe that the first two most important commandments, or laws, of God are to:

1) Love the Lord thy God with all your heart, mind, might and strength.

2) Love thy neighbor as thyself.

The two BEST ways we can show our love to God is to keep His Commandments, and to love and serve our fellow beings! We believe that one of those commandments, or laws of God, is the law of chastity. This law entails that those sexual relations are to be shared only in the bonds of marriage.

We also believe that God intended marriage to be between a man and a woman. With that said, though, one of the tenants of our faith is that we should obey the laws of the land.

Another tenet is that we claim the right to worship God how, where, or when we may. Within that same tenet, we also believe that every human being has the right to believe and worship, or not to worship who, what, or where they may. If we believe differently than the laws of the land or an individual or group of people, we are not to be rude or disrespectful to that law, or that individual or group that is making a choice we do not agree with. We believe that everyone deserves to be treated with dignity and respect! We believe that even if an individual chooses not to obey the commandments of God, that they are still loved by God, and will not be cast off to hell, like some other Christian sects believe.

Although, we *do* believe that there is a consequence for the individual's actions when they choose to obey or to disobey the commandment of chastity. We do believe that choice and the consequence is between God and the individual. We do NOT believe that those consequences for disobeying God's commandments ever involve a withholding of God's love, or a banishment to hell, or outer darkness.

One of our church leaders, Elder Dallin H. Oaks said:

"Because of God's great love for all of His children, those lesser kingdoms are still more wonderful than mortals can comprehend. The Atonement of Jesus Christ makes all of this possible, as He glorifies the Father, and saves all the works of his hands."

My son Joe is gay. I am grateful for the Restoration Doctrine of the different degrees of glory in heaven. My son is NOT GOING TO HELL because he is gay or someday may marry a man, etc. That Restoration Doctrine teaches that he will also live in a glorious kingdom more glorious than I can fathom. Joe is the BEST son any mom could hope to have!! I have been truly, truly blessed. Whoever Joe dates, marries, or lives with, that man will be fully embraced and welcomed into our family circle as our son in law!

Kathy: That would be cool for him.

Amy: I am often asked why the mom of a LGBT child remains a member of The Church of Jesus Christ of Latter-Day-Saints? I stay because I firmly believe that if I turn my back on God and what I have been given countless witnesses as being true doctrine, then I will have taken away the ONE TRUE Defense for ANY of my children that I can have because it is God that I turn to as I pray for their welfare and guidance. 🙏❤️ I know to the core of my very being that there is no mortal group or human being who can succor my children or love them unconditionally, and truly help them other than God. I ABSOLUTELY LOVE JOE with ALL of my heart. Remaining a member of this religion does not compromise or diminish my love for him in any way.

Kathy: I am a 'pro-equality' for all groups of people—gays, Blacks, women, disabled, aged, etc. I am proud of your stance to stand up for inclusion, and I appreciate your sharing your feelings about this important issue with me. I hope you rub off on your cohorts.

Patience is a Virtue

Kathy: I think patience is Amy's middle name. Patience with my 150-minute snafu with a rental car on the first day of our trip. Patience with my never-ending itinerary. Patience with having to hear my constant barrage every day about how Black people are treated in this country. Patience with my aura of anger toward folks who have maltreated us.

My cousin suffers the extreme guilt that many White folks in America feel regarding the terrible things their ancestors have done to Blacks, Native Americans, Asians, Hispanics, Jews ... basically anyone who does not look like them. She does not like identifying with those Marshall ancestors who owned human beings. Our trip would not have been so pleasant had she felt differently.

Our Families

Kathy: I enjoyed learning about your large family, Amy, and how you moved from Indiana to Utah; your parents; your business; daughter; your granddaughter's health issues, etc. You don't look old enough to have been married for thirty-six years with six children and thirteen grandchildren. I appreciate that you are a good listener and always seem to have an upbeat positive attitude which you share with everyone.

Amy: Thank you. Kathy. You ended up carrying the kids as a single mom, while their dad was a firefighter and gone a lot because of his job. After you realized your husband had been using drugs, you gave him time to get cleaned up or get out. It must have been devastating when he died after being hit by a drunk driver.

Kathy: We were divorced, but I grieved his death as a loss to humanity. He was a great man who got caught up in an addictive lifestyle, like many others.

Amy: Even so, you were able to raise your children as a single mom, working for the California Highway Patrol, and as a successful artist too!

Kathy: it has been difficult, but I'm lucky to have two sons in their 30s. Isaac is married. He and his wife have one daughter and two sons. He is a master sergeant in the Marines and will serve his last bill it in Hawaii before he seeks retirement. I was thrilled to be present for Jeremiah's birth in 2016 and visited shortly after Jazmine and Isaiah were born. I am so proud of the man, husband and father Isaac has become. I love visiting them, although it was tough when they were twice stationed in Okinawa, Japan.

My youngest son, Matthew, was always a good student, earning a master's degree in computer science, which he uses on his computer job with the State of California. He was able to buy a house when he turned twenty-four and is a taekwondo master. I've got to brag on him a little as he was the U.S. National Champion in Taekwondo

"FreeStyle" in 2015-2016. That achievement would have led him to the Olympics, but injuries encouraged him to pull back from further competition.

Amy: I remember you told me he had long dreadlocks and you were afraid having the dreadlocks would direct the racial profiling stigma more his way.

Kathy: Yes, and I feared it would be difficult for him to get a job too, but it didn't. He has a likable face and demeanor, is quiet, calm, humble, and exudes competence. He had no problem getting a great job and *earning* his promotions.

Amy: It sounds like he is a straight arrow, and was a bright, hardworking student and an all-around good kid! These amazing family history books you're writing are so your posterity can know who they came from and understand their amazing stories. 🩶

Kathy: What about you, Amy? Have you always lived in Utah?

Amy: No. I went to a community college in Indiana while we lived there for my husband's job, when my youngest daughter, Adrienne, was fifteen years old. I have sixty-four college credits in Human Services but no degree, because a year-and-a-half into my studies I became a grandmother.

Mona Lynn was born with Biliary Atresia. She had a Kasai procedure at three months old, but we knew that she would need a liver transplant. When she was three, her liver began failing. My daughter, Becky, was tested as a live donor for her Mona, so we moved to Utah to help out during the transplant. My daughter had two children at that time and really needed my help. I knew I'd be there for about seven months, away from my husband. Thankfully, Paul was able to change to a position that would allow him to live in Utah. I put college on the shelf, and we moved to Utah in 2014.

Kathy: That sounds hectic and scary for all of you. That's the worst when a child is ill.

Amy: It was. After experiencing a month in the hospital, and so many miracles for both Becky and Mona Lynn, Becky went into cardiac arrest. She needed CPR for fifteen minutes. They weren't sure if she sustained brain damage. Luckily, she was perfectly fine when she woke from the anesthesia. The doctors realized that when they put in my daughter's central intravenous line, they nicked the lining around her heart; the fluid filled it up, causing cardiac arrest. Mona got a new liver in a second transplant operation, which was only five days from the first failed operation. We thought everything would be fine, but one week later, she had an allergic reaction to the anti-rejection drug, Prograph, and had a stroke, paralyzing the right side of her body. Paul and I just couldn't leave Utah after having shared all of this with Becky and her family. Instead of Paul having to move back to Portland, Oregon, he was able to work at the company headquarters in Utah.

We have been in Utah seven years now, and we love it! My parents live in the mother-in-law apartment in our basement and are very happy. Paul was laid off six years ago, but we started our own company and are surviving!

Kathy: I'd love to come through Utah on one of our camping trips and visit with you and your family. I feel I know them already!

Amy: That would be fantastic, Kathy!

Lesson Learned #25: Making a concerted effort to find out about your relatives through DNA testing, traditional genealogical research, and a Welcome to the Table the Table experience can increase the quality of one's life. But perhaps most important is listening and learning from your relative's experiences and family stories to get a better understanding of their truth.

Chapter 13: Another View of Race Relations

The whole point of this book is to encourage people of all races to learn about and communicate with their relatives, whether they be Black, White, or another racial/ ethnic/ political/ religious background. A Welcome to the Table-type of event encourages each cohort to learn about their own and other historical contributions and family stories about each other. The hope is to learn about each other in order to reach a kind of healing.

During the summer of 2021, I sent a draft copy of my The Marshall Legacy in Black and White book to several Marshall cousins whom I met during my yearlong research into the slaveholding Marshalls from Georgia, North Carolina, Virginia, and the United Kingdom.

What follows is an interesting counter story from Cousin Eddie, one of the Caucasian Marshalls whom we found through DNA testing. His family line's experiences growing up in Georgia differ considerably from what I've always read about, namely the difficult race relations in the Deep South. I had no idea a story like his was actually possible and I'm delighted he has gifted me permission to share it with you.

> Eddie: I must say, Kathy, that I am filled with many conflicting thoughts and emotions after reading *The Marshall Legacy*. However, that is not necessarily a bad thing. I think any good creative work should, at its core, elicit an inner response. First of all, I wonder how much of the family details in the book are true, true-to-fact, or just extrapolated from the generic historical record, not the *Marshall* record? If you have been able to glean [prove] those details of your close ancestors, then I bow down to your exemplary skills of research! Your line is obviously an accomplished lot: skilled, intelligent, and successful! I am, frankly, a bit envious!
>
> Let me tell you a little bit about my life. You see, the whole reason why I originally got involved in genealogy was because, even as a

teen, I looked around at our hardships and wondered, "Is this all we are? Is this all we've *ever been*?" It is no secret that people in my Marshall family line were dirt poor. We had no family that we knew of beyond Granddad and Grandma, three aunts and uncles. That was it. They were farmers, and I didn't even know my great-great-grandfather's name. By and by, I learned his name was Jesse W. Marshall. I still don't know what the "W" stood for: "William"? But who knows?

Kathy: I don't know for sure, of course, but "William" is the only name that starts with "W" that I have found in my Marshall research.

Eddie: Well, Jesse W. came to Georgia in about 1810 from North Carolina.

Kathy: Yep, that's where the Marshalls I've investigated came from before Georgia: Halifax, North Carolina.

Eddie: Jesse was a prospector, but obviously not a successful one because we had always been poor dirt farmers, often working as sharecroppers for a living and for a place to live. Most of the rest of the family had eventually moved out west as the frontier opened, but we lost track of them. We didn't re-discover that line until I did my DNA test and started getting names of relatives whose DNA matched mine. So, needless to say, I was very surprised to learn we had ancestors who were "well to do," and shocked to learn that some of them had owned human beings!

My research turned up a connection with the Quaker "Friends" movement back in the generation before, and during the time of Jesse W. I wonder if this became the divide between the "Haves and the Have Nots." If so, their stand against that evil institution caused my family line untold years of poverty and suffering [because we had no enslaved workers who could build our financial coffers]. But that choice made us who we are, and I wouldn't't change it for the world. Quite the opposite: being against slavery is a badge of honor in my eyes …

Kathy: Having heard so many horror stories about the treatment of Blacks in the Deep South, I am always cautious about how much I initially tell people about my enslaved past. I tread lightly until I am confident the person on the other end of the phone won't ban me from further discussion or block me from viewing their online family tree. So, Eddie, I was over-the-moon happy when you were so receptive to speaking to me from the beginning. It was January 2017 when I contacted you about my brother being such a close Y-DNA match to you. Your matching him on 110 out of 111 markers is strong proof that you two share the same Marshall line.

Eddie: The Deep South of my day was predominantly rural. Poverty was the only color that most of us saw. Generations of poverty had created an atmosphere where we all had to be self-sufficient. If your neighbor was in need, you were a good neighbor and helped him out, no matter what their color. You knew that if you ever needed help, your neighbor was the only one you could count on. That was the rule and the code by which we lived. We had to, or else die.

I could tell you firsthand about what it was like growing up so poor we couldn't't afford a phone, or running water, or sometimes electricity. What it was like to go to school with more patches on your knees than pants. Did you know that I was the first Marshall in our line to actually attend college? Ever? I could tell you many true tales of "Life in the Rural South." Most have been positive regarding race relations in my day-to-day life, and the lives of those who came directly before me: stories about neighbor helping neighbor, loving one another, and taking care of one another.

Tales of sitting in [African American] "Ms. Moss" house watching the snow come down through the tin roof. She had some coal to burn, and we didn't, so we stayed with her, and she took care of us like we were her own "White chirdren."

Then there was the story about how we helped Mr. James—never knew if that was his first or last name—plow his garden when his son was sick, or how he and his son later came and helped us dig our well because he heard our old well was dried up. All he asked in return was to be a neighbor if anybody needed one.

In times of plenty, we would pick an extra basket of blackberries, or muscadines, bream, green beans, or tomatoes to take over to the neighbors. They brought us home-made jelly or catfish or squash. Those are the colors of the real Deep South, where hospitality was once a byword. Sadly, those tales are becoming lost forever—never to be told.

Kathy: Honestly, Eddie, I've never heard or read anyone I personally knew portray your perspective of a multiracial village in the Deep South working together for the good of the community. Actually, come to think of it, Eddie, one of my beta-readers reminded me that I *have* studied such communities. My Grandmother Daisy lied about where she was born, and through me off the track for twenty years. Then I found a common cousin who told me about "The Piney Woods" in Noxubee County, Mississippi, where Whites and Blacks were married and had mulatto babies in separate communities that depended on one another. Some people call these multi-racial people "Melungeons." They are groups of people of the Southeastern United States who descend from European settlers and Sub-Saharan African slaves. Tri-racial describes populations who claim to be of mixed European, African and Native American ancestry.

I am delighted and enthralled at the description of how you grew up. I am honored you would share such personal experiences with me. I know your family is very proud of you. And, by the way, you are a compelling writer!

Amy: That is wonderful that Eddie experienced such a tight-knit community while growing up in the South with both his Black and White neighbors! I am sure the poverty that he grew up with as a White child helped that feeling of unity occur more. It put both races on a bit more of an even playing field, demographically speaking.

I grew up in a lower income family, a few times receiving federal welfare assistance, as the child of a single mom who did not receive child support from our father. I grew up in Portland, Oregon, and my mother had a lot of moral and physical support from her middle-income parents. Yet I am fully aware that I was still more privileged because I was born White. I knew a few Black friends growing up, but my school and neighborhood were primarily White. Kathy, your and my discussions during our trip to Georgia has really opened my eyes even more to that reality.

Eddie: Kathy, I committed to you that I would give you my honest assessment of the characterization of the White Marshalls as portrayed in *The Marshall Legacy in Black and White*. Honestly, I find the use of the term "slaveholding Marshalls" to describe me is just a bit offensive (and I am not one who is easily offended). While technically correct, to be defined to the world as such is a bit disconcerting, especially as my direct line held no enslaved people in the past 200 or more years. To have one's entire sixty years boiled down to an event which happened so far in the past just seems a bit unfair. Is that who I am? Is that all I am? No Ma'am.

Kathy: I hope you would not think I believe any of the stereotypes that may be in the book are a direct reflection on you personally. I was speaking about the William Blount Marshall line which intersects with your Marshall line by his great-grandfather, Captain John Marshall, born around 1715 and died in 1782. I knew nothing about the poverty you speak about in your line.

Eddie: As I said, I do not get offended easily. I hope you don't think they [the slaveholding William B. Marshall line] are indicative of everybody in the South. Usually, and I know this from experience, there are always a few loud trouble-makers who ruin it for all of us "quiet, decent folks." Some day they will be judged for their actions...

Kathy: Yes, rabble-rousers cause a lot of trouble. I am glad to hear a different perspective for a change, especially from someone with first-hand experience.

Eddie: Honestly, we just don't know what happened back then, or how our Black and our White roots came together. I would like to think in the absence of empirical proof otherwise, there may have been genuine love there. Daydreamy? Maybe, but who can say? Yes, we as a nation do still have a long way to go towards really, finally, loving our neighbors as our Lord commands us. I would have liked to have seen the book come fuller circle Why not write about how we all—Black, White, or indifferent—worked together to discover this tale, to love one another, and to celebrate not only our differences but our sameness.

Kathy: The reason I sent drafts of Chapter 18 about slaveholder William B. Marshall from *The Marshall Legacy in Black and White* to our White and Black cousins was to get their take on my dream story. It was based on "Slave Narratives"[28] from Georgia, actual Marshall documents like land deeds, probate records, Census records, *A Rockaway in Talbot*, etc. My book takes place during slavery and the centuries before and afterward. I had sent it to you for comment before publishing. I didn't know you were suffering from COVID and never saw the copy I sent to your work email.

Eddie: It would have been nice to see it before it was finalized.

Kathy: Actually, I did make some changes, based on your comments, before it was finalized. I attempted to make it clearer that my comments were directed at those Marshalls who owned people.

I found it interesting that some of our common cousins felt I was way too lenient on the slaveholding Marshalls portrayed in my book. Some of their thoughts differed from the more caring experiences you wrote about occurring after slavery.

You, our common cousins, and other people I've met in Georgia have been nothing but helpful and wonderful to me. However, I'd be surprised if the majority of Black folk in the Deep South were treated as well as Mr. James or Ms. Moss in your story. I am so glad you shared your humanitarian experiences with me. That's why these discussions are so important: to learn the various sides of issues.

Amy: So, I'm a bit confused at Eddie's being offended by his family being referred to as slaveholders. The family he grew up with did not own Black people, according to him, but my and Kathy's William B. Marshall line did. She's writing about the slaver line. Slavery ended or was officially abolished in 1865. That was 156 years ago, not 200 or more years ago. I am trying not to go ballistic when Eddie suggested that perhaps the relationship between our White slaveholding ancestors and your enslaved ancestors was loving or romantic. When a human being is owned by the person who is creating offspring *workers* from them, that is NOT in any way a loving relationship! The owned human being is being used to further the financial interest, and/or pleasure of the owner!

I think that we could, of course, discuss the level of abuse that occurred in order to make that owned-human create said offspring. I feel it is very fair to state that it simply WAS an ABUSIVE ACTION, PERIOD! To create offspring from someone that you own is not the foundation of a loving relationship.

Kathy: From all that I've read and heard from the elders—like my great-great-great-grandmother, Margaret Booker [*The Mystery of Margaret Booker*], whose back received whip marks when she refused to *lie* with her master right after she had born his fifth child. In *most* Mulatto-baby-making cases, I feel it was not a consensual act and there was no love involved, from the point of view of the woman, at least. It was a pure power play from the slaver over the enslaved. However, to Eddie's credit, I have read about cases where there was true love between the master and slave, which sometimes resulted in living unofficially as husband and wife. Those were more likely to be outlier cases, though.

Eddie: Kathy, the work is a wonderful piece: creative and entertaining. I guess it is hard for me to look at certain ugliness and realize that however uninvolved, however distant, however good a man that I try to be, sometimes that ugliness just still clings, even if only in the minds of others. Each of our lives is a tapestry made up of threads of differing origins, colors, and thicknesses. Those tapestries write the tales of not only who we are, but also of how we came to be here. As long as we continue to look at only the colors in the weave, it will take so much longer to finally find the larger, intrinsic beauty to be found within each and every tapestry itself. In the Lord's Peace and Love, and with the greatest gratitude and respect, I am your cousin.

Kathy: You have gifted me with your insights, Eddie. I hope we can continue our conversations to our mutual benefit. It's good to listen and hear each other's point of view. Only then may there possibly be understanding between us. Thank you for allowing me to present your story here.

Kathy: Jennifer K., you've lived in Georgia and Alabama all of your life. What has your experience been with race relations between Blacks and Whites? Will they ever be able to get along in this country?

Jennifer K: Georgia and Alabama were more open to new ideas than, say, Mississippi. Alabama had a hard time with desegregation, but Mississippi did not ratify the 18th Amendment until 1995. Black and White relations is a new concept in this part of the America, and it's going to take a while for us to catch up to the rest of the country. Mixed-marriage is still frowned upon by some. The older the generation, on both sides of the issue, the more diverse the opinion about the topic. There are still Whites in the South who do not accept the advancements that have been made in race relations. They still live in the past, and there is no getting it out of them. To me, acceptance is a choice. You cannot force anyone to make the same choice you do.

Lesson Learned #26: At a reunion, or **Welcome to the Table** event, install a facilitator who would encourage a peaceful exchange of ideas from participants, in order to hear various sides of a story. The facilitator would ensure any conflicting viewpoints don't escalate to sink the ship. The ideal is to hear all sides of an issue without coming to blows.

This concludes my genealogy trip to Georgia with cousins Amy, Jim, Jennifer K., and Jennifer O., and the Car Talk+ issues we discussed during that part of my trip. I've highlighted the many lessons I learned on the way in Chapter 22, with the hope you can benefit from them *before* you arrange a similar get together for your family.

Part II discusses my journey to Alabama to try to uncover information about my Smith and Ligon great-great-grandparents who married into the Marshall line.

Part III contains concrete hints and tips for planning your get-together, as well as a *Solving Your Mystery* Appendix that lays out doable steps *you* can take to write a book about *your* family roots.

Chapter 14: Guess Who's Coming to Dinner?

At about 4:30 p.m. Thursday night, I arrived at the Hampton Inn Hotel in Auburn, Alabama. It was the closest hotel I could find to Tuskegee Institute, about twenty minutes away. Originally, Clevlyn, a cousin on my paternal grandmother's side, was supposed to share the room and travel with me for research at the Tuskegee Archives. At the last minute, she had to cancel her trip due to a family medical emergency. So I was left with two beds to spread out my research, a table near the window as a mini office, a refrigerator for healthy snacks, a microwave, and a coffee pot. My room was next to the elevator, but its mechanical noises didn't bother me.

I began filling out the daily journal from my last day with Amy in Georgia, while the events were still fresh in my head. Then I reviewed my goals and itinerary, got my clothes ready for the next day, ate a bite of my protein bar for dinner, then lay face down on the bed for just a moment ... but the rigors of the past days caught up with me and I fell into a deep sleep.

Ring! Ring! "What's that?" I murmured from some faraway dream place, splayed out on my stomach. Without thinking, I fumbled for my smartphone within arm's reach on the bed. Still half asleep, I pressed the green talk button, and slurred, "Yes?"

"You don't know who I am, but I know who you are," the voice blared out of my phone. "I'm cousin Gloria Hardnett ..."

My exhausted brain struggled to wake. When I heard the name "Hardnett," it triggered a recent memory. On Wednesday, Mike Buckner drove Amy, his wife, and me to a trailer in Talbotton. He introduced us to a woman with a t-shirt labelled "Hardnett Reunion." I left my business card with the lady, hoping she would give it to someone who knew more about their family than she did. I sat up, reached for my water glass on the bedside table, and gulped a swig, shaking my head awake. I somehow managed to say, "Oh, you must be related to Maybelle. I am so glad to hear from you." Each word brought me closer to full consciousness.

Gloria was talking a mile a minute, reciting her family ties: "My mother was a Marshall and my father was a Hardnett. I started working on the Hardnett side first, because it was too confusing to research both sides at the same time."

Giggling, I replied, "Yes, Girl, I know what you mean. That's why I am concentrating on my Marshall family for this book. The oldest ancestor I know about is Samuel Marshall, born around 1830. He had a daughter with the unusual name of Josephine, and sons with the uncommon names of Austin, Wright, and Searcy. I think those were the last names of the slaveholder's friends. I thought it would be easier to find connections to my family because those first names were so unusual. Other sons were given the more common names of Henry and Sam."

She said, "Uh-huh. Searcy sounds familiar. And you also said Austin?"

"Yes," I responded. "My grandfather's name was Austin Henry Marshall Sr. and his son was Austin Henry Jr., who had a son named Austin David Marshall. Austin was a popular name in my direct paternal line.

A confounding puzzle is that a marriage certificate says Henry A. Marshall was married to my great-grandmother, Mary Smith. However, the death certificates for four of Mary's five children say "Austin" Marshall was their father, not Henry. The 1870 Talbot Census says Sam Marshall had sons named Searcy, Henry, Wright, Austin (born in 1864), then Sam. But the 1880 Talbot Census doesn't mention an "Austin" but does mention an "Oscar" Marshall born in 1864. I wonder if the 1880 Census taker wrote down the wrong name."

Gloria commiserated with my confusing name dilemma. With a Southern drawl, she continued, "My mother talked about her Uncle Cap Marshall, but I think that was a nickname. His real name could have been Henry or Austin. I don't know."

I replied, "I found a marriage record for a Sam Marshall and a Maria Wilkinson from 1867. But there's also an 1874 Marriage License for a Sam Marshall and an Emeline Bunkley, who was living as his wife in 1880. Do either of these names—Maria or Mary, Emeline or Emma—sound familiar to you?"

"Well, it's hard to say, really. But Kathy, you might be interested in this. Almost every year, there's a big reunion and parade in Talbotton with Marshalls and Hardnetts, and other families that intermarried with them. One year, I counted 300 people and got tons of pictures, including my Uncle D. Hudson Marshall. They all have the same physical characteristics, like almond eyes. And there's lots of twins in the family."

"Twins, really?" I asked, "My dad's younger brother, Bruce Marshall, had twin boys and I read there's more twins in the White Marshall family than one would normally expect." *Does this lend some credence that we might descend genetically from those slaveholding Marshalls?*

I continued. "I was so shocked that Mike Buckner had so many things to show us that afternoon. Meeting Maybelle was such a nice surprise. By then, though, I was so tired and hungry that I was babbling like an idiot. Anyway, Mike said Maybelle had a cousin who was a family historian. That must have been you he was talking about."

Chuckling, Gloria said, "Well, my family tells me to stop digging, because I might find out they're married to their close cousin!"

Laughing with her, I said, "That's why we had to start doing genealogy because some of my maternal cousins unknowingly did get married and their kids had a lot of health problems."

"Yeah, there's twins on the Marshall side and some double cousins. For example, Maybelle's mama married my uncle, and my uncle is my mama's brother."

"That gets confusing," I added.

"You better believe it!" Gloria snorted.

Sitting up in bed now, I reached for my iPad on the nightstand and was thumbing through my family tree on Ancestry.com as we were talking. "Girl, I am going to tell you something you may not believe... Right now, I am looking at my online tree. There's a Sam

Marshall who was born in 1899. His father was Henry Marshall and mother was called Mariah. Sam was married to Annie Marshall, and their children were Millie, Ethel, Merdis, Sam, D. Hudson, and Roy."

"That's my mama, Ethel Mae!" She cried, excited that I was fishing in the right pond.

"Gloria, you won't believe this, but today I was having lunch with *your* relative, and you didn't even know it. Her name is Jennifer Owens, and her people are from Henry and Mariah Bunkley, just like yours! And she's got Marshalls in her family too. Yesterday, Cousin Amy and I went with Mike Buckner to the Bunkley's house off Highway 36 or 208, I can't remember which right now."

Gloria replied, "Oh wow! My mama always thought we were related to the Bunkleys."

"Yep, I guess you are," I confirmed. "I believe that your

Finding Gloria Hardnett's Marshall family in Kathy's family tree

Henry Marshall is *my* Samuel Marshall's brother, both born about the same time around 1830, perhaps in Talbot or maybe in Putnam County, Georgia. My great-grandfather's name was *Henry*, and my grandpa was Austin *Henry*, and his son was Austin *Henry,* too. Were my Henrys named in honor of your Henry, or did their owner name them after one of his friends named Henry? There were a LOT of enslaved with the last name Marshall, but I don't know how many of them were related. Do you know?"

"Well, there were some Mulatto Marshalls who all had almond-shaped eyes..." Gloria revealed.

"Girl! For fifty some-odd years, I denied having anything but African blood coursing through my veins, but my first DNA test in 2012 told me I was mixed, just about half-White and half-Black. I only had to look in the mirror to know that, but I wouldn't believe it until DNA proved it. Have any of you done DNA testing?"

Gloria said, "Yes, I've done a test and had my dad's baby brother tested. Our ancestry was very strong in West Africa."

I got really excited at the thought that we might have genetic proof of our family connection. "What was your dad's brother's name?"

"Melvin Hardnett."

I quickly checked my DNA matches, as well as those of my siblings and two Marshall cousins to see if we matched any Hardnetts. Nope for me and my siblings

"Gloria! My first-cousin Michal has two Hardnett matches who were born in Perry, *Houston* County, Georgia. The young woman who matches Michal lives in the United Kingdom and her father was from the Congo, in Africa! It looks like the African married a woman whose family came from *Houston*, Georgia. My first-cousin Jocelyn matches a lady who has a George Hardnett from Tallapoosa, Alabama, in her tree. But right now, it doesn't look like you and I have enough shared DNA to prove anything other than a distant cousin relationship."

"Aw, that's too bad," Gloria sighed. "But we'll keep in touch alright?"

"Wait a minute. Last year, I found an 1867 Work Contract from *Houston* County, Georgia.

The boss was Madison Marshall who had "employees" named Sam, Austin, Henry, Albert, the latter of which could have been concubine Rosa Marshall's son. In 1850, my great-great-grandfather, Samuel, would have been about 20. There's a 21-year-old male on the census. The Austin, Henry, and Albert that I knew about would not have been born by 1850. So perhaps Madison

Marshall did not own my kin after all. Who was Madison Marshall? Was he related to Stephen B. Marshall who died in 1831 in Putnam County, Georgia? I'll need to do some homework to be sure."

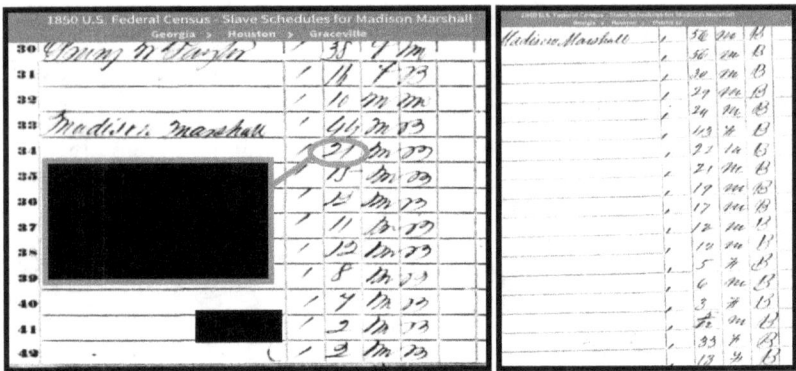

In Houston, GA, Madison Marshall's enslaved in 1850 (left) and 1860

"Sounds promising. I'll check to see if I can dig up any Obituaries for you for my Marshalls."

"That would be great, Gloria. And yes, let's stay in touch. What do you think about having a Zoom session with all of our cousins when I get back home?"

"I'd love that!" she replied.

"Ok, I'll work on that when I get back home. I really appreciate your calling me. I'm excited to meet you!"

"Me too. Bye now cuz. Drive safe!" Gloria hung up.

I was reinvigorated, ate more of my protein bar dinner, many cups of water, and hit the sack by 11:30 p.m.

> Lesson Learned #27: Be open to listening to someone else's point of view and try not to be judgmental if their stance differs from yours.

PART II: ALABAMA

Chapter 15: The Alabama Backstory

The trip to Georgia with Amy and other paternal Black and White Marshall cousins was a primary reason for my May 2021 pilgrimage. I couldn't be happier with our Car Talks and other travel experiences we shared. But traveling in Georgia wasn't the only motivation. Grandpa Austin's maternal lineage was just as important.

Here's the backstory. Great-grandpa Henry A. Marshall married Mary Smith in 1888 in Columbus, Georgia. They had five children born between 1889 and 1898: Clifford (1890-1964), Israel (1891-1961), Grandpa Austin Henry (1892-1967), Thomas Alphonso (1895-1968), and Cora Lee (1898-1919). But I couldn't figure out what happened to Henry after Cora Lee was born.

By 1900, Mary and her children were living on Fifth Avenue near 17th Street in Columbus with her parents, the Reverend Israel Smith and Laura Ligon. I wanted to know more about Israel and Laura, who their parents were, who their owner was, whether they toiled outdoors in Cotton Valley or worked at a trade in Tuskegee. I had many theories but needed more facts.

My *The Marshall Legacy in Black and White* presented a number of fascinating facts found online which I wanted to verify in Macon County, Alabama. I hoped by traveling to Macon County, Alabama, where they were living by the end of slavery, their spiritual essence would guide me to their truth.

Laura Ligon

The 1870 Census from Tuskegee, Macon County, Alabama, indicated Israel Smith was a bootmaker and his wife, Laura, was keeping house. Their daughter Mary—who would become my first great-grandmother—was fourteen, their son Milo was four, and their year-old daughter, Lula, rounded out their family a mere five years after slavery ended. I didn't know whether Laura was born in

Macon, Alabama, nor who her owner was. I wasn't sure whether Israel was Mary's father, or it someone else.

I found a DNA match to a living woman named Leslye Smith, who was sure of her lineage to Amanda Woods *Ligon* Boyd. According to the following graphic, Amanda's slaveholder had an association with Robert Fulwood Ligon. I eventually gravitated toward believing R.F. Ligon could have been my Laura's owner.

Amanda Woods			Posted on MyKindred.com, Person ID I63726, Source ID S1099, Family ID F21559.
Aug 1850	Georgia, USA [2]		
Female			
Mar 04, 1917	Cotton Valley, Alabama, USA [2]		

- Amanda Woods was purchased by James C. Boyd from Georgia. She was a beautiful black lady and was purchased to be the wife of the plantation overseer who at the time was Hilliard Boyd. Amanda's mother was from GA and her was father from Virginia.
According to the 1860 slave Schedule in Southern District of Macon County, William Wood owned a large number of slaves. Among the females, there were two age 50; two age 40; one age 35; twenty-one age 33; two age22; one age 20; eight age 18; three age 15; two age 13; three age 7; one age 11; one age 9; two age 7; and three age 3. Many of male and female slaves came from Georgia. Therefore, it is possible that Amanda was on this plantation when James C. Boyd bought her. She would have been 10 years old at this time.
Robert Fulwood Ligon who was born in Clarke County, Georgia in 1824 owned a plantation in the Southern District of Macon County. He owned the following slaves: one female age 60: one male age 50: three males age 45:one male age 40: two males age 30; five males age 27; three males age 20; four males age 16; three females age 35; four females age 30; two females age 25; one females age 21; three females age 18; four females age 12; three females age 7; two females age 5; one female age 3; two females age1; one male age 16; three males age 10; four males age 18; three males age 5; two males age 4; and six males age 1/2 year. Many of these slaves were born in Georgia. Again, it is possible that Amanda had relatives on this plantation.
A metal gate that was installed in the fence around Amanda's house fell on her. She died as a result of the injury in 1917.
Dr. E. A. Ligon also in the Southern District of Macon County owned the following slaves: one female age 40; four males age 27; two females age22; one female age 20; one female age 5; and one male age 1.
F. M. Ligon (b. 5 Oct 1863, d. 28 April 1893) the son of T. B. Ligon had a plantation in the Northern District (Tuskegee) of Macon County and owned the following slaves: one female age 30; one male age 13; one male age 11; two males age 9 and one male age 7. It is possible that the 30 year old female is Amanda's mother.
A relationship existed between the Wood and Ligon plantation owners because on 29 October 1853, William P. Wood signed his consent for his under age daughter, Eugennia R. Wood to marry Edward A. Ligon.
On 8 January 1848, Robert F. Ligon was appointed Guardian of Edward A.Ligon and Amanda Ligon minor heirs of Robert Ligon deceased. (Bond Book2, page 216).

Biography of Lt. Governor Robert Fulwood Ligon by Dr. Shari Williams

What Was Reverend Israel Smith's Story?

I wasn't sure whether Israel had always been a skilled worker, or whether he was a typical field hand on a farm before becoming a shoemaker by 1866 in Tuskegee. I didn't know for sure whether Israel was born in Macon, Alabama, or who his owner was, but there were four possibilities which I reviewed with intensity:

1. Israel C. Smith, born in 1810 in Vermont, who was a merchant in Mobile, Alabama, in 1850. His mother's maiden name was Austin (like my grandfather and great-uncle's first name).
2. Thomas Smith, who had a son named Clifford. My grandfather's eldest brother was given the uncommon name of Clifford.
3. Guy Puy Smith, a fellow who is in the ancestral trees of several of my DNA matches.
4. Neil Cassius Smith, who was a carriage maker in Tuskegee, with roots in South Carolina and might have been related to Neil A. Smith.

I found a Slave Manifest record indicating that a five-foot five-inch, 17-year-old Black teenager named Israel Smith arrived in New Orleans on the *Tippecanoe* domestic slave ship on January 17, 1842. The shipper was listed as H. H. Slatter, a notorious slave trader from Baltimore, Maryland. If that teenager was *my* Israel, was he forced to board the ship in Baltimore, or Charleston, or some other port?

Was Israel sold at auction in New Orleans to White Israel C. Smith, who sailed him to his home base in Mobile, Alabama, then sold him to another Smith or some other slaver?

There were so many possibilities, but no proof. That's why I had to go to Macon, Alabama. I hoped the ancestors would somehow reach out to me and lead me into the light.

There was quite a bit of documentation of Israel and Mary's existence after slavery ended in 1865. An 1866 Colored Population Schedule listed Israel Smith in Tuskegee, and he registered to vote in 1867. He and Mary officially tied the knot that same year, but I believe they had been a family unit since 1856, when my great-grandmother, Mary Smith, was likely born.

I found an *incredible* story about Israel in an 1870 Congressional Investigation into voter tampering. It is well documented that the Reconstruction Era between 1865 and 1877, was an astounding time in American history when Black people were finally free to determine their own lives, vote in elections for the first time, own property, and theoretically work where they wanted. Black folk could legally be married and send their children to school for the first time.

But White Southern Democrats wanted to keep colored people as an underclass, by revoking our voting privilege and instituting Black codes and Jim Crow Laws to keep them in their former subservient place. Whites feared most newly-freed Blacks would vote with President Lincoln's Republican party, and they did everything in their power to stop the Black vote.

My shoemaker ancestor, Israel Smith, became an activist, along with many other Black movers and shakers, like Lewis Adams who was a shoemaker, tinsmith, and future founder of Tuskegee Institute. They created Central Club of Macon County to organize Black folk into a powerful voting bloc. Meetings were held at a ramshackle church building, which became the focal point for a multi-year grass-roots project. It united and empowered African Americans, rural and urban, educated, and uneducated people, to fight for the right to vote.

Butler Chapel A.M.E. Zion Church, an imposing brick building located on a hill west of downtown Tuskegee, was built on the site of that former church. It is a prominent landmark in the historically Black neighborhood known as Zion Hill.

During that period of activism, the KKK was lynching and burning Blacks and their property, trying to scare them from voting. The violence climaxed the month before the 1870 election. Republican speakers at the courthouse were heckled by local Southern Democrats who carried pistols. There was plenty of disagreement within the Black population on how to vote, perhaps from bribes or fear of White retaliation.

Fights broke out in the Zion Church during a Central Club meeting and my brave ancestor, Israel Smith (who may have been a reverend by then) stood up to the mob to quell the violence. How do I know that? Because once the 1870 votes were counted, William A. Handley, the Southern Democratic candidate, won Macon's Congressional election. However, the Republican candidate, Benjamin W. Norris, accused Handley's election goons of terrorizing Black voters and intentionally miscounting hundreds of Negro votes, illegally attributing them to Handley's camp instead.

Visiting the location where Reverend Israel Smith provided testimony in a Congressional Record about 1870 voting irregularities.

A Congressional investigation was convened, and *my* Israel Smith's deposition described the events that unfolded in the church when Whites stormed inside, shooting every which way. Partly due to the testimony of Israel and others, there was a recount of votes which changed the election outcome. Norris, the Republican, was declared the winner. Most Negroes cheered and looked forward to a brand-new day in America: equality for all its citizens.

But like many of the Black leaders, Israel and his family had to leave Tuskegee immediately or be lynched. That's how the family ended up in Columbus, Georgia. I hoped to find more evidence of Israel's life in Tuskegee by visiting the courthouse, or the building which housed Woodson's Shoe Shop where Israel may have worked, Butler Chapel and the Zion Hill area, Tuskegee Institute, houses where Smith and Ligon slaveholders lived, etc. I searched Google Earth and other mapping programs to find those places in advance, but they were occupied over 150 years ago and have since been destroyed or refurbished as something else. Would the ancestors direct me to the truth once I drove to Tuskegee?

> Lesson Learned #27: Try to retrieve as much information as possible about family places before a genealogy trip (e.g., places the family lived and worked, churches, cemeteries). Ensure the itinerary reflects many different options to visit, and that corresponding travel routes are mapped out in advance.!

Chapter 16: The Archivist

After the enlightening Thursday night telephone call from new cousin Gloria Hardnett, I got off my hotel room bed and prepared myself for a long Friday in Tuskegee. I laid out my clothes and reviewed my itinerary. Oops! I forgot to remind Dana Chandler, the archivist at Tuskegee Institute, about my 10 A.M. appointment with him before I left home. Even though it was very late Thursday night, I emailed:

> *Hello Dana,*
>
> *Are we still a "go" for 10 AM? Clevlyn was unable to make it this time, but I am still interested in finding out more about my great-great-grandfather, Reverend Israel Smith, Lewis Adams, and/or the lives of Black folk in the City of Tuskegee in the 1860s. If you really feel there is no information in the Institute's files about the City of Tuskegee's history prior to 1881, perhaps we should cancel our meeting and I'll try the County Courthouse instead.*

Upon reflection, I probably *should* have apologized for not confirming the date sooner.

It would take 25 minutes on Highway 85 to reach Tuskegee Institute. As usual, I got lost a bunch of times; but that's not necessarily a bad thing. GPS directed me to turn onto Montgomery Road, which took me to a residential neighborhood. It was interesting seeing those older homes with street signs named for important African Americans, like (Booker T) Washington Street, (Lewis) Adams Street, (Ralph) Ellison Avenue, (Phyllis) Wheatley Street, (John Hope) Franklin Road, and Martin Luther King Highway. Hmm, I figured out I had input the incorrect address into the Maps app! Silly me. I was going to be late, and I hate being late because it continues the old "CP Time" stereotype that "colored people" are never on time. I plugged in the correct address, which indicated I was six minutes away from my destination. But the GPS instructions took me to a locked gate on the Tuskegee campus. Arghh! I kept driving until I found a parking lot, which luckily happened to be for the Main Library. Is this where Dana's office was?

After parking the car, I noticed that Dana had responded to my query. His response—"I'm "not sure I can help you much, but come if you like, before 11"—came after leaving the hotel that morning.

When I entered the Library building, a Black man in a crisp white shirt was talking into his cell phone on the stairs in front of me. Maybe cellular reception was a problem in that old building and he'd have to position himself close to an exit door for his call. The gentleman noticed my damsel-in-distress stare, finished his call, then asked if he could help me.

After explaining I was from California and traveled there to meet with Dana Chandler, he sighed, revealing his desire to live in California. I replied that the beauty and tranquility of the Tuskegee campus was *my* idea of divine. Fluffy words aside, he walked me toward my car and described how to get to the Archives building where Dana worked. Pointing, "Just go to straight down that road until you come to an intersection. Look to the left and you'll see a big building. Park in that lot, enter the side door, walk down a long hall, then turn right into Dana's office. Simple. You can't miss it."

I nodded and smiled, knowing there was no way Miss Misdirection would ever be able to remember all of his instructions. I thanked the man and gave him one of my business cards.

Calling Dana again to see if he was still in his office, he was a bit curt on the phone, probably because I didn't reaffirm our appointment before I left home. He said to come over anyway. I turned on the engine, exited the parking lot, turned left through the main entrance to Tuskegee Institute, and hoped I was going in the right direction. The road wasn't straight in the least.

The Tuskegee Institute campus is beautiful. The trees and lawn are perfectly coiffed. The black, curving roads are smooth. The old-fashioned streetlamps with Black posts and golden globes are charming. The emotive bronze statue of Booker T. Washington removing the shroud of ignorance from a seated Black man is powerful. It is easy to get sidetracked in such a bucolic setting. I could imagine myself being a happy student there.

I drove along the winding pavement, surrounded by leafy-green trees, admiring the Colonial Revival, red-brick buildings with their pristine white trim. The undulating road was mesmerizing. Window open, I could hear the trill of birds. The cloudy sky and slight breeze was a welcome respite from the hot, sunny days I'd experienced thus far on my pilgrimage. I held up my camera with my left hand, shooting video through the opened passenger and driver windows.

I marveled that this campus was founded by Lewis Adams, a former enslaved man who had no formal education, yet could read, write, and speak several languages.

Lewis Adams, founder of
Tuskegee Institute

Lewis was an experienced tinsmith, harness-maker, and shoemaker. As presented in the exciting Chapter 4 of *The Marshall Legacy in Black and White*, I wondered if he had taught my great-great-grandfather, Israel Smith, the bookmaking trade. It is documented in the Congressional Record that they were both activists in the mid-to-late-1860s at Butler Chapel A.M.E. Zion Church, successfully encouraging Black residents to vote. It seems likely Lewis and Israel's families were good friends too? Did my

Israel look like the photograph of the slightly younger Lewis in 1905?

Tuskegee University campus, Tuskegee, Alabama. May 2021.

Oh, the Tuskegee History Museum came into view. I maneuvered the car to the closest parking lot then walked toward the building. Darn! The Museum was closed due to the COVID pandemic.

Something guided my head to look to the left. I noticed a placard on the building: John A. Kenny Hall. Bingo! That's where the helpful guy at the Main Library told me to go. The small entry door labelled "Archives" opened into a long, cream-colored hallway, bisected every fifteen-feet or so by a closed doorway. A sign at the end of the hall indicated the University Archives were to the right. The corridor was dark, save for a yellow light coming from an open door on the right. I peeked in. A large man at a desk looked up. He reminded me of George R. R. Martin, author of the wildly popular "Game of Thrones" series of books (and I have the complete set of series DVDs at my home).

"Dana?" I hesitated.

"Yes, I'm Dana Chandler. Come on in," he beckoned, with his blue paper mask obscuring his lips. I pointed to the mask over my mouth and mentioned I was fully vaccinated. He said he was too and invited me to de-mask if I felt comfortable doing so.

In 2020 and 2021 much of America mandated the wearing of face masks and staying six feet away from other people in public, to reduce the spread of COVID-19 infections—infections which had killed 500,000 Americans by February 2021. Taking off one's mask almost felt like being naked in front of a stranger.

I introduced myself and apologized profusely for sending my meeting confirmation so late. The air seemed to clear with that admission, and both of us relaxed. I couldn't help but gaze around the crowded room peppered with incredible artifacts: rocks of every shape and hue, small stone sculptures with a Central American flavor, wooden bowls, rows and rows of books, certificates on the wall, and much more in every nook and cranny.

"This is amazing!" I admired. "Where do these artifacts come from?" One of my many unrequited desires was to be an archaeologist, so I really wanted to know the provenance of these treasures.

"These are from different Mayan sites that I've been to or worked at," he said nonchalantly, as I panned my video camera around the petite room. "And that is *not* a German Swastika," he pointed at an object on the bookshelf. "It's from India." I guess he didn't want me to think he was a Nazi.

I was feeling quite comfortable by then and asked, "Are you a Dan Brown fan?"

"Yes, I like Dan Brown."

"Well, your mention of 'not-a-swastika' came up in his *The DaVinci Code* when Brown's protagonist, Robert Langdon, played by Tom Hanks in the movie, was speaking at a conference about the importance of understanding symbology. He talked about the origins of the symbol that we know as a swastika.

Dana smiled and explained, "Even before that story came out, I was talking about symbology."

My camera trained onto some small pottery bowls on a low bookshelf. The vessels looked really old.

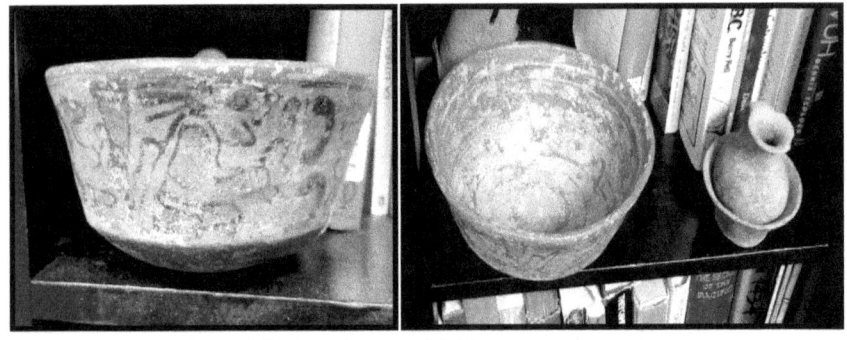

Thousand-year-old Mayan pottery

"That bowl is Mayan, not your'n," he quipped.

I laughed out loud and volleyed, "I'm not touch'n," but I don't think he got my joke.

He said, "That's all right. You can touch it. The bowl on the left has a rabbit scribe on it. I have it here for my students to examine."

I stroked the exterior of the perhaps thousand-year-old piece of painted pottery, made by Mayan people who no longer exist. It was smooth to the touch, and the Chino orange and iron-oxide colors were still vibrant. "I'm a potter, so this is especially cool to me."

"The little pitcher next to it is for cacao, or cocal, as they called it. They mixed it with honey and peppers and drank it as a frothy drink."

My camera scanned to the top shelf. "Oh, that's wooden," I exclaimed out loud.

"Yep, care to guess what it is?" he dared. "You may pick it up and smell it."

"Ooh, is it some kind of fruit?" I guessed, looking more closely at the twelve-inch diameter, five-inch-tall wooden bowl.

He said, "It's from Peru, from the Andean region. When you look at the bowl, what do you notice about it?"

"Well, it looks burnished. What are those two carved somethings—are they two feet? And what's that thing on the top that connects them? Okay, I give up."

Time was ticking away, and he probably knew I had no clue and would guess wrong forever, so he told me the answer. "It's two oxen yoked. What does that usually mean in the context of cultures?" We could hear crickets in the otherwise quiet room, meaning, I was still stumped.

I admitted, "I don't know much about religious symbology…" But I guessed, "Togetherness?"

"Marriage!" he replied rather loudly, probably thinking I was a pretty dull girl. *Cousin Amy would have known that answer!*

To redeem myself, I added, "I guess I didn't win the $10,000 prize."

Dana explained. "It's a marriage bowl and it had chicha in it, a purple corn liquor. It was made by their women who chewed up corn and spat it back in the bowl to let it ferment. That particular bowl was used at a marriage ceremony I attended in Peru, and I had to drink out of it. As a gift, they gave me the bowl."

"Wow!" is all I could think to say. The ceremonial process was similar to one I had read about in the "Clan of the Cave Bear" book series.

When I returned home, I was so glad I had videotaped some of our conversations for this book.

> Lesson Learned #28: Document your pilgrimage with video, audio, and still photographs. Take copies of announcements, maps, and other printed materials from each visited location. This information will spark your memories, as well as make it possible for you to create videos that your family can watch, so they can feel like they are there with you.

It was difficult to pull myself away from the extraordinary artifacts, but I was on a mission. I restated my desire to find information about my Black family who had lived in Tuskegee before the institute was only a kernel of an idea in Lewis Adam's fertile mind. Dana reiterated that he didn't think he could help me and reminded me he had to leave in thirty minutes.

The formalities out of the way, Dana rose up and signaled me to follow him. He turned to the right out of his office, down the darkened, empty hallway. I thought of Amy, and her concern about the White male guides who showed us around different parts of Georgia. We had read so many horror stories suggesting some Southern men couldn't be trusted to keep their hands to themselves. But I had been on the track team in school and knew I could run fast if I had to… Smile.

A single, dull light emanated from around the corner, illuminating several industrial metal bookshelves which contained stacks of brown boxes. Dana reached into one box and pulled out a book: *A Century of Agriculture in the 1890 Land-Grant Institutions and Tuskegee University—1890-1990*. "This might help you understand the experience of Native Americans and Black people here at Tuskegee." We walked back to his office and chatted some more about his interesting adventures, with him looking at his watch every five minutes, as a reminder of the time.

Everyone I've met on this trip has given me something useful to forward my research. Dana was no different. He said, "I've got a friend who may be able to help you. Her name in Shari L. Williams. She is a Ph.D. Graduate from Auburn University, one of the state's two public flagship universities." He gave me her contact information. I thanked him again, retraced my steps down the hall, exited the side door into the blinding sunlight, regained my car, and prepared to drive to my next adventure.

> Lesson Learned #29: Even if you're late to an appointment, go anyway, apologize for your tardiness, and enjoy the moment. Better still, confirm meeting dates days in advance and *don't* be late!

I drove around the Tuskegee campus and started weeping with pride when I saw two dozen male and female students exiting a brick building. They wore White medical lab coats over suits, or shirts and pants, or pretty dresses, or even mini dresses. Some women wore high-heeled shoes, some wore practical, low pumps. The students were smiling, but still professional. There was no buffoonery. They are our future doctors taking a lunch break in this gorgeous campus dedicated to Black excellence." It made me feel proud to experience this moment, knowing they will make an important difference in the lives of so many Americans. I thought of their ancestors who toiled in Macon, Alabama, and other places in this country. I know they would be crying tears of joy, just like me.

Chapter 17: Tuskegee Courthouse

My car found its way to the Tuskegee Institute exit gate. I almost hated to leave that beautiful campus full of important African American history, but I had dozens of plans for today. I keyed "Tuskegee Courthouse" into the Maps app and followed the instructions to the County seat of Macon, about five minutes away.

In the middle of the town square is an architectural wonder—an example of Romanesque Revival architecture, designed by J.W. Golucke, completed in 1906.

Macon County, Alabama, Courthouse, in Tuskegee. Kathy Marshall. 2021.

I parked the car, then stood on the steps of what I thought was the front door. I looked around for another entrance. This tiny square of buildings was the Macon County seat. It felt surreal. My ancestors, Reverend Israel Smith and Laura Ligon, lived somewhere near here, perhaps even within a few blocks, or perhaps they got around town by horse and buggy. Where was the market where they shopped? Where was their church? Did they live in town with their owners, or did they migrate to Tuskegee only after they were free? This is why genealogy trips like this are so important: to see, smell, hear, touch, and feel what your blood kin might have experienced hundreds of years ago. I savored the moment and snapped several photographs.

Now back to business. What? The front courthouse door was locked. This is a huge building. How do I get inside? Walking down the steps, I looked to the left and right and took a 50/50 chance that the left would be right. Booyah! I was right.

A dozen people were waiting in a line outside the building in the hot sun. Evidently, COVID precautions only allowed a few customers inside the building at a time. They wanted to renew driver's licenses and pay bills, but I was there for research. It was too muggy to be standing outside if I didn't have to. I asked several folks if there was another way to get inside. They said no but being obstinate and not wanting to wait one more minute outside, I called the probate office, hoping to gain entry right away.

I heard a beep at a small door at my right. I briefly thought of Alice fumbling through Wonderland. The door clicked opened and I escaped inside the building.

> Lesson Learned #30: Never accept "no" for an answer. If things aren't going according to plan (like avoiding a long line), come up with a creative solution, like calling or emailing various sources to help you achieve your goals.

Oh my! I felt transported back to the seventies; had I actually fallen down the rabbit hole? There were gray metal desks, gray metal filing cabinets, and gray metal chairs with hunter green seat cushions. The walls were avocado green. I think they still even had typewriters.

The front of the Probate Office was surrounded by clear plexiglass—perhaps bullet-proof—with a foot high-and-wide opening to accept transactions, like in a bank. I signed in with the date and time of my arrival on the visitor logbook. *Oops! I'm just now thinking that I never signed out when I left. Oh well!*

"Down the hall to the left," an office person instructed. I passed a hallway lined with 70s-style brown wood panels which led to an open-door stack of the familiar, red-bound books: the same books found in every courthouse I've visited from the Deep South to Ohio.

A gym membership isn't needed if one does research in courthouses. Each book feels like it weighs thirty pounds. One must reach up on tippy-toes or stoop down low to pull out the weighty court record books. On the plus side, it is a lot easier to read handwritten documents in the original large size, compared to my small computer screen at home. But boy are those tomes heavy! Some record books are now printed in a more manageable 8.5x11 size, but those require a magnifying glass to read the text. "It's always somethin'," as Roseanne Roseanna Danna used to say on the *Saturday Night Live* TV Show."

I went down the hall to the main clerk to ask whether they had separate files for Blacks and Whites, as some states did. She said no, but when I went back into the deed/probate room I found separate volumes for colored marriages and White marriages. Unfortunately, those volumes were for later years than I was interested in. It was time to move on and do something else today.

I found several land deed transactions by R.F. Ligon, but none mentioned the names of his human property. It was wonderful to see the original deeds, land records, marriage certificates, etc. Thanks to LDS volunteers, most of the records have been digitized and are available online from the comfort of our homes.

I'm pretty sure I can do more research at home online, so I didn't spend the whole afternoon in the courthouse.

After an unproductive two-hour visit to the courthouse, I drove around the charming city center square because it was too muggy to walk. I could only find Tuskegee maps dated after 1885.

Tuskegee Courthouse Records, Tuskegee, Alabama. May 2021.

Where were Israel and Laura's owners living and plying their trades? Was Israel working as a shoemaker at Woodson's Shoe Store at 3222 South State Street, and was that located in downtown Tuskegee?

Downtown Tuskegee, Alabama. Kathy Marshall. 2021.

A Final Word from Tuskegee

As I wrote this text right after Independence Day, a Montgomery Advertiser news report flashed on my internet browser: "Councilman Johnny Ford talks about his attempt to take down confederate monument in Tuskegee."[29]

Evidently, Councilman Ford tried to ignore the many confederate statues that still existed everywhere I've traveled on this Deep South pilgrimage. Even though some states have removed those celebrations of the "Lost Cause" of slavery crumbling to dust, many places still hold onto them for dear life. I had to read about the story of this brave man who had the gumption to remove the statue. The news article presents the pain that many of us feel when those vestiges of atrocities sneer at us every day, reinforcing to all what they really represent: enforced White superiority overs Blacks. The article stated:

Before Johnny Ford drove into downtown Tuskegee and climbed into an electronic lift bucket with a saw on Wednesday, he prayed. He remembered his childhood friend, Sammy Younge, a Black Navy veteran, and civil rights worker gunned down in 1966 after asking to use a Whites-only bathroom. Ford remembered Tuskegee University students streaming into town streets when Younge's accused killer was acquitted, attaching chains and ropes to the towering monument to the Confederacy in a failed effort to pull it from its pedestal. Ford attempted to fulfill his pledge to remove the painful Confederate memorial from the heart of his hometown. County Sheriff Brunson got wind of the plan and stopped him from completing his task. Ford said the town had attempted to relocate the contentious monument to a Confederate cemetery in the past, but the plan fell through.

"The citizens in my district have said enough," Ford said. "We want to promote downtown, historical Tuskegee, and we don't want a Confederate statue in our midst." Brunson said Ford and others could face multiple charges, including destruction of property. "I welcome that. Sometimes you have to get into good trouble in order to bring about change," Ford said, referencing a familiar refrain from the late civil rights leader John Lewis.

I, for one, will gladly donate to Councilman Ford's legal fees.

Guess what the all-Black staff at the Talbot County, GA, Courthouse answered when asked if they minded having a huge Confederate statue looming in front of their courthouse every day? One woman said she didn't even notice it anymore. On my pilgrimage, I refused to sully my camera with any photos of those failed-Confederate reminders. In my opinion, those statues are valid historical representations, but they need to be in a museum, not in a public space funded by taxpayers.

Chapter 18: Serendipity Strikes in Cotton Valley

A big storm was projected to hit in a few hours. Please, ancestors, point me in the right direction to find answers to my questions while the weather holds.

DNA cousin Leslye S. maintained that her Amanda Ligon Woods Boyd ancestor might be related to my two-times great-grandmother, Laura Ligon who married Reverend Israel Smith. Leslye said the Boyd and Ligon slaveholders intermarried in Cotton Valley, along SR-29 in Macon County, Alabama. She thought their enslaved might have been traded or gifted amongst their families, enticing me to learn whether those forced workers might be related to my Ligon family. Perchance a clue will somehow present itself through the heart of Cotton Valley. Let's explore!

I drove onto on State Route 29 from downtown Tuskegee, hoping the ancestors would whisper where to go. I took lots of videos along the road, narrating my thoughts and feelings as I passed.

Longleaf pine forests along SR-29 in Cotton Valley, Alabama. Kathy Marshall. 2021.

"Look at these weird trees," I dictated into my smartphone, as my car sped underneath graying clouds. "Look at those leafless branches. They look like sticks, like something sharp sticking up out of the ground. They reminded me of black arms reaching up, praying to God for help and mercy, but receiving none. All these little pine trees we see along the road, were probably cotton fields back in the day. But cotton ain't king no mo' here. Timber farming is now the main crop."

Panning the scene from right to left as I drove, I imagined in my mind's eye the thousands of forced laborers who were once right here, picking cotton in the bright sun, with few trees back then to shade their sweaty brows. I could feel their essence, their pain, their anger, their despair. It was unsettling, but I couldn't take my eyes away. *My people were likely right here almost two hundred years ago!* Do you hear me? I felt a heaviness in my breath. I couldn't reconcile the beautiful parts of that roadway with the horror of what Cotton Valley stood for.

One of the experts from Talbot, Georgia, had told me a surprising thing. "There is no irrigation of fields except what the good Lord gives us." How did the crops grow if the farmers depended wholly on the rains to irrigate the crop?

There are a lot of things that don't make sense to me, a visitor in 2021. But they happened. They happened right here in Cotton Valley and in many parts of the Deep, Mid, and Upper South.

Did slaveholder Robert Fulwood Ligon have a house in Cotton Valley, as well as in Tuskegee? I observed his land transactions in the Courthouse and found a township plat map of Macon County indicating who owned which plats. But it was difficult to determine exactly *where* Ligon's properties were on a 2021 map. According to the following plat map, they owned the yellow-tinted properties surrounded by a gray box in the southernmost part of Macon County. *Ancestors! Tell me where you were!* I soundlessly pleaded in the car.

What's that? There was an interesting little building on the left side of the road, so I pulled over. It was actually a defunct post office. Just as I was about to get back on SR-29, my smartphone rang. It was the woman Dana Chandler mentioned at the end of our appointment. He must have asked her to call me. What a doll!

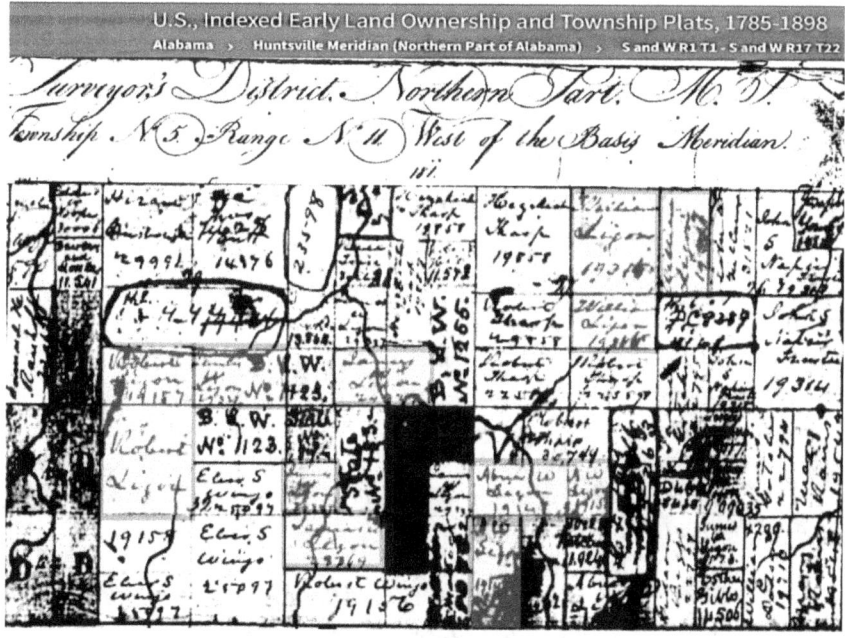

Plat map of land ownership in Alabama. Ligon-owned land is yellow.

> Lesson Learned #31: Be curious. Stop and smell the roses. Explore unforeseen opportunities to obtain more data, photographs, or other qualitative experiences.

After a few minutes of introductions and explaining to her what I was searching for, she volunteered to look through her research. Dr. Shari L. Williams was the first African American female to have earned her doctorate in History at Auburn University. She had written a publication about Robert Fulwood Ligon for inclusion in the Alabama Encyclopedia.[30] The following day, Dr. Williams emailed me a map of Tuskegee which contained the location of his home, as well as the 1974 survey information for that home located at 1108 S. Perry Street. It's not clear, though, whether that was the home of our potential R.F. Ligon owner (1823-1901), or his son with the same name (1864-1939).

> Lesson Learned #32: Obtain a plat map showing which land lots were purchased by various landowners during the period where your family lived. Attempt to overlay a present-day map over the plat map so you may visit the places your ancestors owned. If necessary, consult local experts who can help you with this.

I asked whether Dr. Williams had any information about my Black Ligons from Alabama. She wrote in the *Encyclopedia of Alabama* that:

> *"Robert Fulwood Ligon (1823-1901) served as Alabama's fourth lieutenant governor from 1874 to 1876, and then as a US representative for Alabama's fifth congressional district. He was also a planter, lawyer, and veteran of the Mexican war and the Civil War. Ligon was born in Oconee County, GA."*
>
> *[Note: Oconee County was just north of Putnam County, GA, where many of the Marshall owners lived and some moved to Talbot County, GA].*
>
> *"Ligon relocated to Tuskegee, Macon County in 1844, studying law under Judge David Clapton; both of their parents came from Halifax County, Virginia. In 1854, he obtained a land patent for 319 acres in Macon County about nine miles south of Tuskegee, known as Cotton Valley and by 1860, he owned sixty-four slaves. His plantation encompassed 1200 acres on which he raised livestock and cultivated cotton, vegetables, and hay. Ligon was a Methodist, Mason, and a member of the Democratic Party."*[31]

My Laura Ligon and her parents and siblings may have been counted among R.F. Ligon's enslaved property. There were many bits of data which seemed to corroborate a connection between R.F. and my great-great-grandmother, Laura Ligon. He had a daughter named Laura. He also had a daughter named Amanda, like Cousin

Leslye's ancestor. A Black cook named Alice Ligon was listed next to R.F.'s household in Tuskegee in the 1870 Census. Were Alice and my Laura sisters, born between 1840 and 1846? My great-great-grandparents, Laura Ligon and Israel Smith, were living very close to R.F. in 1870.

If my Laura worked in R.F.'s house as a maid or cook, she may have benefitted more than some other Black folks. She and her family may have received hand-me-downs from the owners, better food, an indoor job, easier access to church and education, etc.

Another documented fact is that R.F. Ligon did business with carriage maker Neil Cassius Smith, who may have owned my Reverend Israel Smith. That association may have initially brought Laura and Israel together and allowed them to act as husband and wife during slavery before they were able to officially wed in 1866.

I had hoped to find documentation at the Tuskegee courthouse solidifying my theories, but to no avail. I'll have to revisit the topic in a future Second Edition of *The Marshall Legacy in Black and White*.

Fort Dixon Railroad Depot, Macon County, Alabama. Kathy Marshall. 2021.

Another stop along SR-29 brought me to the Fort Dixon Railroad Depot. The depot was constructed in 1892, approximately the time that the Savannah-Americas-Montgomery railroad came through the community. It was in use until 1975. The depot served as the cornerstone of the community for over 100 years and is still a well-known landmark for south Macon and north Bullock Counties.

I took a little side jaunt off the main SR-29 to escape the speeding cars. I wanted to take my time and savor the experience in this part of the world. Tall, slender pine trees, planted in rows, paralleled a creek which is perhaps used to irrigate the forest trees. No logging trucks were allowed on the road. Trees after trees after trees, maybe eight- to twelve-inches in diameter and thirty feet tall, as far as the eye could see. Greener-than-green grasses were a carpet at their feet. Someone told me the forests were grown for the paper pulp industry. Hundreds of trunks had been cut down, denuded of branches and leaves, laid in a disorganized heap, perhaps to dry out.

After a mile of this leafy scenery, I realized that if my car conked out there, way in the boonies of nowheresville, I'd be in big trouble. Who knows what could be lurking over the top of the next hill. Paranoia had set in, big time. Flashbacks to the movie "Deliverance" and "squealing like a pig" slapped some sense into me. I turned around quickly and got my brown buns back to Tuskegee.

Honestly, Cotton Valley gave me the creeps, mostly because of what it stood for. While my emotional brain had a burning desire to get away from that place, the genealogist in me cringed never knowing for sure where my kin lived. I flew my silver steed up the road, because other cars would have rear-ended me driving less than 75 MPH. It only took about ten minutes to get back to civilization.

I was hungry and remembered seeing a smoothie place across the plaza from the courthouse. Darn! It was closed. Oh! My itinerary reminded me to look for 3224 State Street where a Black shoemaker might have apprenticed my ancestor, Israel Smith. Sigh. There was no State Street on the Maps app. Could it now be State Road 29, which connects Alabama to Florida?

A sweet smoothie wasn't enough sustenance, so I kept driving, finally seeing a modern strip mall in the distance, containing a Dollar Tree and a couple of restaurants. But I took yet another wrong turn. Or was it? The next street on the right was *Church Street*. I made a U-turn in the church parking lot. Wait a minute! A big sign read "Butler Chapel." Oh my Gosh! Is this really Butler Chapel A.M.E. Zion Church that was a "must" on my itinerary? In all the excitement of being in Tuskegee, having that great experience with Dr. Shari, and being scared to death on SR-29, I had forgotten about this very important stop. But the ancestors came to the rescue once again, guiding my hands on the steering wheel to find this important historical place in my family story. I parked, and ran to a placard which explained the importance of this place to my family and to Alabama as a whole:

> "Before the mid-1960s, Tuskegee's Black population faced challenges when attempting to register to vote. Furthermore, the State of Alabama re-drew the towns political boundaries in an effort to prevent registered Blacks from voting in local elections. In response to this discrimination, several thousand people gathered at Butler Chapel African Methodist Episcopal Zion church on June 25, 1957, for the first meeting of the Tuskegee Civic Associations "Crusade for Citizenship." Reverend Kenneth Albuterol, minister of Butler Chapel, with several other speakers, urged their listeners to boycott White businesses. Local citizens challenged the restrictions in court and won. National court case legislation eventually secured for Black people the right to register to vote. By February 1964, Macon County had a predominantly Black electorate and several Black citizens have been elected to offices, including Reverend Kenneth L Beaufort who served on the Tuskegee City Council."

Wait a minute! That sign was describing voting restrictions from the 1960s, but exactly the same thing is happening in many states in 2021, as well as in the mid-1860s in Tuskegee. And my ancestor, Reverend Israel Smith, helped a momentous effort happen right here at the Butler Chapel location, almost exactly one-hundred years ago. As mentioned earlier, that's when Israel Smith was an agitator of sorts, working with Lewis Adams and Mr. Alford, President of the Club of Macon County. They got Black residents on Saturday evenings to formulate an action plan, and they helped foster a sense of fearlessness to register to vote. This was in the face of constant intimidation from the KKK. Reverend Israel Smith's testimony in an 1870 Congressional investigation provided detailed conversations about that era, allowing me to write his incredible story in *The Marshall Legacy in Black and White*. Thanks, Google, for uncovering this priceless story!

I wondered if Reverend Israel Smith's ministry was in the A.M.E. or Baptist, or some other Christian denomination.

Enough of history. I was hungry!

> Lesson Learned #33: Use Google and other online search tools to look up your ancestor's names and places. You might find helpful newspaper articles, family stories, or other narratives which will give interesting tidbits about your ancestors' lives.

Retracing my steps back to the strip mall I had noticed before visiting Butler Chapel, I stopped at a Mexican restaurant to relax with a huge platter of enchiladas, beans, and rice. The service was slow, but that was all right by me since it gave me the time to write today's happenings in my daily journal. After lunch, the next-door Dollar Store beckoned. Candy time and the price was right. Yep! You guessed it: one dollar for each box.

Stomach full, snacks in my purse, videos and photos documenting the day's adventure, I decided to go back to my hotel room. That was more appealing than driving fifty miles in the opposite direction to Montgomery to search the Archives (which hadn't been helpful to me the last time I visited them for my *Finding Daisy: From the Deep South to the Promised Land* book project.)

The skies had been looking more and more ominous as the hours passed. My steed returned me home in the nick of time. I bought a frozen dinner from the lobby store and cooked it in the comfort of my room. After this incredible week of discovery, I turned the TV on for the first time.

In the background, I heard a strange roaring sound. Turning down the TV volume isolated a vacuum-cleaner-like noise. A flash of light caught my eye from the drawn blinds. I looked outside and felt like Dorothy Gale caught in the twister. Jagged lightning bolts crackled down from the heavens, windows were splashed with large droplets, tree branches blowing fiercely in the blustery wind.

What luck that this didn't hit during the day because I didn't bring a rain jacket. Blinds closed, I turned the TV back on, and went on about my business until 11 p.m., when the storm lulled me into a blissful sleep.

Chapter 19: Six Degrees of Separation

Are you ready for another crazy story? When I finished the research portion of my trip and am driving on Interstate 85 north, to get back to my cousin's house near Atlanta. I see a Visitor Center, park, and saunter inside to pick up some travel brochures.

The clerk asked, "May I help you find anything in particular?"

"I'm really at the end of my trip but thought there might be some information for my research files."

"What areas are you interested in?" the clerk asked.

"Putnam and Talbot County."

"Oh, we have those brochures over here." We started talking about my genealogy trip. When mentioning the Marshalls from Harris and Talbot County, he began to weep. *Oh my, what did I say?*

After a moment, he was able to control his emotions. He revealed an incredible story. A Black woman named Susie Marshall took care of him in Harris County, near where my enslaved family was living in the 1800s. He described a touching story about *Miss Susie* who had never seen the ocean before. His family took her with them on an oceanside vacation. *Oh, how nice.* The invite wasn't for Susie to relax wading in the water, but to take care of this guy while his parents enjoyed themselves. Then the clerk said something about Highway 36.

"Highway 36?" I asked. "By any chance, was she buried at Bluff Springs C.M.E. Church?" He nodded, still a bit choked up. "Well, I was just there a couple of days ago. And believe it or not, I took a picture of Susie Marshall's headstone. I didn't know who she was, but because she held the name Marshall, I wanted to remember her with a photo.

"That's crazy, right? Me stopping at this Visitor Center, 3,000 miles from my home in California, meeting you, and learning that I had taken a photo of your beloved Susie? The ancestors are working overtime, right? Thank goodness!"

He uttered, "Six Degrees of Separation." I gave him a big hug, then reentered my car, got back on I-85 North, and wondered what additional miracles might be in store for me on this eventful trip.

So many people in Georgia and Alabama put me in touch with others who might know about my Marshall family from Talbot and Putnam, Georgia, or my Smiths and Ligons from Macon, Alabama.

I had one more month to connect all the owner and parentage dots before *The Marshall Legacy* manuscript was due to my editor. The ancestors wanted me to get their story right and, as always, I vowed to fulfill their mandate.

> Lesson Learned #34: Don't be afraid to talk to strangers about your family. Say their names and places in conversations. You might just meet someone who is related, or who knows someone who might have information about your family or the places they lived.

PART III: WELCOME FAMILY TO THE TABLE

Chapter 20: Plan Your Family Gathering

Traveling back to my cousin's house in Lawrenceville gave me time to reflect on what I had learned during the trip and what would increase the success of future gatherings. The process could be similar to scheduling a family reunion.

What follows are potential steps people could consider for convening a family event. I did most of these steps by myself over a couple of weeks of preparation, for what turned out to be two gatherings that were smaller than originally planned. If you expect more than a dozen attendees, you'll probably want to have several people helping to make the event a success. Here are some ideas:

1. **Select one family member or family line to study**.

2. **Bring together a small family group** to discuss action steps. Feel free to modify the following as appropriate.

3. **Encourage family to DNA test** to find more cousins (mention that unexpected secrets might be uncovered). My *Finding Otho: The Search for Our Enslaved Williams Ancestors* has four chapters about DNA, to help readers learn what DNA is and how to use it to find more relatives. You can also search Facebook or YouTube.com for DNA-related social media sources.

4. **Research the selected family line** by gathering stories from relatives about their daily lives. Collect Census records; birth, marriage, and death certificates; probate records; and other documents mentioned in the "Gather More Information" section of Appendix G.

5. **Develop a family tree chart** that clearly shows how family members are related to one another. A sample is shown in Appendix C. Include as many family members in the tree as possible, up to the present day. Build the tree up (ancestors),

down (descendants), and wide (siblings). The more accurate and broader your family tree, the more DNA finds more relatives.

6. **Create a private social media page** (like Facebook) **or a blog** which contains information about your family research. Invite family to become members. Encourage your relatives to share their stories and documents about the family. Begin to talk about having a family get-together to meet everyone and further discuss family lineage.

7. **Assign a Cultural Coordinator** to handle issues that might arise from finding that your family line has mixed-race family members. The coordinator should be aware of the ethical and emotional issues that might arise during the event. It's recommended the coordinator review the discussions in Chapter 12, "Car Talk," https://comingtothetable.org, and read *Gather at the Table* by Sharon Morgan. Moderate differences of opinion about race, politics, and religion should they become disruptive topics. Chapter 13 shared the unexpected opinion of a Caucasian Marshall descendant.

8. **Collect contact information and family data** for all family members in that selected family line, for example: cell and home phone numbers; emails; social media account names; home addresses; birthdates; birthplaces; parent's names and birthdates and birthplaces; and children's names and birthdates and birthplaces. A sample in shown in Appendix B.

9. **Select a gathering date** with several months lead time for people to plan to attend.

10. **Select a convenient location**, like a State Park, or hotel with amenities like a pool, meeting rooms, a restaurant, and free parking. Selecting a meeting location near where the ancestors lived makes it easier to visit the family homesite, cemeteries,

libraries, and historical centers which could provide more information or photo opportunities.

11. **Develop a Schedule of Events itinerary** that will be posted on the private social media page. A sample is in Appendix A.

12. **Write a letter** explaining the purpose for the gathering, the date, the place, cost, instructions, and deadline for reservations, and the Schedule of Events itinerary.

13. **Ask for volunteers to help** you with the planning and execution of the meeting, such as:

    A. **Master of ceremonies** to open the meeting/program, introduce the speakers, and make sure the program flows well.
    B. **Storytellers** (the elders?) to tell some interesting and fun family stories (not the controversial tales).

    C. **Family historian(s)** and helpers who will collect the contact information and family data in advance and type it into a booklet for each family group and make the information available in a secure online place.

    D. **Site coordinator** to handle issues dealing with the accommodations, meals on site, etc.

    E. **Photographer(s)/videographer(s)** to record all aspects of the event. Ensure they record family names as the photos/videos are being taken. Ideally, they would interview elders and others to capture their stories. You'll appreciate those remembrances when you're sitting at home trying to remember what so-and-so said and how the house looked and the yard smelled like, etc. Trust me, this is one of the most important parts of any pilgrimage and gathering of people.

F. **Babysitter(s)** to supervise young children while the adults circulate with each other.

G. **Food coordinator(s)** to plan and execute food needs away from the hotel site.

H. **People to develop games** related to family history.

14. **Social Media Coordinator** to document the event on the social media site and/or in a book that family may purchase. That book could be a paperback, photo book, three-hole-punch book in a binder, saddle-stitch stapled book, or e-book. Appendix G has ideas on how to organize and self-publish a paperback or print a photo book.

15. **Zoom meeting coordinator**: Schedule a Zoom call with family members before and after Welcome to the Table events.
    A. Create an agenda and email/send it in advance.
    B. Assign a moderator to admit attendees, handle technical Zoom issues, and record the session.
    C. Show a family tree to living descendants.
    D. Show images of the event for those who could not attend.

16. **Archiver**: Have someone print the results of the event: agenda, photos, attendee contact information, etc.

> Lesson Learned #35: Gather a group of family members to fine-tune this list and assign people for each task. Remember, for small events, one person might be able to handle all these tasks.

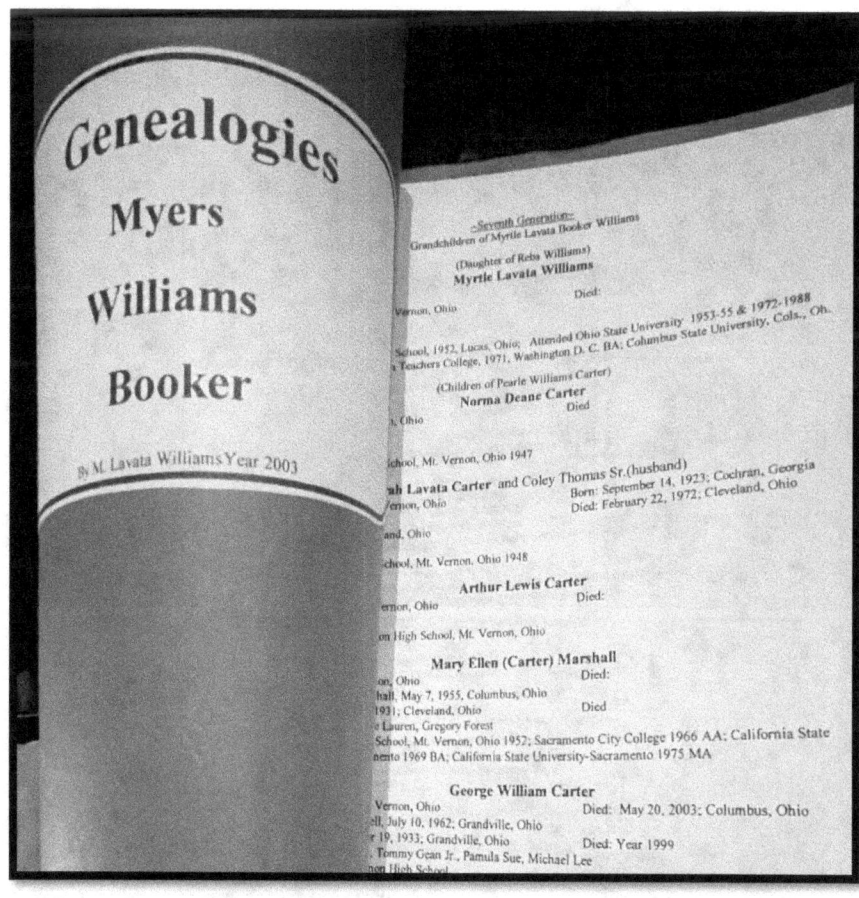

Sample of what Kathy Marshall calls the Genesis version of genealogy family records, i.e., who begat who, dates, and places. Archivists/ historians could be more creative with the addition of pictures, contacts information, and actual family stories, etc.

MARSHALL-RELATED COUSINS

Chapter 21: Zoom Call With Cousins

One of the benefits of writing about this genealogy trip has been meeting new cousins and introducing them to existing cousins. During this time of COVID, fewer face-to-face meetings were recommended to diminish the chance that COVID would spread. Digital communications became all the rage, increasing exponentially in 2020, and continuing that explosion in 2021.

Returning home after the successful genealogy trip to Georgia and Alabama, I decided to convene a Zoom meeting of old and new relatives, with my Brother Greg's technical help. I quickly put together a summary of my trip experience, a chart of how family members are related, and a loose agenda that was emailed to all my Marshall-related relatives.

A few weeks later, our Marshall clan experienced a wonderful two-hour Zoom meeting. This was the first time meeting each other, for most of the attendees. Some cousins I've known all my life, some were found over the past few years via DNA and family trees, and some were met during my May pilgrimage to Georgia and Alabama. I served as the moderator, introducing myself and briefly explaining how and why the get together came to be.

The egghead in me started by showing a chart of how we were related (see Chapter 3), explaining how to read the chart. Then, we discussed the following map illustrating the Marshall Migration, coming from the United Kingdom. Greg zoomed in on Robert Marshall Sr., our common ancestor from England, born in 1642. Everyone could visualize the Marshall's migration to the Isle of Wight, then Brunswick, Virginia, then further south to Halifax, North Carolina, then Warren, Georgia, into Putnam, Georgia, ending in Talbot, Georgia. My direct line ended up in Cleveland, Ohio, where I was born. Then each person chatted a bit about themselves, so we could learn about each other. It was a great first start, which resulted in many continued chats and messages with all participants afterward.

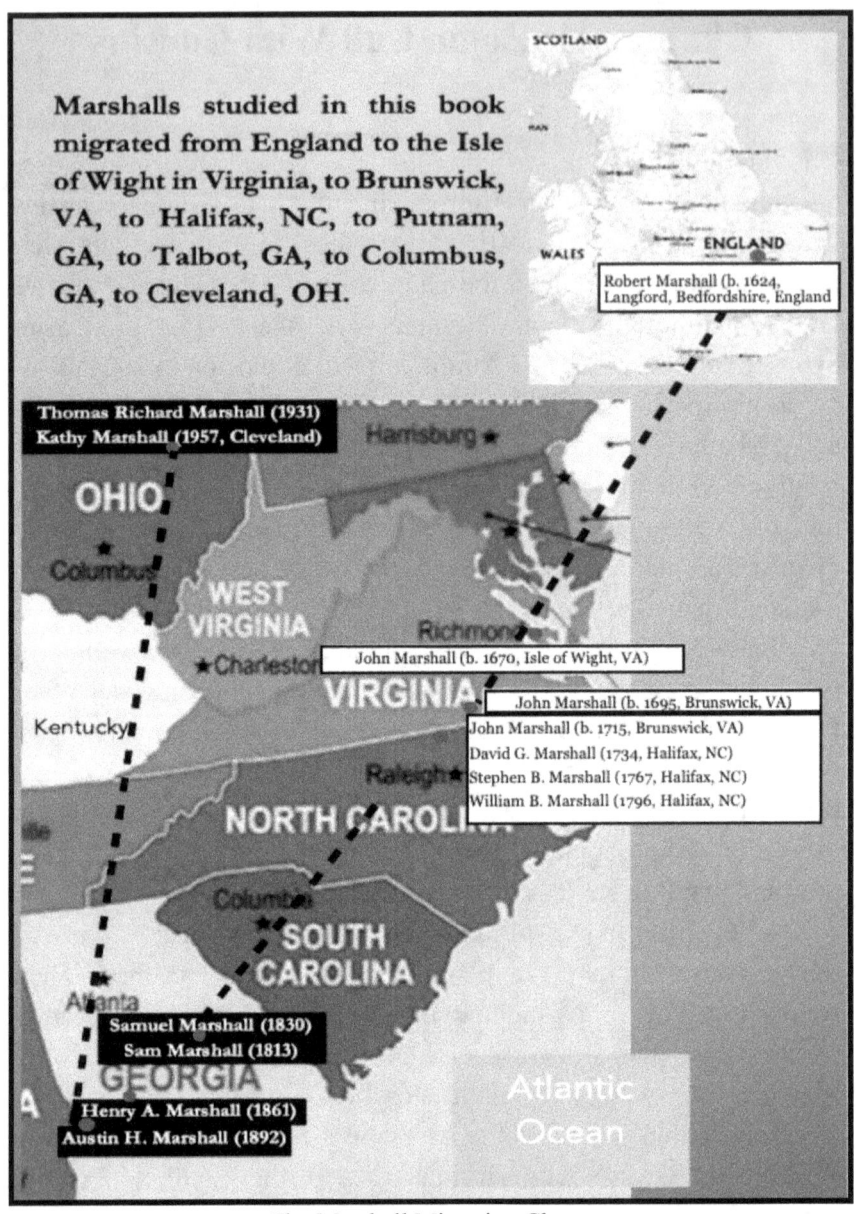

The Marshall Migration Chart

The following chapters present some helpful hints on how you can do this for your family!

Chapter 22: Lessons Learned

Here's a recap of the lessons I learned from my trip to Georgia and Alabama in May 2021. They may help you in preparing for your own genealogy trip and/or Welcome to the Table event. They are listed by chapter in this book.

Chapter 1:

Lesson Learned #1: Examine maps from the places where your family lived. County boundaries often changed. Your family may have lived in the same house, but documents may have been stored in nearby county offices.

Lesson Learned #2: Keep documents organized in one place, by family, and chronologically by person within the family, so the information can be analyzed to help the ancestral story shine through.

Lesson Learned #3: Get yourself, your parents, your eldest elders, and first and second cousins DNA-tested NOW. This is especially critical for the descendants of the enslaved, and adoptees, who don't know much about their family history. DNA, in combination with traditional genealogical research, is a winning combination to find your ancestors.

Lesson Learned #4: Examine the documents of people who married into the family you're researching. Dowries often included enslaved people as gifts. Those records may be pertinent to your research.

Chapter 2:

Lesson Learned #5: When the ancestors want their stories told, they will pave the way for you to get the job done, come sleet, or snow, or COVID plight! Their mandate is for you to do the research, writing, printing, and distributing their stories no matter what.

Chapter 3:

Lesson Learned #6: Develop an itinerary of the places and people you want to visit before your genealogy trip (Appendix A). Ensure you determine the hours of operation and availability of venues, as well as make appointments in advance of the visit. Share your plans with family in case they want to join you on the trip, or give ideas for more places and people to visit.

Lesson Learned #7: Develop specific questions you wish to ask local experts and notify them in advance of your trip so they may have answers available during your visit (Appendix B).

Chapter 4:

Lesson Learned #8: Ensure that you fully understand the car rental process for your destination airport, as practices may differ from place to place. Also, ensure that the people who provide You with information actually know what they're talking about. Bottom line: I will never use Dollar Rental Car again; at least not at the Atlanta airport.

Lesson Learned #9: Ensure that you have multiple ways to contact your relatives, such as: cell and home phone numbers, email, home address, Ancestry account name, Facebook page, Instagram account, etc.

Lesson Learned #10: Keep a daily diary of your adventures (sample in Appendix E). Describe your feelings and emotions, sights, sounds, and smells, as you found places where your family lived, or documents that contained family information. Typing your notes into a computer, laptop, or smartphone every day, instead of writing them longhand, saves you from having to retype them later. Use the photographs you took during the day to refresh the memory of your experiences. Most of all, enjoy the journey.

Chapter 5:

Lesson Learned #11: Black Lives and Deaths did not matter in this cemetery.

Lesson Learned #12: Fried pickles are tasty! Trying local delicacies can enhance your experience.

Lesson Learned #13: Take lots of photos and videos. Don't discount any information gleaned from a genealogy pilgrimage. Note: Weeks later, after finding more corroborating DNA information, it seemed that Stephen Jr., who died in 1864, might have had more to do with my family than I originally thought.

Chapter 6:

Lesson Learned #14: Trust your Spidey Sense and always be aware of new places and people. Remember where you parked your car. Look at though you know what you're doing. Don't be a victim.

Lesson Learned #15: Be aware of particular animals, insects, flora, fauna, foods that you might be allergic to. Be sure to bring an inhaler or allergy medicines, or other medications with you on your trip. Consider packing a small first-aid kit and sewing kit.

Chapter 7:

Lesson Learned #16: Bring plenty of water and snacks with you each day of the trip.

Lesson Learned #17: Be sure to give into serendipity once in a while, even though it is not on the itinerary. Ask locals what their favorite restaurant is, or where they would take their visiting family, take a side trip to a local attraction. Leave some wiggle room in the itinerary to take advantage of unplanned experiences.

Lesson Learned #18: Visit some cemeteries and take pictures to honor the ancestors.

Chapter 8:

Lesson Learned #19: Purchase something that reminds you of the local places you visited. This includes taking selfies of yourself in front of well-known monuments and buildings, etc., to record your visit.

Chapter 9:

Lesson Learned #20: Stay hydrated at all times and eat nutritious food snacks during the day to be at your maximum performance.

Lesson Learned #21: If you are lucky enough to secure an expert guide (contact the local Historical Society or local library for recommendations) be sure to record, photograph, and videotape the tour. When you're back at home, you'll be happy you did.

Chapter 10:

Lesson Learned #22: Ensure that you have done all you can to give advance notice of itinerary timetables; in this case, I should have reminded her about our 9:30 a.m. appointment when we woke up. Exercise patience and understanding to keep tempers cool.

Lesson Learned #23: Be more empathetic to the customs, sights, sounds, eatables, sanitation systems, people, etc., that I encountered on a genealogy or pleasure travel trip. Their ways are no less valid than mine.

Chapter 11:

Lesson Learned #24: A face-to-face or online meeting can go very far in fostering a loving, familial relationship with people of different backgrounds. Stories maybe shared, differing upbringings brought to light, and the healing of wounds caused by racial divides secured.

Chapter 12:
Lesson Learned #25: Making a concerted effort to find out about your relatives through DNA testing, traditional genealogical research, and a WelcometotheTableexperience, greatly increases the quality of one's life.

Chapter 13:
Lesson Learned #26: At a reunion, and/or WelcometotheTable event, install a facilitator who would encourage a peaceful exchange of ideas from friends and relatives, in order to hear various sides of a story. The facilitator would ensure any conflicting viewpoints don't escalate to sink the ship.

Chapter 14:
Lesson Learned #27: Always be open to listening to someone else's point of view and try not to be judgmental if their view differs from yours.

Chapter 15:
Lesson Learned #28: Try to retrieve as much research and information as possible on each genealogy trip. Ensure the itinerary reflects the many options available and corresponding travel routes are mapped out in advance.

Chapter 16:
Lesson Learned #29: Document your pilgrimage with video, audio, and still photographs. Take copies of announcements, maps, and other printed materials from each visited location. This information will spark your memories, as well as make it possible for you to create videos that your family can watch, so they can feel like they are there with you.

Lesson Learned #30: Even if you're late to an appointment, go anyway, apologize for your tardiness, and enjoy the moment. Better still, confirm the meeting date in advance and *don't* be late!

Chapter 17:

Lesson Learned #31: Never accept "no" for an answer. If things aren't going according to plan (like avoiding a long line), come up with creative solutions, like calling or emailing information sources to help you achieve your goals.

Chapter 18:

Lesson Learned #32: Be curious. Stop and smell the roses. Explore unforeseen opportunities to obtain more data or qualitative experiences.

Lesson Learned #33: Obtain a plat map showing which land lots were purchased by various landowners. Attempt to overlay a present-day map over the plat map so you may visit the places your ancestors owned. If necessary, consult local experts who can help you with this.

Chapter 19:

Lesson Learned #34: Don't be so afraid to talk to strangers about your family. Say their names and places. You might just meet someone who is related, or who knows someone who might have information about your family or the places they lived.

Chapter 20:

Lesson Learned #35: Gather a group of family members to fine-tune this list, assign people for each task.

Chapter 23: Epilogue

What an adventure! Thanks to DNA research, I have met new Black and White cousins, researched, and commiserated with them and previously-known family members, written half-a-dozen books about my genealogy travels, family history findings, and stories I've synthesized from those facts. But in May 2021, during the Coronavirus pandemic, my data gathering experiences were enhanced by a serendipitous trip to Georgia and Alabama.

You see, I am the descendant of many Caucasians, as confirmed by one look in the mirror and the ethnic identity proclaimed by my DNA test results. Through research, I found that several of my three-times great-grandparents were European progenitors. But one particular owner, William Blount Marshall, became the focus of my book *The Marshall Legacy in Black and White* released in August 2021.

My brother, Greg Marshall, took a 111-marker Y-DNA test that proved beyond a doubt that my paternal line was genetically descended from Marshall-surnamed males. They were men who hailed from the United Kingdom in the 1600s to what is now called America. This investigative process, which was forty years in the making, led me to particular cousins—White and Black—who wanted to figure out how we intersected.

One of those new cousins, Amy Peacock, was the sixth-great-granddaughter of slaveholder David Gregg Marshall, who was born around 1734 in Halifax, North Carolina. Through DNA, I theorized that David Gregg Marshall could be my fifth great-grandfather, and Captain John Marshall my sixth, but the chart in Appendix B shows many other possibilities. I was excited that John and David were veterans of the Revolutionary War and hoped to prove my lineage through documentation, so the Daughters of the American Revolution would accept me as a member. That became a goal of *The Marshall Legacy* book which, as of this writing, is still a mystery until I can prove which White Marshall "did the deed."

Amy said she was the first cousin, six-times removed from David's grandson, William Blount Marshall. William was the only Marshall-surnamed slaveholder in Talbot County, Georgia, where my first- and second-great-grandfathers—Samuel and Henry A.—were enslaved. William fathered four children by his slave, Rosa Marshall, who in 1870, lived next-door to my Samuel's family with her Black husband and their five children, along with her four Mulatto children from their former enslaver, William.

Amy learned that she, and a Black cousin named Erika Thomas were both related to William and Rosa's son, called Marshall Marshall. He was Amy's second cousin five-times removed and Erika's three-times great-grandfather.

Amy and I met several new cousins and friends who have helped us in our detective work! We gathered at the physical and digital table, sharing tender feelings, tears, and laughter.

The ancestors are smiling!

ACKNOWLEDGEMENTS

A book like this does not happen in a vacuum. Numerous individuals not only made my trip to Georgia and Alabama possible, but fruitful and enjoyable.

First, I'd like to include a special acknowledgement to Cousin Amy Peacock for the camaraderie, laughs, serious discussions, understanding, and friendship she provided as we toured Georgia together. And many thanks to her husband, Paul, who suggested that Amy follow her heart and join me, a stranger, on the trip of a lifetime in the Deep South.

I appreciate the time Cousin James P. Marshall, President of the Putnam County Historical Society, took to fully immerse Amy and me in the history of our Marshall family in Putnam County. Meeting Cousin Jennifer K. was a plus, helping us all experience our first Welcome to the Table event, and sharing her considerable ancestral knowledge with me after the trip.

Chief Deputy Clerks Terri Jenkins and Shattara Powell at the Talbot County Courthouse, and Clerk Lisa McMillan at the Putnam Courthouse were knowledgeable and helpful.

What an incredible adventure Mike Buckner and his wife, Debbie, took Amy and me on in Talbot and Harris Counties! I can't choose which was the most special: sleuthing along Highway 36 for owner William Blount Marshall's plantation home, visiting Mike's two-story renovation project in progress, perusing actual farm records, watching a working grist mill, or exploring the pottery kiln he built. Or was it experiencing the Buckner's expansive 1830 property which contained a cotton field, and many outbuildings brought to their site for historical preservation. All those things made for an energizing afternoon.

Maybelle Hardnett welcomed us into her home in Talbot County and her cousin, Gloria Hardnett, has been in touch with me many times since returning back home.

Dana Chandler, an archivist at the Tuskegee Institute, let me live my dream of being an archeologist on a Mayan dig, exploring the artifacts he has collected over a lifetime. He also put me in contact with Dr. Shari L. Williams, who spoke with me about my possible connection to former Lieutenant Governor Robert Fulwood Ligon.

Delightful Cousin Jennifer Owens was able to join Amy and me for a meeting-of-the-minds during our last full day in Georgia. And Cousin Erika Thomas chatted with us on a video phone call from Texas.

DNA Cousins Eddie Marshall and Lori Ligon Hughes were unable to join us in Georgia for several reasons, but they were there in spirit and via email and Facebook before and after the trip.

My siblings, Greg and Carrie, agreed to be the "tech support" for conducting a rousing Zoom chat with old and new cousins, which included Austin David, Pershell Marshall, and Mike Chick, as well as Amy, Jennifer Owens, and Gloria Hardnett.

What would I do without the support of my Elk Grove Senior Center and Elk Grove Writing Guild writing/critique groups who patiently listened to my musings every Monday afternoon and the first Friday of every month? I am especially indebted to author/beta-readers Penelope Clark, George Hahn, Loy Holder, Betsy Schwarzentraub, Robin Roberts Harris, Judy Knott, and Jacquelyn Howard who provided invaluable feedback. Genoa Barrow, journalist for the *Sacramento Observer* Magazine gave her thoughts about the book title.

And finally, to the enslaved ancestors mentioned in this book and to those who have not yet been named, Amy said it beautifully:

> *"You have not been forgotten. We honor you and your ability to endure. So today, I wish these roses for the many enslaved human beings born without a birth certificate and died without death certificates. We apologize for such a sin that our ancestors inflicted upon you and your descendants. We make a pledge to do our personal best to eradicate hate and racism each day. We pledge our lives to Love and Lift those around us."*

ABOUT THE AUTHOR

Kathy Lynne Marshall was a researcher, analyst, and technical writer with the California Patrol for 36 years. She has been exploring her family roots for over four decades. Since 2016, Marshall has written a series of family heritage books which investigate her enslaved ancestors and their descendants. The research has taken her to visit the Deep South, Mid-west, East Coast, and Europe. Marshall truly believes that *The Ancestors Are Smiling!* If you enjoyed this heritage book and would like to support Marshall's writing, feel free to:

" Post reviews of Marshall's books on goodreads.com and amazon.com.

" If you purchase books on her KanikaMarshall.com website, Marshall will gladly autograph them for you.

" Sign up to receive Marshall's monthly newsletter. A link is at the bottom of each KanikaMarshall.com webpage.

" Marshall has Facebook Pages for each of her books. Feel free to "Like" them if you enjoy the insights she posts about her theories, research, photographs, DNA finds, genealogy trips. She hopes you will become motivated to write your family's stories.

" Follow Marshall on Instagram: KanikaMarshallArtBooks

Published by Kathy Lynne Marshall

Award-winning how-to book for uncovering slave history, using DNA and tips on structuring and self-publishing *your* own book.

Short stories from the descendants of former slave Otho Williams speak their truths and prove the human spirit can beat adversity.

Lots of *Roots* investigation led Kathy Marshall on a thrilling journey into her Grandpa Austin Henry Marshall's tangled historical past in Georgia and Alabama, finding Black and White ancestors she'd never known, leading to places she'd never been, and uncovering secrets that did not want to be told.

Award-winning story about a formidable woman who lied about her southern birthplace to make her mark in the Promised Land. The ending is not to be missed.

Margaret's journey from slave to fifty years free is told with gusto, as is her father's heroic trip to a political convention in 1855 which changed their lives.

Appendix A - Itinerary Example

Date	Day	Where Activity	Open hours	Address & Phone
May 23	Sun	Delta 783 Sacramento to Atlanta	7AM Takeoff	SMF, 6900 Airport Blvd, Sac, CA 95837
May 23	Sun	Pickup Dollar Rental car #J75516101A0	3:15 PM	2300 Rental Pkwy, College Pk, GA
May 23	Sun	**Meet with cousin Eddie at Holiday Inn**	5 PM?	520 John B. Wilson Court, Lawrenceville, GA
May 23	Sun	Spend the Night at Julie's		Lawrenceville GA 30045
May 24	Mon	Pick up Amy. Drive 68 miles SE to Eatonton.	9:30 AM	520 John B. Wilson Court, Lawrenceville, GA
May 24	Mon	**Meet with cousin James Marshall**	11:00 AM?	104 Church Street, Eatonton, Putnam, GA
May 24	Mon	Drive to Eatonton County Clerk: plat, slaves	8:00-5:00 PM	100 South Jefferson Ave, Eatonton, GA
May 24/26	Mon	Find Marshall plantation site on Hwy 36		Bluff Springs Church & Marshall plantation site.
May 24	Mon	Drive to Hampton Inn	6:00 PM?	Hampton Inn, 7390 Bear Lane, Columbus, GA
May 25	Tues	Explore Talbotton courthouse **Vault**: deeds	9:30-5 appt	26 S. Washington Ave, Talbotton, GA, 31827
May 26	Weds	After lunch, chat with **Michael Buckner.**	1-4 PM?	Fielders Mill Road, Junction City, GA
May 26	Weds	Visit Waverly Hall cemetery		Highway 208, east of US-27, west of Talbotton
May 27	Thurs	Visit Marshall home in Columbus, GA		1710 Fifth Ave. Columbus, GA
May 27	Thurs	Visit 6th Ave. Train Station?		6th Ave and 10th Street, Columbus, GA
May 27	Thurs	Visit St. James AME Church Archives	Closed 1-2 PM	1002 Sixth Ave, Columbus, 706-322-8043
May 27	Thurs	Visit 1st African Baptist Church??		901 Fifth Ave., Columbus, 706-323-3367
May 27	Thurs	Walk around 10th and Broadway area.		10th and Broadway area, Columbus, GA
May 27	Thurs	**Early dinner with cousins**	2 PM	BoneFish, Veterans Parkway, Columbus, GA

Appendix B - 3X Great-Grandfather?

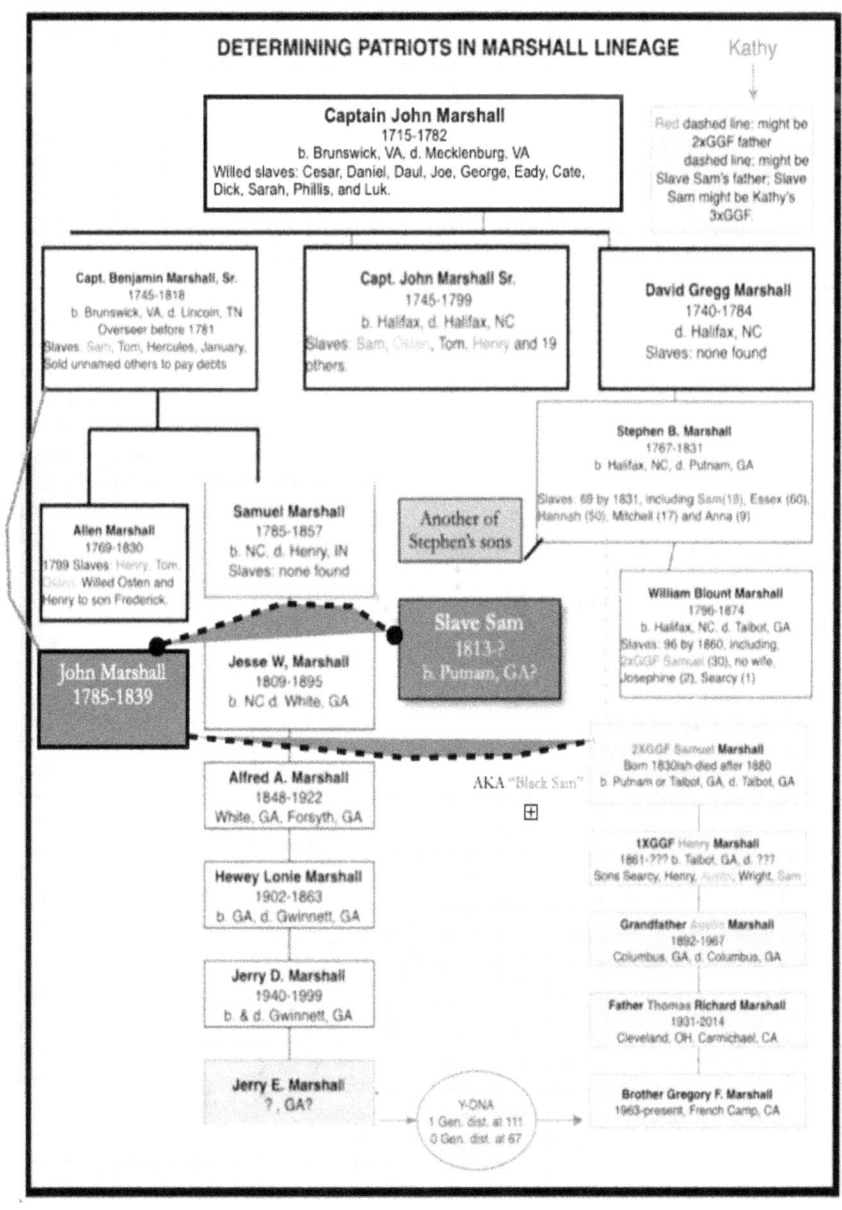

Appendix C - Trip Questions Example

Questions to Ask Locals on Genealogy Trip			
Person to ask	Person Contact Info	Day	Question

Sample Research Questions from Kathy's May 2021 Trip:

Questions about the Marshall lineage

Person to ask	Day	Questions about the Marshall lineage
Eddie Marshall	May 23	What kind of family stories had you heard about growing up within 200 miles of our first Marshall ancestor?
Eddie Marshall	May 23	Did you only do the Y-DNA test with FTDNA? Tested with other company?
Eddie Marshall	May 23	Have you messaged other Y-DNA matches to find the common ancestor, like the one who has George Abner Marshall?
Eddie Marshall	May 23	Do you know which CHRs are for the Marshall line?
James Marshall	May 24	Who are your up-line Marshalls?
James Marshall	May 24	Some bios say William B. Marshall was a judge. Where would one go for higher education in Warren or Putnam?
James Marshall	May 24	Is the Farm Book and ANY mentions of slaves available from the Stephen B. Marshall (Sr. and Jr.) estate available?
James Marshall	May 24	Is there a plat map available for Stephen B. Marshall & Peter F Mahone?
James Marshall	May 24	Do you know what William B. Marshall looked like? Likely he had a gray beard?
James Marshall	May 24	What type of crops were grown in Putnam in the 1820s?
James Marshall	May 24	Was Tony Marshall's ancestor, John Marshall, the last son of David G. Marshall, born in about 1785? Is that why he moved Rebecca Burt to Putnam in 1810?
Michael Buckner	May 26	Where's Marshall plantation? Hwy 36 and Sarah Marshall Rd. Why Sarah?
Michael Buckner	May 26	Trying to figure out why my great uncles were named Wright, Searcy, Austin.
Michael Buckner	May 26	Any info about Marshall slaves? When did they leave? Any still here?
Michael Buckner	May 26	He said corn was planted for livestock. How much?

Appendix D - Family Tree Chart Examples

There are several ways to present family tree lineage. Blank forms may be purchased from EasyGenie.org, Etsy.com, Amazon.com, among other sources. Useful chart examples follow.

Common Ancestor Chart. The row at the bottom includes living people who took a DNA test. Their parents are listed in the second row from the bottom, grandparents the third from the bottom, etc. Their common ancestor would be at the top of the chart, e.g., Robert Marshall, in this example.

Common Ancestor: Robert Marshall Sr. (1642-1698, Bedfordshire, England)			
John Joseph? Marshall & Sarah Malone (1661?-1728)	John Marshall & Sarah Malone (1695?-1733, Isle of Wight to Brunswick, VA)	John Marshall & Sarah Malone (1695-1733, Isle of Wight to Brunswick, VA)	John Marshall & Sarah Malone (1695-1733, Isle of Wight to Brunswick, VA)
Capt John Marshall & Mary Malone (1725-1782)	Capt John Marshall & Mary Malone?(1725-1782)	Capt John Marshall & Mary Malone (1725-1782)	Capt John Marshall & Mary Malone (1725-1782)
Benjamin Marshall Sr. (1745-1818, TN)	David G. Marshall? (1740-1784, Halifax, NC)	David G. Marshall (1740-1784, Halifax, NC). Amy's 6xGGF	David G. Marshall (1740-1784, Halifax, NC)
Samuel Marshall (1785-1857)	**Stephen B. Marshall?** (1767-1831, Putnam) & Slave Hannah? (1781)	Lucy Marshall (1758-1829) & William Blount 1755-1825)	**Stephen B. Marshall** (1767,NC-1831,GA)
2x Jesse W. Marshall (1809 NC-1895, GA)	William B. Marshall (1796) or Slave Sam (1813) or Jesse Marshall (1809)?	Richard Blount (1790-1841) & Ruth	**William B. Marshall** (1796-1874) & **Rosa Marshall**
1x Alfred A. Marshall (1846-1922, GA)	2x=Samuel Marshall (1830-?) & Mary Wilkinson or Emeline Bunkley	William Blount (1823,GA-1884,TX) & Martha (1823-1870)	Albert Marshall & Clara Marshall
Hewey L. Marshall (1902-1963)	1x Henry A. Marshall (or Austin Marshall)? & Mary Smith	Oliver Marshall Blount (1857,GA-1924,TX) Emma(1865-1900,TX)	**Mariah Marshall &** John Walton
Jerry D. Marshall	Austin H. Marshall & Daisy Dooley	John F. Blount (1888-1969, TX) & Dora (1897-1981)	Walker Carter & Amelia Walton
Private	Thomas Marshall & Mary Carter	Emma Blount & John Lyles	Private
EDDIE __ Y-DNA to Greg 110/111 **Tony & Jennifer K** from Benjamin Marshall	**KATHY**, Greg, Carrie, Pershell, Austin, Jocelyn, Lori, Michal, Carolyn, Matthew **AZMINA**, 11 cM to KM	**AMY** __ 4.1 cM to KM **JP** & Nancy descend from Mathew Marshall and Rhoda	**ERIKA** __ 6.9 cM to KM

Pedigree Chart tracks your individual family history back through time. This means that every person listed on the chart is directly related to you: your parents, their parents, and so on, usually going back six or seven generations shown on the screen. Here's an example:

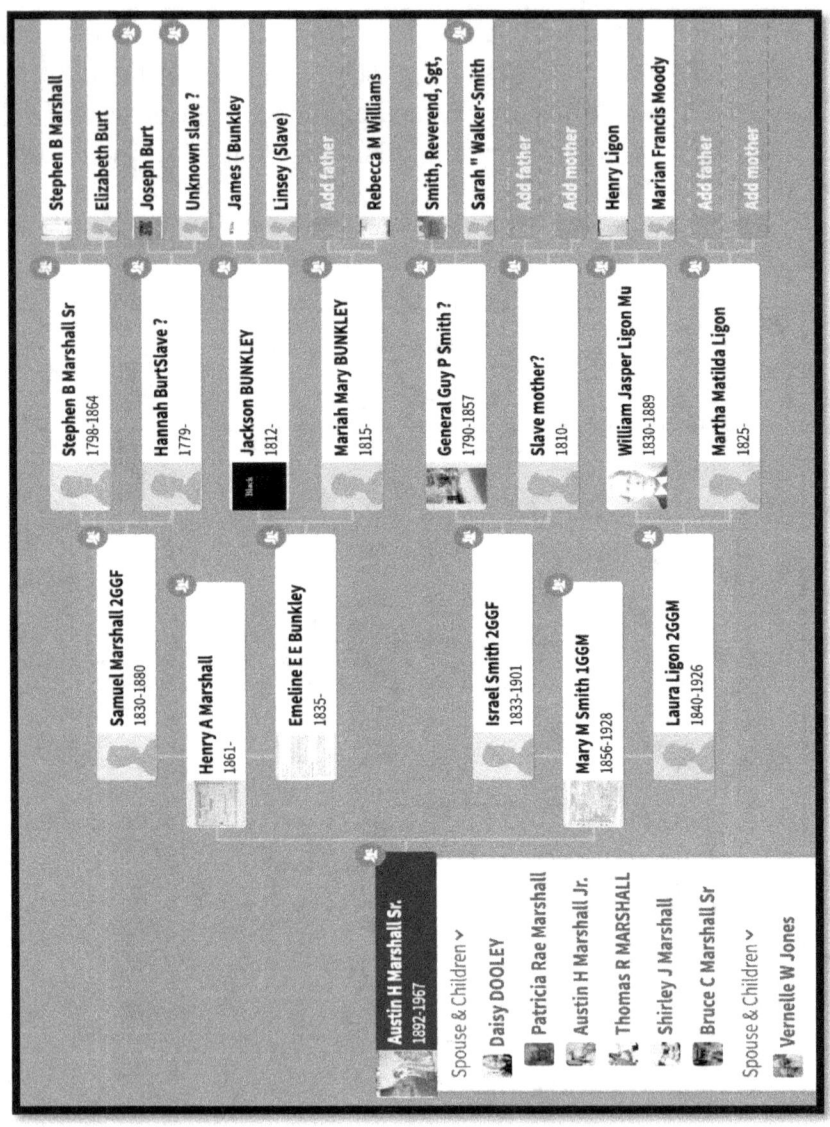

Family Group Sheet example from Ancestry.com is a view of parents and children in a family, and is designed to show names, dates, and places of birth, marriages, and deaths in an easy-to-read format.

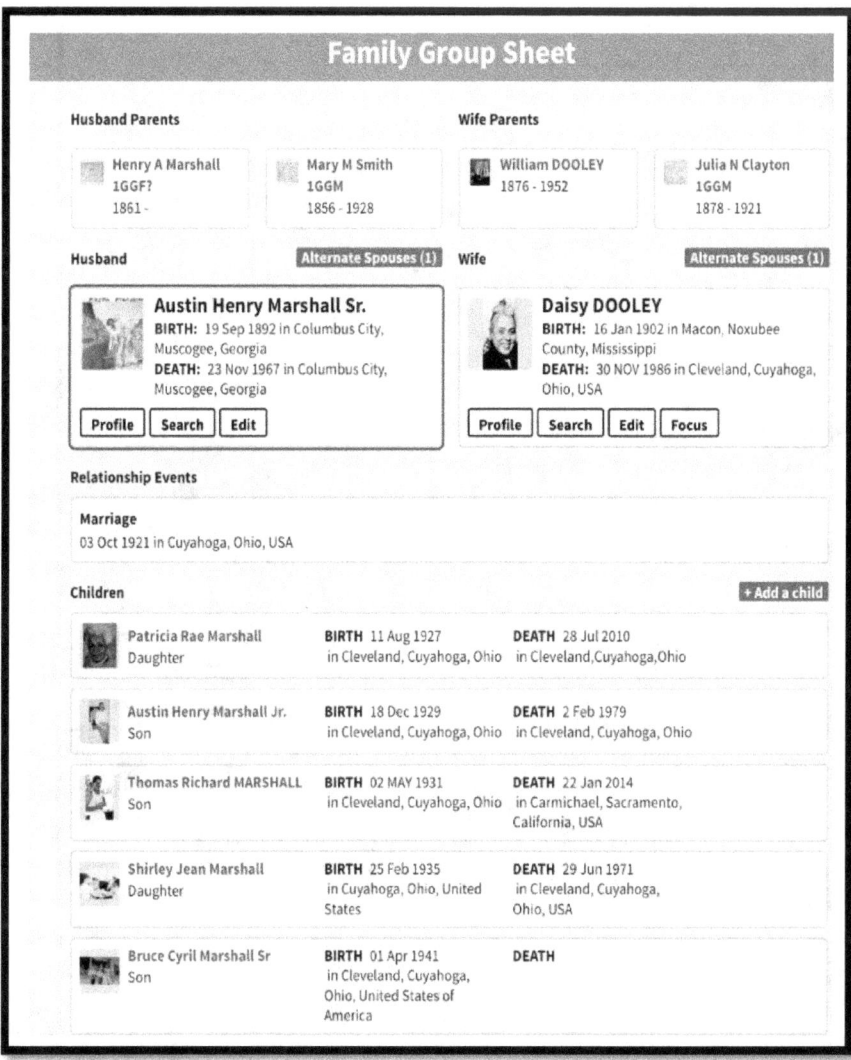

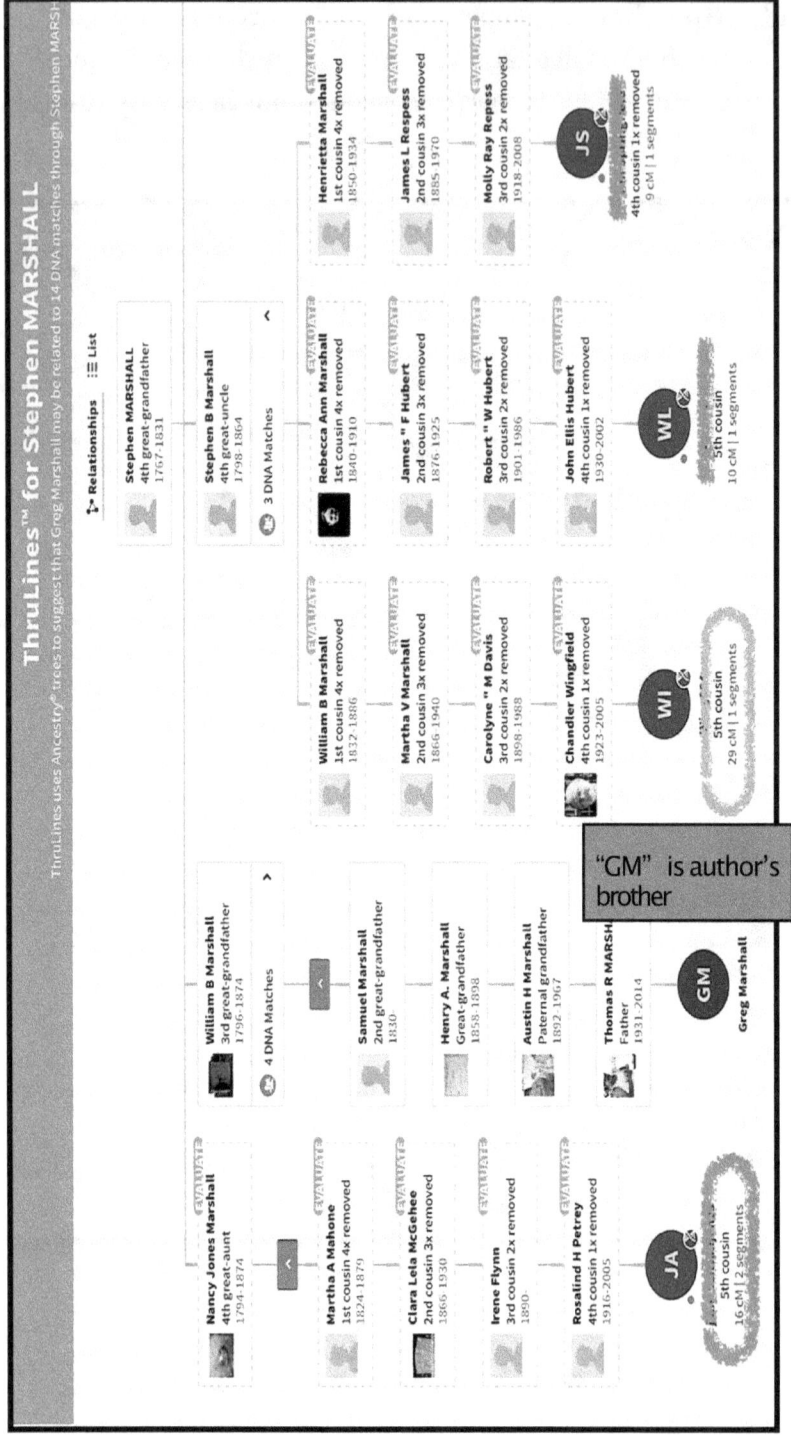

Appendix E - Explore DNA ThruLines

Note: This and the previous page should be joined as one chart. !GM" is the author"s brother. The people at the bottom of each column are living, genetic/DNA relatives who have Stephen B. Marshall in their family trees. Is he their common ancestor?

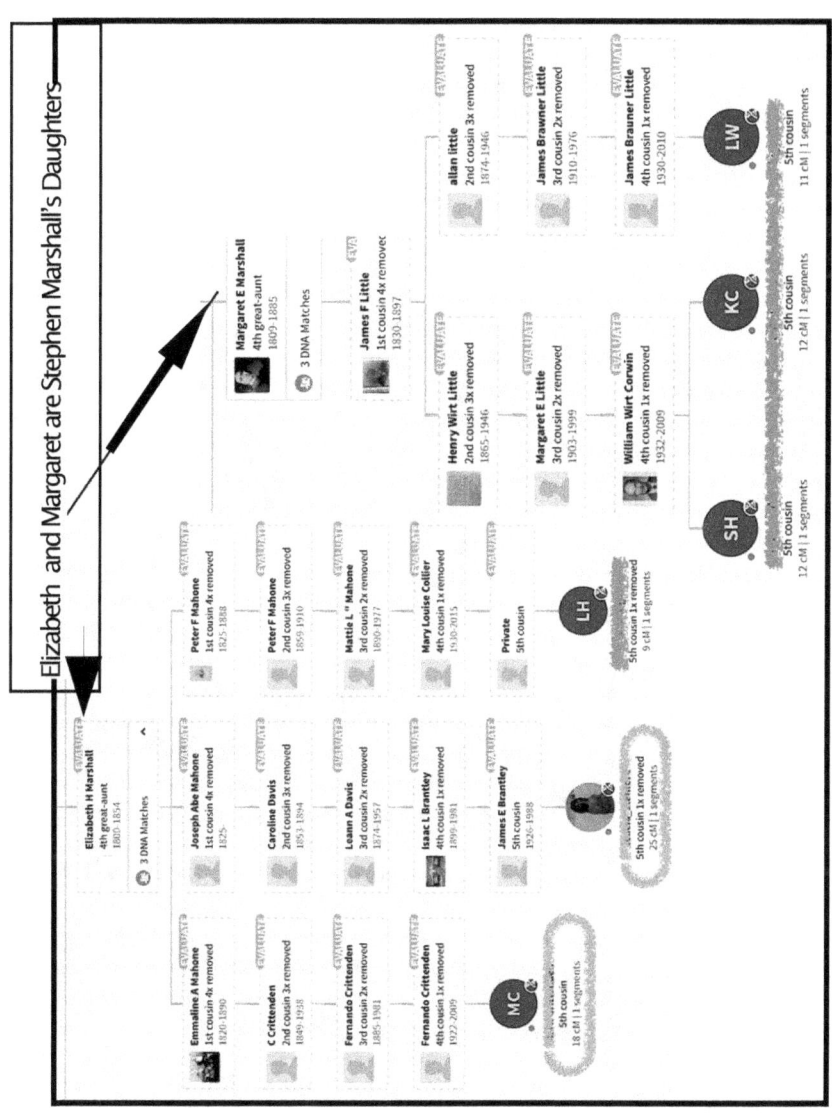

Appendix F - Keep a Daily Diary

It's helpful to jot down your thoughts, feelings, and emotions that generally accompany a genealogy trip into the land of the ancestors. In the long run, it is easier if the day's adventures are typed into a digital device, such as a smartphone or electronic tablet or a laptop, but an old-fashioned pad of paper works too. You can also dictate the day's events into a voice memo-type App or another recording device. Taking photographs of the day's activities is a must, including selfies in front of pertinent historical places. A video recording is particularly beneficial for it combines sight and sound in a way that is difficult to achieve through words or pictures alone. Whichever method you choose, consider collecting something like the following to help write the story of your visit.

Option 1: Trip Diary for <u>Date</u> in <u>County</u> , <u>State</u>

Time	Location	Who with?	What experienced?	Describe/Felt

Sample Daily Diary

1BOOKER Genealogy Journal_2019 West Virginia Trip.pages

Oct 5: Sacramento to BWI to Hagerstown
Oct 6: Hagerstown, Antietam, Boonsboro, Funkstown, Maryland, to Elkins, West Virginia
Oct 7: Elkins and Beverly

I couldn't believe it was Time to get up when is the alarm sounded at 8 AM.

But I got up, opened the Roman blinds to let light into the room, then took a shower period

I didn't get dressed until about 845, then took my camera in my room key downstairs to the breakfast room. The hotel had a nice enough set up for a continental breakfast. Hot and cold drinks, an oatmeal stand with walnuts and cranberries and brown sugar, a heated chafing dish for egg white omelets'n veggies or scrambled eggs, a chafing dish for bacon and sausage, and another chafing dish for sausage gravy and biscuits. There was also a couple of types of cold cereal, several different types of breads and muffins, and cinnamon rolls. I had the egg omelette, two pieces of bacon, oatmeal with cranberries in walnuts, some kind of fruit juice, and I took a banana. The breakfast room is double duty for the Office room with tables and chairs and some bench seats.

I went back up to the room, brushed my teeth, then packed my research binder and computer in the computer bag, put the banana in my "purse" along with some electronic devices, put on my heavy Black on one side, white on the other fake sheepskin coat, wrapped my head in a kind of turbin, and exited the hotel for my little ford fiesta. I plugged in the coordinates into the Apple maps program, started up the car, turn on the lights, it Turned on the windshield wipers, then made my way the three blocks to the Elkins public library.

Entering the library I saw that there was a separate genealogy room right next to the receptionist desk. I entered, without having to speak with anyone. The small, maybe eight by 10 foot room with floor to ceiling books on three sides. I soon found that the books were not in any particular order, except that the top two shelves were for Pearl S Buck books – I imagine she is a local author. Since there was no order, I had to look at every single book. That was tedious but it did give me an idea of what is important here in Randolph County, West Virginia. That was explicitly about Black people. Other than that, I took some photographs of some pages of some books, but there wasn't much of benefit to that trip. I left the library at about 1230.

I opened the Apple maps app and programmed in the location for Beverly Historical Center. It started raining as I pulled out of Elkins. I took some video as I went and about 15 minutes later arrived in the town of Beverly. I saw a sign for a cemetery as I passed this narrow, one car Lane that seemed to lead to the cemetery. So I drove around the corner and again and again, trying to find a way to get the car into the cemetery. The residential area next to the main road only had these little one car lanes between the houses, which looked like mobile homes with vinyl siding. There was so much traffic on the main road. Being only one lane each side certainly didn't help. Having logging trucks in cars And every other type of vehicle on the road of the same time didn't help either. I finally figured out how to get into the Chenowith/Beverly Cemetery. Parked the car halfway around the backside, got out, marveled at the beauty of before foliage bordering the cemetery, took lots of pictures, walked up and down half of the cemetery looking for familiar names such as Early (found none), Bucky, and __.

Appendix G - Solving Your Mystery

I have been researching the lives of my African American family for four decades, creating the requisite genealogy binders full of vital records, census, and other documents for six of my family lines, including the Williams, Bookers, Marshalls, Dooley, Carters, and Myers family lines.

An alarming thought entered my head in May 2016 when I began my sixtieth year of life. There are only three people older than me in my mother's family and three older in my father's. Soon I may be the matriarch of the family. If I don't write a book about my ancestors, who will? Now is the time to commemorate the lives of those enslaved and free people who have gone before me, and of those still living who are their proud descendants. I have a burning desire to ensure that my family is remembered in a tangible, written way.

After a gentle push from my spirited ancestors, I began writing *The Ancestors Are Smiling!* on October 1, 2016 and published it in July 2017. The next 15 months were spent solving the mystery of my enslaved relatives in *Finding Otho: The Search for Our Williams Ancestors*. Then came *Finding Daisy: From the Deep South to the Promised Land* in 2019, *The Mystery of Margaret Booker* in 2020, then *The Marshall Legacy in Black and White* in 2021.

Listen up, dear reader. There are a number of reasons why I was finally able to successfully accomplish my family story book goals. I had heard many of the following how-to tips numerous times over the years in various genealogy classes and conferences, but I finally started DOING WHAT WAS SUGGESTED by experts.

Please note that the following ideas are only *one* way to write a paperback or electronic book, but they are steps that have worked well for me.

You don't feel comfortable creating a standard paperback? No problem, I'll present other ideas and video links for communicating your stories. Will any or all of these concepts work for you? Why not give them a try? See if they will help *you* get started (and finished) with *your* book.

Focus Your Book

The first step is to determine who or what the book will be about. Pretend you have a magic wand which would allow you to interview ONE of your relatives (or another subject for a book), past or present, during an entire 24-hour period. The wand will take care of all your responsibilities—spouse, children, job—so you can fully concentrate on the questions you want to ask that relative.

WHO would that one person be that you would love to spend 24 hours with, to help you write a book about them? For example, your WHO person could be a great-grandparent, an unknown biological parent, a formerly enslaved relative, or a slaveholder. Write down the name of your WHO. If you can't think of anyone, write your own name as the WHO. Writing a book about significant events in your own life can be the best way to learn how to write a book.

WHY did you choose that WHO person to write a book about? For example, if I wanted to write a book about my Marshall ancestors, I had to first learn about Grandpa Austin Henry Marshall.

What three (or more) things do you already **KNOW** about that WHO person? For example, I knew my Grandpa Austin was born in Columbus, Georgia, was a Pullman Porter, and owned the Marshall Funeral Home in Cleveland, OH.

WHERE did your WHO person live? List all the known places.

WHAT do you want to find out about your WHO person? I usually want to know the parents of my WHO person, their descendants up to the present day (so DNA can work its magic), the slaveholder, and whether DNA can help me find more relatives with family trees.

It is critically important to this process to write down your answers to the WHO, WHY, KNOW, WHERE and WHAT questions. Kathy Marshall's quick-start process for writing *your* book won't work well unless you perform the focus exercise above. Of course, you may want to customize the following steps, and rearrange any of the chapters, but the following will give you an idea of how to start your project.

"SO WHAT?" says genealogist Dr. Shelley Murphy. **Why bother doing that exercise?**

- The "**WHO**" refers to the protagonist, the heroine/hero, or relative who the book is about. I prefer to mention my WHO as the Book Title and present her/him/them in the Introduction.

- The "**WHY**" is your inspiration for writing the book. It could be discussed in the Introduction and the first chapter. The WHY sets the stage for the story and clues the reader to your inspiration for the book.

- The "What I already **KNOW**" information could be presented in the second chapter.

- The "**WHERE**" could be the third chapter, describing the locations where your WHO lived, how people were treated there, what the opportunities and issues were in that locale.

- The "**WHAT**" is the meat and potatoes—your goals for the book. What are you seeking to learn or present about your WHO in the book? Each of those WHAT questions could become separate chapters in your book.

I wrote an Introduction right away, indicating my fifth book would primarily be about my paternal grandfather, Austin Henry Marshall, why I chose him, and what my goals were. I wanted to prove with documents and DNA testing who his parents and ancestors' owners were, and what his life was like in the Deep South and Cleveland. Writing an Introduction at the beginning of the process, and reviewing it periodically kept me on track to finish writing, editing, and publishing that book. I wanted to get *The Marshall Legacy in Black and White* story into the hands of my family, bookstores, genealogists, and the research libraries where my Marshall family had lived.

Self-publishing one book per year is the mandate from *my* ancestor bosses. I don't intend to let them down.

Now let's put into practice how I used this method. Your may customize the techniques however you wish. The following contains a sample outline for *The Marshall Legacy in Black and White* book. It was the inspiration for this *Finding Marshalls: Genealogy Trip with A Black and White Twist*.

NOTE: You can use the basic steps of this Quick-Start process, even if you want to write a book of short stories, poems, a book of fiction, or a how-to book.

Quick-Start Process for *The Marshall Legacy* Book

WHO is the book about? Austin Marshall, his ancestors and descendants.

WHY write about Austin? To commemorate my ancestor's existence as part of the American historical record.

WHERE did Austin live? Columbus, GA, and Cleveland, OH.

What do you already KNOW about Austin? (Background)

- He's my paternal grandfather, born 1892 in Columbus, Georgia.
- His parents were Henry A. Marshall and Mary Smith.
- His siblings were Clifford, Israel, Thomas, and Cora Marshall.
- He was a Pullman porter by 1917, working New York to Chicago.
- He served in France during World War I.
- He married Daisy Dooley in 1921 in Cleveland, OH.
- He and Daisy bought a house in Cleveland in 1923.
- He and Daisy bought a Funeral Home at 8115 Cedar Ave. in 1939.
- His and Daisy's kids: Pat, Austin, Thomas, Shirley Jean, and Bruce.
- His grandson, Greg Marshall's Y-DNA, confirms Marshall blood.
- He married Vernelle Jones probably in the mid-1950s.
- He died in 1967 in Columbus, GA, buried in Porterdale cemetery.
- The 1900-1940 Censuses indicated who lived with him.

WHAT more do you want to learn? (Goals)

- Austin's father, Henry's owner's full name and his family's history.
- Was there more than one owner?
- Exactly (house) where did Samuel and Henry live?
- Who was Austin's grandmother (Samuel's wife)?
- What happened to Henry after 1897?
- What happened to Samuel's children?
- Who were Samuel's parents?
- Can DNA prove enough genetic connections to a specific patriot Marshall to apply for membership in the Daughters of the American Revolution?

Plan to Write Your Book

1. Adopt an **ATTITUDE THAT YOU MUST PUBLISH YOUR BOOK**, before all else. Your mantra must be: "I live and breathe to publish a book about my family." Otherwise, any mundane activity will divert you from your goal to leave a written legacy for your family.

2. **FOCUS ON ONE** specific family line, or one person, or one specific aspect of the family, for example, a specific enslaved ancestor from one of your family lines.

3. Determine the **SCOPE** (extent) of the book. I wanted to find my grandfather's parents and grandparents, write about their lives, then publish this book. What, specifically, do you want YOUR book to be about?

4. Develop a **LIST OF QUESTIONS** you want to answer (e.g., who were my third great-grandparents, what jobs did they do, where did they live, who were their slave masters?).

5. Understand that you may not be able to answer all your questions but accept that it is OK. Write about the **steps you DID take** and present what you *did* and *did not* find. Indicate that you may resume your inquiry in the Second Edition when more information becomes available.

6. Decide on the **AUDIENCE** for your book (e.g., children, family, genealogists, the public) and use appropriate words for that audience.

Create the Framework & Type as You Research

7. Decide on a computer **WORD PROCESSING PROGRAM** for your book, such as Microsoft Word or Apple Pages.

8. **OPEN A NEW DOCUMENT** and initially **NAME IT** with the WHO name or whatever other name you wish (e.g.,

AustinMarshall.docx) and **SAVE** it to a folder on your computer. You can change the name later.

9. Be sure to **SAVE** your word processing manuscript every ten minutes or so and **BACK UP** your book file every day (e.g., keep a copy on the Internet cloud or on a portable backup drive).

10. Develop a **BOOK OUTLINE** in your new word document, like the following:

11. Title Page: **Type the WHO and the Author Name** on the first page.

12. Type **Copyright** on the second page (see copyright.gov for sample verbiage).

13. Type a **Dedication** on the third page.

14. Include a **Filler** on the 4th page, like adding a picture, or a quote, or a poem, or a **Foreword** from a professional.

15. (If desired) On an odd-numbered page, include a **Table of Contents** (TOC). Note: Microsoft Word and Apple Pages can be configured to automatically generate the TOC with the "Styles" Function.

16. (If desired) Insert an **Acknowledgments** page, thanking people who helped you write your book.

17. (If desired) Add an **Introduction** that explains what the book is about; write it early in the process, then refine it.

18. (If desired) Include a **Timeline** of historical events, if desired.

19. Add ten or more **Chapters** to include certain characters or topics (e.g., chapters labelled "What I Know," "Where the WHO lived," "Mother," "Father," "DNA results," NOTE: Start chapters in the printed book on an odd-numbered page (so chapter headings in the header or footer will be on odd pages).

20. (If desired) Add an **Epilogue**/Conclusion/Coda/Wrap up to summarize your efforts.

21. (If desired) Include **Appendices**, lists of tables, maps, etc..

22. (If desired) Add a **Bibliography** listing which sources you used to develop your ideas in the book.

23. (If desired) Include **End Notes** with complete citations, using this basic format: Author, *Title*, (Publisher State, Publisher, Year), page number.

24. **Refine the book layout** after fifty or so pages have been typed. Print a draft copy so you'll have proof you are actually writing a book. This will motivate you to finish your manuscript and print the final copy.

Write Your Manuscript

25. **START WRITING TODAY** with what you already know (e.g., your life story, parents, grandparents, documents collected).

26. **DON'T WORRY ABOUT PERFECT SENTENCES**. Type broad ideas and the gist of stories. You can revise them later.

27. **COPY AND PASTE** into the correct chapter any documentation that has already been written. For example, a memory about your fifth birthday party would go into your chapter; your grandparents' wedding picture would go into their chapter, etc.

28. **TYPE THE BOOK** as you are conducting your research and getting stories. Include your emotions at that time when they are fresh.

29. **BACKUP** your work periodically, saving the document often in the computer, as well as saving the manuscript to a thumb drive, or external back up drive stored away from the computer. In case your computer fails, you'll want to have another copy on a backup drive.

30. Include **FOOTNOTES/CITATIONS** citing your information sources as you write.

31. **RECHECK YOUR FOCUS** and scope often, to remain on track with what your book is about.

32. Consider writing the passages as though you are telling the story directly to your audience or writing the stories from the **POINT OF VIEW** of your family members.

33. **READ OUT LOUD** what you have written to uncover awkward sentence structure or to notice missing words and to hear whether the text is too conversational or too technical, keeping in mind your audience.

Gather More Information

34. **INTERVIEW YOUR ELDERS** and other family members. Type their stories in the appropriate chapter in the manuscript.

35. Do **DNA TESTING NOW** for yourself, your elders, and other family members. The major DNA companies are: ancestry.com, 23andMe.com, FamilyTreeDNA.com, My Heritage, and Living DNA. For more information, check https://isogg.org/wiki/List_of_DNA_testing_companies.

36. Gather **FAMILY PHOTOGRAPHS**, using your camera or smartphone to take high-resolution photos. Copy the photos to a folder on your computer. Save them as 300 dots-per-inch (dpi) resolution for printing. Label the photos in the manuscript with the date, place, and names of the subjects.

37. Read **PROBATE, CENSUS, and LAND RECORD** documents pertinent to your family research.

38. Visit family **HOME SITES** and **CEMETERIES** (search Findagrave.com), take photographs and type your findings, and **YOUR FEELINGS,** about visiting these places in your manuscript.

39. **PRINT DOCUMENTS** within each family line and organize them into separately named **GENEALOGY BINDERS**.

40. Start an **ONLINE FAMILY TREE** (e.g., **ancestry.com, familysearch.org**) with names, dates, locations, etc., and **KEEP IT PUBLIC** so others may connect with you and share information about your family, and so DNA testing tools can find more relatives.

41. Keep **FAMILY TREE DATA ON YOUR COMPUTER** (e.g., Family Tree Maker).

42. Use **ONLINE GENEALOGY SITES** (e.g., ancestry.com, familysearch.org, USGenWeb.com, WikiTree.com, newspapers.com, fold3.com, and Genetic Genealogy Tips and Techniques.

43. Become a member of **GENEALOGY FACEBOOK PAGES** and other web pages (e.g., Our Black Ancestry, Our Black Legacy, Genealogy Adventures, Black ProGen Live).

44. Watch free **GENEALOGY HOW-TO VIDEOS** from ancestry.com or youtube.com.

45. Do a simple **online Google search on your ancestors' names and states** to see if any books or other resources contain your kin's names. Recheck these resources often.

46. Take **GENEALOGY COURSES** like the Midwest African American Genealogy Institute, enroll in genealogy conventions, and join genealogy guilds to learn the best genealogy practices. Conduct an exhaustive search. Document accurate citations. Analyze information. Resolve conflicting evidence. Develop a reasoned written conclusion.

47. **DEVELOP THEORIES** and prove or disprove them with actual documents and DNA, but do not be too rigid. Review and revise theories and update the book accordingly. Avoid obsessing on preconceived ideas from family lore.

48. Discuss your book ideas and theories with other authors, editors, and family, and **ASK THEM TO GIVE FEEDBACK** on your work in progress.

Try Self-Publishing

49. Have the book professionally **COPY EDITED** and **PROOFREAD** to ensure the manuscript is perfect before publishing.

50. Hire someone to **PERFECT THE LAYOUT** of your book (e.g., ensure the font sizes are consistent for headings, captions, and text)

51. Export your book manuscript to a **.pdf FILE** on your computer. Check all pages for layout, spelling, etc.

52. If you want to sell your books, obtain an International Standard Book Number (**ISBN**) through **bowker.com** ($295 for ten or $125 for one). Leave 1.5 inches wide by 2.0 inches tall on the lower right back jacket of your book cover for the ISBN bar code..

53. **COPYRIGHT** your book (e.g., copyright.gov).

54. Create an online account with a **SELF-PUBLISHING WEBSITE** (e.g., **lulu.com** or **Kindle Direct Publishing** KDP.com, **IngramSpark.com, or Apple**) and read their online instructions for uploading a .pdf copy of your book. Choose whether to create an e-book, paperback, or hardback book. Choose a book size, keywords (see Kindlepreneur.com for great information), book categories, number of pages. Upload the .pdf of your manuscript.

55. Prepare a blurb for the cover back jacket and for the online **DESCRIPTION** of your book (you may use the text on the back jacket of your book). Look at several amazon.com memoir book examples to see what kinds of things are written in the book description. Make it pop!

56. Paying someone to make a cover will likely be the best option for a high quality cover, albeit hundreds of dollars. Instead, if desired, use

the self-publishing website's **BOOK COVER CREATOR** (front, back, and spine). Or make your own cover on your computer. Be sure to use the precise height and width measurements supplied by the self-publishing service. Export your book cover to a .pdf file.

57. After your book manuscript is perfected, export it to a .pdf file, then **UPLOAD THE MANUSCRIPT AND COVER .pdf** to the self-publishing website. Make sure you review any corrections the book website suggests (like ensuring the photos are 300 dpi), make the changes, then upload the .pdf files again.

58. Decide on a retail **PRICE** for your book. The book service will tell you how much revenue you will earn depending on your retail price, the book size, and number of pages. The lower the price the less revenue you'll receive, but more people may buy the book.

59. Once the manuscript is submitted for printing, order an **ADVANCED READER COPY**. Carefully **REVIEW** the printed book, make corrections, create a new .pdf, re-upload the file, recheck the uploaded file, order another Advanced Reader Copy. When you are absolutely certain there are no errors in your manuscript submit it for **FINAL PRINTING**. It takes 24-72 hours for book approval and about a week to print the book(s).

60. If using Amazon.com's Kindle Direct Publishing, choose **MARKETING CHANNELS** for your book (e.g., Amazon in America and/or Europe, resellers, research channels).

61. **MARKET** your published book (e.g., **amazon.com**, Facebook page, webpage, newsletter, blog, local bookstores, donate to research libraries, and/or offer to be a volunteer speaker at local networking groups and service clubs).

Alternatives to Printing Paperbacks and E-Books

Photo Book: Instead of a narrative, self-published book as described in the previous steps, you could create hard-cover, photo album style books. Simply upload your high-resolution (300 dpi or more) .jpg family photos, charts, graphs, or maps to shutterfly.com or photo.walgreens.com or costco.com or other online photo book services. Get on their mailing lists to get periodic discounts. This is an easy way to commemorate your ancestors' lives, and/or to write poetry or story books of any kind.

Hire a Ghostwriter to Write, Print and/or Publish Your Book: Ghost writers are writers-for-hire who take money, but none of the credit, for the work they produce for you for a fee. The "ghost" is usually paid in advance of completing the job. The lowest costs *may* start at $6 per page, or $60 per hour. Expect to pay *many* thousands of dollars for a ghostwriter. Be sure to sign a work proposal that includes costs and a payment schedule for each stage of the work. You could seek recommendations for a "Ghostwriter" on Google, Facebook pages, and the "LinkedIn.com" website. Also check the local Northern California Publishers and Authors group for ghostwriters in our area (https://www.norcalpa.org).

Use a Local Commercial Printer: Your manuscript must be in digital format, either emailed to your home printer from a computer, or downloaded to a portable thumb drive and taken to a printer.

Traditional Publisher: Truly, it is difficult to get a traditional publisher. You have to look for a publisher, find a literary agent, sign a contract, and hope your book gets published within a year, and that you earn more than $2 per book sold. A winning idea is to join the Northern California Publishers and Authors group and write a short story for inclusion in one of their anthologies to become a published author. Several of our Senior Center writers have become first-time authors this way. You could also contract with one of the NCPA editors or publishers. (https://www.norcalpa.org)

Always Remember

Be so passionate about commemorating your ancestor's stories that you have an overwhelming need to publish your book. Be focused on writing about a specific person or family line. Create a book template and begin typing what you already know about your ancestors into it and type all your new findings into it. Include source citations as you enter information. These important actions will result in the quick development of a manuscript that looks like a ready-for-printing **real book**.

I hope these lessons I learned will help you write and self-publish your own family stories. Remember, when the ancestors call, we must listen.

The Ancestors Are Smiling!

BIBLIOGRAPHY

Barfield, Louise Calhoun. History of Harris County, Georgia, 1827-1961. Harris County, 1961.

Business and Professional Directory of the Cities and Towns of Georgia, 1909-1910. Young and Co. Publishers, Atlanta, GA, p. 265, https://archive.org/stream/youngcosbusiness01unse/youngcosbusiness01unse_djvu.txt.

Carrington, Wirt Johnson. A History of Halifax County, Virginia. Richmond, VA, 1924.

Crumpton, Daniel Nathan. Warren County, Georgia Land Records, Volume One, Warrenton, Georgia. D.N., Crumpton, 2002, p. 194.

Daniels, Margie, compiler. Talbot Counties, GA Marriages, 1826-52. 2004. http://www.usgennet.org/usa/ga/county/taylor/talbot/Talbot%20Marriages/marriage.htm.

Davidson, William H. A Rockaway in Talbot: Travels in an Old Georgia County, Volumes I-IV. W. H. Davidson Publisher, 1983.

Elliott, Dan. A Cool Plantation in Talbot County, Georgia, in Mister Soapstone [blog] https://danelliott.wordpress.com/2014/09/05/need-a-cool-plantation-in-talbot-countygeorgia/#comment-1757.

Federal Writers Project. "Georgia Narratives." Slave Narratives: A Folk History of Slavery in the United States from Interviews with Former Slaves, v. 4, p. 20-27. https://www.loc.gov/resource/mesn.041/?st=gallery.

Fire Insurance Map of Columbus, Georgia No. 24. Sanborn Map and Publishing Co., New York, New York. 1889.

Georgia, U.S., Property Tax Digests, 1793-1892, https://www.ancestry.com/search/collections/1729/

Gass, Christofer. "A Walk Through Columbus# Past." The Odyssey Online, 27 Aug. 2017, www.theodysseyonline.com/walk-through-columbus-past.

Georgia Historical Society. "Historic Markers Across Georgia." https://georgiahistory.com/education-outreach/historical-markers/.

Muscogiana: Journal of the Muscogee Genealogical Society, all volumes from 1989 to 2019, https://csuepress.columbusstate.edu/muscogiana.

Harris, Joel Chandler. Uncle Remus and His Friends: Old Plantation Stories, Songs and Ballads with Sketches of Negro Characters. Houghton Mifflin, Boston, and New York, 1893.

Lawrence, Betty. Marshall Family History in Talbot County. Transcribed by Wesley Culpepper, the GAGenweb Project, Accessed June 24, 2021, http://www.thegagenweb.com/gatalbot/bio/marshall.htm.

!Marshall Family," in Colonial Families of the USA, 1607-1775, p.355-356. https://www.ancestry.com/imageviewer/collections/61175/images/colonialfamiliesi-000574_355?pld=6580.

Mayberry, B.D. A Century of Agriculture in the 1890 Land-Grant Institutions and Tuskegee University, 1890-1990. VintagePress, NY, 1991.

Murphy, Ric, Arrival of the First Africans in Virginia, The History Press (August 31, 2020)

!Race & Slavery Petitions Project," University of North Carolina at Greensboro, Maintained by ERIT, University Libraries, 2000-2009.

!Slave Ship Manifests filed at New Orleans, 1807-1860," in Slave Manifests of Coastwise Vessels Filed at New Orleans, Louisiana, 1807-1860, National Archives. Accessed August 17, 2021. https://www.ancestry.com/imageviewer/collections/1562/images/31204_188992-00254?pld=26642.

Smith, George Gillman. Putnam County, Georgia History, The Story of Georgia and the Georgia People 1732 to 1860. 1901. Submitted to Genealogy Trails by K. Torp in 2007.

Talbot County, GA, Cemeteries map: http://www.dot.ga.gov/DriveSmart/MapsData/Documents/CountyMaps/Talbot.pdf.

!Visit Columbus, Georgia." Heritage Park | Things to Do in Columbus, GA | Visit Columbus, GA, visitcolumbusga.com/visit/things-to-do/heritage_tour_and_park.

Williams, Shari L. !Robert Fulwood Ligon," Encyclopedia of Alabama (1823-1901), http://encyclopediaofalabama.org/article/h-3901.

END NOTES

[1] The Coming to the Table concept could also be used to foster an environment of listening, understanding, and common ground for any group suffering from divisiveness (e.g., political, religious). Resources are available at: https://www.comingtothetable.org/resources.

[2] The 1619 Project is a long-form journalism endeavor developed by Nikole Hannah-Jones, writers from The New York Times, and The New York Times Magazine which "aims to reframe the country's history by placing the consequences of slavery and the contributions of Black Americans at the very center of the United States' national narrative.: https://en.wikipedia.org/wiki/The_1619_Project

[3] A 110/111 DNA match indicates a very close ancestral relationship. Most one-off matches are fifth or more recent cousins, and over half are second cousins or closer. In this case, the author's brother, Greg, and her cousin, Eddie Marshall, are proven to share a male Marshall-surnamed ancestor, who was perhaps Revolutionary War Captain John Marshall, born in around 1721 and died in 1782 in Mecklenburg, Virginia. For more information on how to interpret Y-DNA relationships, view: https://learn.familytreedna.com/y-dna-testing/y-str/two-men-share-surname-genetic-distance-111-y-chromosome-str-markers-interpreted/

[4] Biography of Donald Trump, the one-term 45th United States President, who received the most electoral votes in 2016. https://en.wikipedia.org/wiki/Donald_Trump

[5] Joseph Biden was the 46th United States President elected in 2020: https://en.wikipedia.org/wiki/Joe_Biden

[6] COVID-19 was deemed by some as fake news and a conspiracy: https://www.pewresearch.org/journalism/2020/06/29/most-americans-have-heard-of-the-conspiracy-theory-that-the-covid-19-outbreak-was-planned-and-about-one-third-of-those-aware-of-it-say-it-might-be-true/. Some refused to get Covid vaccine because they thought it was poisonous, but there were numerous articles that disproved the allegation, including: https://www.usatoday.com/story/news/factcheck/2021/05/25/fact-check-moderna-vaccine-not-poisonous/5152680001/

[7] 2016 United States Presidential election results indicated Hillary Clinton won the population vote, versus the defacto outcome for Donald Trump from the Electoral College: https://en.wikipedia.org/wiki/2016_United_States_presidential_election

[8] Barack Obama was the 44th United States President elected in 2008 and again in 2012: https://www.Whitehouse.gov/about-the-Whitehouse/presidents/barack-obama/

[9] Domestic Terrorism attack on the U.S. Capitol on January 6, 2020, in protest of Donald Trump losing the 2020 election: https://www.congress.gov/event/117th-congress/house-event/LC65965/text?q=%7B%22search%22%3A%5B%22capitol+attack%22%5D%7D&s=1&r=7

[10] From the superpower of the fictional character Spider-Man (introduced by Marvel Comics in August 1962), nicknamed Spidey – an ability to sense danger before it can be perceived by other senses.

[11] Siri: is a virtual assistant that is part of Apple Computer devices. The assistant uses voice queries and gesture-based control, to answer questions, make recommendations, and perform actions, etc.

[12] Emojis are small digital images or icons used to express an idea, emotion, etc.

[13] Headrights were grants of land to settlers and played a significant role in the expansion of the American colonies in North America prior to the American Revolution. Both the Virginia Company and Plymouth Company offered headrights to settlers as an incentive to come to the American colonies.

[14] From the superpower of the fictional character Spider-Man (introduced by Marvel Comics in August 1962), nicknamed Spidey – an ability to sense danger before it can be perceived by other senses.

[15] Dope: a drug taken illegally for recreational purposes, especially marijuana or heroin. Marijuana was decriminalized in most states by 2016. https://en.wikipedia.org/wiki/Timeline_of_cannabis_laws_in_the_United_States

[16] Susie Marshall becomes unexpectedly pertinent during my last leg of this trip (Chapter 19).

[17]Centimorgan: As a foot and yard measure length, a centimorgan is a unit that measures genetic (DNA) linkage. Each human receives about 3400 centimorgans from their father and 3400 centimorgans from their mother. The smaller the number of centimorgans two people share, the less likely they are close relatives. Statistically speaking, some DNA testing companies believe less than seven centimorgans is not a significantly close relationship to be valid. One centimorgan equals a one percent chance that a marker on a chromosome will become separated from a second marker on the same chromosome due to crossing over in a single generation.

[18]Kathy Marshall's Kanika African Sculptures art business was started in 1993, expanding her repertoire with a MIG welder in 2010. Images are available at www.KanikaMarshall.com.

[19]The Claflin School for African American children was located at 1532 5th Ave, in Columbus, GA, and was converted into low-income housing. https://www.georgiatrust.org/places-in-peril/claflin-school/

[20]City Directories from Columbus, GA, indicated Israel Smith was working as a shoemaker and living at 1714 5th Avenue as early as 1894. His descendants are listed in City Directories between 1894 and 1928, as living at 1710 Fifth Avenue.

[21]High Five: a gesture of celebration or greeting in which two people slap each other's open palm with their arms raised.

[22]Lech: lecherous.

[23]Jump the broom: In some African-American communities, marrying couples will end their ceremony by jumping over a broomstick, either together or separately. This practice is well attested for as a marriage ceremony for enslaved people in the Southern United States in the 1840s and 1850s who were often not permitted to wed legally.

[24]Ancestry ThruLines® shows how the test taker may be related to their DNA matches. ThruLines are based on information from family trees; they don't change the information in trees. If there's inaccurate information in your tree, you may receive inaccurate ThruLines.

[25]Convict leasing, also called peonage, also felt to be another name for slavery by some African Americans because it makes convicted Black

people work for free, like slavery days: https://eji.org/news/history-racial-injustice-convict-leasing/

[26] The Columbus Consolidated Government saves $10.5 million with their work prison: https://www.columbusga.gov/mcp/?fbclid=IwAR3OonLxM1Lrjy5M7IGmZlGLX0B4FMU9spvi0BdZ8sS1lvPqygci_U0Mwbc

[27] Skin Tone and Stratification in the Black Community clarifies how systemic racism and residual slavery which pitted lighter-skinned from darker-skinned Black people against each other, Verna M. Keith, Arizona State University: https://www.jstor.org/stable/2781783

[28] Born in Slavery: Slave Narratives from the Federal Writers' Project, 1936-1938 contains more than 2,300 first-person accounts of slavery and 500 black-and-white photographs of former slaves. These narratives were collected in the 1930s as part of the Federal Writers' Project (FWP) of the Works Progress Administration, later renamed Work Projects Administration (WPA). https://www.loc.gov/collections/slave-narratives-from-the-federal-writers-project-1936-to-1938/about-this-collection/.

[29] Councilman Johnny Ford attempts to take down Confederate monument in Tuskegee. https://www.montgomeryadvertiser.com/story/news/2021/07/07/tuskegee-councilman-johnny-ford-takes-saw-confederate-monument-town-square/7894987002/

[30] Robert Fulwood Ligon, by Shari L. Williams, Auburn University, Encyclopedia of Alabama, http://encyclopediaofalabama.org/article/h-3901

www.ingramcontent.com/pod-product-compliance
Lightning Source LLC
Chambersburg PA
CBHW070648120526
44590CB00013BA/871